Additional Praise for *Enterprise Risk Management*

"It's hard to imagine a more timely book. James Lam provides us with an excellent overview of enterprise risk management. A worthwhile read for professionals in a wide range of industries—from financial institutions to energy firms."

Richard L. Sandor, Ph.D.
Chairman and Chief Executive Officer
Chicago Climate Exchange, Inc.

"This book provides highly user-friendly insights into the many theoretical and practical aspects of enterprise-wide risk management. The case studies are particularly timely and provide a deeper understanding of the day-to-day real world complexities of implementing an effective risk management program."

Dr. Robert Mark
Chief Executive Officer
Black Diamond

"While enterprise risk management has been a hot topic for discussion and debate, Lam manages to provide us with the first fully developed framework on the subject. Essential reading for anyone interested in the subject of risk and the successful implementation of risk management."

Tobey J. Russ
President & Chief Executive Officer
Chubb Financial Solutions, LLC

"*Enterprise Risk Management* is managerial science. James Lam has been a consistent voice for the business benefits of risk management and has thoughtfully and clearly articulated the business case for ERM. Long at the forefront of the profession, even having coined the title "Chief Risk Officer," James uses real-life examples, practical suggestions and insights from his many years of practice to simplify risk management without being simplistic. This is a must-read for CEOs, CFOs, board members and others who want and need to know of this modern discipline to business management."

David R. Koenig
Chair of the Board of Directors
Professional Risk Managers' International Association

"Our bank has greatly benefited from the implementation of enterprise-wide risk management. The concepts introduced by James Lam through case studies, theory, and his business experiences provide insightful analysis and form the foundation for any broad based risk management program. This book is an excellent read for managers of all levels responsible for risk management."

William C. Nelson
Vice Chairman and Chief Risk Officer
Bank of Hawaii Corporation

John Wiley & Sons

Founded in 1807, John Wiley & Sons is the oldest independent publishing company in the United States. With offices in North America, Europe, Australia, and Asia, Wiley is globally committed to developing and marketing print and electronic products and services for our customers' professional and personal knowledge and understanding.

The Wiley Finance series contains books written specifically for finance and investment professionals as well as sophisticated individual investors and their financial advisors. Book topics range from portfolio management to e-commerce, risk management, financial engineering, valuation and financial instrument analysis, as well as much more.

For a list of available titles, please visit our Web site at www.WileyFinance.com.

Enterprise Risk Management

From Incentives to Controls

JAMES LAM

WILEY

John Wiley & Sons, Inc.

Published by John Wiley & Sons, Inc., Hoboken, New Jersey
Published simultaneously in Canada

For general information on our other products and services, or technical support, please contact our Customer Care Department within the United States at 800-762-2974, outside the United States at 317-572-3993 or fax 317-572-4002.

Wiley also publishes its books in a variety of electronic formats. Some content that appears in print may not be available in electronic books.

Library of Congress Cataloging-in-Publication Data:

Lam, James.
  Enterprise risk management : from incentives to controls. / James Lam.
      p.   cm.—(Wiley finance series)
    ISBN 0-471-43000-5 (cloth : alk. paper)
    1. Risk management.   I. Title.   II. Series.
    HD61 .L36 2003
    658.15'5—dc

                                                                2002155494

Printed in the United States of America

10   9

To my parents, Kwan Lun and Mary, who took the greatest risk of their lives when they gave up their comfortable teaching careers in Macao, China and moved our family to New York City in 1971. While their lives became harder, their decision opened up a whole new world of opportunities for me and my sister Lily. With deepest love and appreciation I dedicate this book to my dad and mom.

Contents

Preface

It has been said that every man should have a son, plant a tree, and write a book. Well, with my wife Pam we have three sons, 10-year-old Brandon and 8-year-old twins Austin and Garrett. I've planted several trees, mostly with the help of my gardener. And this is my first book, and it is on risk management.

I have spent my entire career of 20 years in risk management. About half of that time I've worked as a consultant, preaching the gospel of "best practices" in risk management. The other half of my career I've spent in industry, trying to practice what I've preached under the realities of day-to-day business. My rotations through these two roles, as consultant and manager, have taught me that successful risk management is all about balance.

First, risk management is about balancing risk and reward. Interestingly, the Chinese character for danger is actually the combination of the characters for opportunity and risk. Business leaders are natural risk takers because they were put into leadership positions as a result of past success. The challenge for leaders is to take *intelligent* risks. Running a successful business is all about pursuing the right business opportunities given the company's financial and managerial capabilities.

Risk management is also about balancing art and science. Considerable attention has been directed to advances in quantitative risk management—perhaps too much attention. Pick up the average risk management book or journal and the major focus is typically on derivatives or risk measurement techniques. Risk products and models play an important part in risk management, but it can be dangerous to put too much emphasis on them. Witness the collapse of Long-Term Capital Management (LTCM), a hedge fund managed by Nobel Prize winners whose mastery of the most sophisticated risk products and models was second to none. As LTCM's troubles reminded the world, the scenarios that lead to financial disasters happen, almost by their nature, when there is an unexpected confluence of events. Such scenarios are very difficult for models to predict. So there remains an element of art in risk management, an art based on management experience and judgment.

Finally, risk management is about balancing processes and people. A company can survive and may even thrive if it has good people and bad processes, but it cannot if the reverse is true. At the end of the day, a company's risk profile is driven by the decisions and actions of its employees. While risk management processes such as risk reporting and audit can provide useful monitoring, it is more important to ensure that the right people are in place to begin with, and that they are motivated by the right culture and incentives. Risk management is ultimately about people.

Enterprise Risk Management is organized into four main sections. The first, Risk Management in Context, provides an introduction and foundation for the book. In this section, we will first review why a company should strike a balance between risk and return, including some basic reasons why risk management is an important management issue. As has been wisely said, history tends to repeat itself unless we learn from it. So we will go on to discuss the lessons to be learned from the major financial disasters of years past. The reader may be familiar with some of these cases discussed throughout the book, while others will hopefully be new. While the particular circumstances of these financial disasters differ significantly, there are uncanny similarities in their themes and causes, which will be distilled into seven essential lessons to be learned. After drawing lessons from the past, we will discuss the key concepts, processes, and tools underlying risk management.

In the second section, The Enterprise Risk Management Framework, we will begin by discussing the business rationale for integrating risk management processes, as well as the seven building blocks for developing an enterprise risk management program. We will also discuss the role of a "chief risk officer." In the rest of Section II, we will examine each of the building blocks in greater detail, specifically the control processes and practical approaches that apply to each building block.

In the third section, Risk Management Applications, we will discuss the applications of risk management in two dimensions: functions and industries. We will begin by discussing the functional requirements for credit, market, and operational risks. We then discuss how risk management has evolved from a control function strictly concerned about minimizing downside risk to one that enables performance optimization. In the rest of this section, we discuss risk management in four key industry segments: financial institutions, energy firms, asset management firms, and nonfinancial corporations. In each industry segment, we will discuss major business and risk management trends, as well as contrast financial disasters and bestpractice applications.

In the final section of the book, A Look to the Future, we will discuss emerging topics in risk management with respect to people and technology. We will close the book with a fun story of how best-practice risk management might look like in the year 2010.

Acknowledgments

This book is a reflection of my 20-year career in risk management. As such, I should first thank two of my early mentors. Charlotte Chamberlain, of Jefferies & Company, contributed to my professional development by challenging me to improve my writing and presentation skills. Charlotte was also a risk taker when she hired me, at age 23, as vice-president in charge of asset/liability management for Glendale Federal (then a $15 billion bank). Jon Moynihan, of PA Consulting, taught me that a successful professional must develop a "T" skills set with both broad general management skills (the horizontal line) and deep technical expertise (the vertical line). Based on Jon's advice, I've strived to develop business management and risk management as my "T."

Effective risk management is driven by not only sound theory, but also sound practice. "Best practices" in risk management can only emerge when sound theories and models are tested in the confines of the real world. Two individuals provided me with significant opportunities in this regard. Rick Price hired me in 1993 to help set up a new capital markets business at GE Capital, and gave me the first opportunity to define the role of a "chief risk officer" in managing market, credit, and operational risks. Jerry Lieberman was very supportive of the enterprise-wide risk management program that I established at Fidelity Investments between 1995 and 1998, especially in managing operational risks and balancing the "hard" and "soft" side of risk management.

This book features several case studies that illustrate the approaches to implementing best practices. In order of appearance, I would like to thank Jim Brockbank of EDC for the case study on credit risk, Leslie Daniels-Webster of JP Morgan Chase for the case study on market risk, Mike Litwin of Heller (now with Merrill Lynch Capital) for the case study on operational risk, and Bob Mark, formerly chief risk officer of CIBC, for the case study on enterprise risk management at financial institutions.

I would also like to thank the partners and consultants who provided invaluable input to me while we worked together at Oliver, Wyman & Company and ERisk. Special thanks go to Marlyn Bilodeau, Kim Birkbeck, Alexia Dorozynski, John Drzik, Jennifer Pence, Anna Lewis, Rob Mackay,

Duncan Martin, Rebecca Prout, Anna Liu, George Morris, Peter Nakada, Curtis Tange, and Tom Yu. I am especially grateful to Sumit Paul-Choudhury, who provided extensive editorial support and input. His contributions are reflected throughout this book.

Finally, I would like to thank my editor Bill Fallon and his editorial assistant Melissa Scuereb from John Wiley & Sons. Bill has been involved in the risk management field for many years and it is truly a pleasure to work with someone who understands the subject matter.

Risk Management
in Context

Introduction

One evening in the autumn of 1995, I flew into Boston to have dinner with Denis McCarthy, then the chief financial officer of Fidelity Investments. McCarthy was the person to whom I would report if I accepted an offer to become the first chief risk officer for the corporation. I asked him what the main objective would be for this new position. His reply: "We want to operate in an environment in control, not a controlled environment."

I took that job with the understanding that Fidelity wanted to improve its risk management practices, but not at the price of destroying the entrepreneurial spirit and product innovation that had made it the largest mutual fund company in the United States.

Fidelity was not alone then and is not alone now. Every business faces the parallel challenges of growing earnings and managing risks. A thriving business must identify and meet customer needs with quality services and products; recruit and retain talented people; and correctly make business and investment decisions that will lead to future profit opportunities. However, the pursuit of new profit opportunities means that a business must take on a variety of risks. All of these risks must be effectively measured and managed across the business enterprise.

Otherwise, today's promising business ventures may end up being tomorrow's financial disasters. As I am fond of telling audiences when speaking on the importance of risk management, over the longer term, the only alternative to risk management is crisis management—and crisis management is much more expensive, time consuming, and embarrassing. The majority of such audiences have experienced one or more crises in their time, so this is a message that rings true.

Every business decision involves an element of risk. There are risks involved in making investments, hedging with derivatives, or extending credit to a retail customer or business entity. There are also risks involved when developing and pricing new products, hiring and training new employees, aligning performance measurement and incentives with business objectives, and establishing a culture that balances revenue growth and risk management.

Over time, individual business decisions and risks collectively build up into a company's overall risk portfolio, which will have a unique *risk profile*. This risk profile will determine the company's earnings—and earnings volatility—over the business cycle. Some decisions will be winners and some will be losers. Some risks will offset each other, some risks will be unrelated to each other, and some will compound each other. In order to manage risk effectively, a business must address not only its underlying risks, but also the interrelationships between them.

As we will see from the numerous case studies discussed in this book, ineffective risk management can lead to reduced earnings or even bankruptcy. However, risk management means different things to different people. In this book, risk management is defined in its broadest business sense. Risk management is not just about using derivatives to manage interest rate and foreign exchange exposures—it is about using a portfolio approach to manage the full range of risks faced by an enterprise. Nor is risk management only about establishing the right control systems and processes—it is also about having the right people and risk culture. And although the term has come to bear some negative connotations, risk management is not only about reducing downside potential or the probability of pain, but also about increasing upside opportunity or the prospects for gain.

Individual investors managing their investments must be careful when it comes to the amount of risk that they take on. If they take on too much risk, perhaps by making aggressive investments, the losses could exceed their risk tolerance, or be too uncertain for comfort. On the other hand, if they fail to take on *enough* risk, by making conservative investments, they may earn returns that are stable, but inadequate for achieving the investor's financial objectives.

Striking an optimal balance between risk and return is not only important to the individual investor, it is also an imperative for business management. The concept of "no risk, no return" is widely accepted in the business world. A corollary to that concept is "higher risk, higher return," a positive relationship illustrated in Figure 1.1. This is how many people think about the trade-off between risk and return, and it has the virtue of simplicity. However, it is certainly not valid if risk is put into its proper perspective.

A better way to think about risk and return is illustrated in Figure 1.2. The focus is no longer on the relationship between risk and *absolute* return, but about the *relative* or *risk-adjusted* return. A company in zone 1 is not taking enough risk, and its capital is being underutilized. This company would be better off increasing risk through a growth or acquisition strategy, or reducing capital through higher dividends. In zone 3, however, the company is taking too much risk. This company's risk level is above and beyond its risk absorption capability in terms of capital, and/or its risk management capability in terms of people and systems.

FIGURE 1.1   Risk and absolute return.

In zone 2, the company has found the "sweet spot" that optimizes its risk/return profile. The problem is that most companies do not even have good information on enterprise-wide risk exposures (which is to say, where they are on the horizontal axis), let alone where they are on the risk-adjusted return curve. To make matters worse, the net present value and economic value-added models frequently used in strategic planning naturally favor higher-risk investments unless proper adjustments are made to account for risk. Over time, investments guided by these unadjusted models may inadvertently lead a company to drift into zone 3.

A principal message of this book is that a company should develop an integrated approach to measuring and managing all of its risks in order to optimize its risk/return profile. A key management requirement for risk/return optimization is to integrate risk management in the business processes of the company.

We've seen, then, that risk is an inescapable part of doing business and

FIGURE 1.2   Risk and relative return.

argued that a business should strive toward its optimal risk/return profile. However, there is another question that deserves examination: why manage risk? Indeed, why read this book?

A company could conceivably agree that it bears risks but feels it inappropriate to manage them, rather than simply live with them. Risk management may seem to be irrelevant, too costly, or not in accordance with the interests of the company's stakeholders. Some academics have argued positions close to these, as we will see. Certainly, before a company invests money and other valuable resources into risk management (and before the reader spends any more time reading this book), the "value proposition" of risk management needs to be clearly established.

Perhaps the best way to answer the question "why manage risk?" is to borrow a popular technique used by diet and other self-improvement programs. That simple but effective technique is to paint a clear picture of the *gain of action* along with an equally clear picture of the *pain of inaction*. In the next section, we'll paint the happy picture: the benefits of effective risk management in terms of the expected benefits and gains. In the section thereafter, we'll paint the dire picture of the severe negative consequences—the pain—that may be suffered if effective risk management is not in place.

THE BENEFITS OF RISK MANAGEMENT

Numerous academic papers have established the theoretical basis for managing risk, arguing that it can reduce taxes, reduce transaction costs, and improve investment decisions.[1] However, beyond the theory there are at least four practical reasons why risk management should be of paramount importance to the management of a firm. In this practical context, risk management should be defined more broadly, to include internal controls as well as hedging.

Let's now take a look at these four reasons in turn.

Reason #1. Managing risk is management's job.   One notion in modern finance theory is that managing risk, or more specifically hedging, is not necessary because an investor can reduce risk through a diversified investment portfolio. Regardless of what some theoreticians may argue, you will never in the real world hear a fund manager or individual investor tell a company's management, "Don't worry about managing risk or bankrupting the company—I have a large diversified portfolio."

Managing the risks of a business enterprise is the direct responsibility of

---

[1]S. Waite Rawls III and Charles W. Smithson, "Strategic Risk Management," *Journal of Applied Corporate Finance* 2, no. 4, winter 1990.

its management, not of its shareholders. While modern portfolio theory is a major contributor to the theory and practice of finance and risk management today, the argument that the investor can better manage or diversify risks does not ring true in the real world. The average individual investor probably spends more time buying a new car than addressing the risks of his or her investment portfolio. Even the professional fund manager is several degrees away from the "insider knowledge" required for effective risk management, which includes:

- Historical data on risk/return results, volatilities, and correlations
- Current risk exposures and concentrations in the business
- Future business and investment plans that may alter the firm's risk profile

Given the complexity of the above information, as well as the lack of full transparency to outsiders, the shareholder cannot be expected to make optimal risk/return decisions. Measuring and managing enterprise-wide risks is a great challenge even for the enterprise's management, which has superior access to information and support from risk management professionals. The most that shareholders can do is to elect an independent and risk-astute board that will represent their interests, and walk away with their investment dollars if they are not happy with management's performance. In the meantime, it remains management's job to ensure that the company achieves its business objectives and is not exposed to excessive risks.

Reason #2. Managing risk can reduce earnings volatility. One of the key objectives of risk management is to reduce the sensitivity of a firm's earnings and market value to external variables. For example, the stock prices of companies that are more active in, say, market risk management should exhibit lower sensitivity to market prices. This is borne out by the empirical evidence. For example, a study published in 1998 by Peter Tufano of the Harvard Business School[2] ranked gold producers in terms of the intensity of their hedging activities. The conclusion was that the stock prices of those in the top quartile were about 23 percent less sensitive to gold price changes than those of the bottom quartile. Companies exposed to interest rates, foreign exchange rates, energy prices, and other market variables can better manage earnings volatility through risk management. Managing earnings volatility today is more important than ever given that the stock market severely punishes stocks that fail to meet earnings expectations. At the same time, the Securities and Exchange Commission (SEC) and other regulatory bodies are cracking down

---

[2]P. Tufano, "The Determinants of Stock Price Exposure: Financial Engineering and the Gold Mining Industry," *Journal of Finance* 53, 1998, pp. 1015–1052

on "earnings management" practices that use accounting techniques to smooth out earnings. In this business environment, management must pay more attention to managing the underlying risks of the business.

Reason #3. Managing risk can maximize shareholder value.   In addition to managing earnings volatility, risk management can help a business enterprise to achieve its business objectives and maximize shareholder value. Companies that undertake a risk-based program for shareholder value management typically identify opportunities for risk management and business optimization that can add 20 to 30 percent or more to shareholder value. Such improvements can be achieved by ensuring that:

- Target investment returns and product pricing are established at levels that reflect the underlying risks.
- Capital is allocated to projects and businesses with the most attractive risk-adjusted returns, and risk-transfer strategies are executed to optimize portfolio risk and return.
- The company has the appropriate skills to manage all of its risks, in order to protect against large financial losses or damage to its reputation or brand.
- Performance metrics and incentives, at both the individual and business unit levels, are in congruence with the enterprise's business and risk objectives.
- Key management decisions, such as mergers and acquisitions and business planning, explicitly incorporate the element of risk.

Strategies for achieving these objectives, and case studies of how they work in practice, will be discussed in the main sections of the book.

A 1998 study by George Allayannis and James Weston of the University of Virginia[3] has supported the notion that active risk management contributes to shareholder value. Allayannis and Weston compared the ratio of market value to book value for companies that were more or less active in market risk management between 1990 and 1995, as measured by their hedging activities. They found that the more active companies were rewarded with an average increase of 20 percent in market value. Risk management adds value not only to individual companies, but also supports overall economic growth by lowering the cost of capital and reducing the uncertainty of commercial activities.

Reason #4. Risk management promotes job and financial security.   On an individual level, perhaps the most compelling benefit of risk management is that it

---

[3]G. Allayannis and J. Weston, "The Use of Foreign Exchange Derivatives and Firm Market Value," working paper, University of Virginia, January 1998.

promotes job and financial security, especially for senior managers. In the aftermath of the fall 1998 turmoil in financial markets, a significant number of chief executive officers (CEOs), chief operating officers, chief risk officers, and business group heads of financial institutions lost their jobs because of poor risk management performance. Senior executives in other industries have faced a similar fate in the wake of risk management problems. More recently, senior executives involved in corporate frauds and accounting scandals have appeared on national television being led away in handcuffs and face the potential of severe criminal sentences.

In addition to "career risks," senior executives with a significant portion of their wealth tied up in company stocks and options have a direct financial interest in the success and survival of the firm. These incentives, if structured appropriately, work to put the "skin in the game" for managers, resulting in a strong alignment between management and shareholder interests. Risk management provides managers with a higher degree of job security and protects their financial interests in their firm.

CAUTIONARY TALES

Ultimately, however, the arguments above may not sway skeptical managers. Arguments based on the potential gains of improved risk management can be supported by those that point out the potential pain of ineffective risk management. However, these are often rebutted by the sentiment that "it couldn't happen here." In these cases, it is worth reminding the skeptics that history has repeatedly demonstrated how bad things can and do happen to good companies.

If anyone ever doubts that risk management is a critical issue for any business enterprise, they should take a hard look at Figure 1.3: The Wheel of Misfortune. The Wheel of Misfortune illustrates that risk management disasters can come in many different forms, and can strike any company within any industry. Beyond purely financial losses, the mismanagement of risks can result in damage to the reputation of the individual companies, or a setback for the careers of individual executives. The damage can quickly escalate until a previously healthy firm suddenly faces bankruptcy; indeed, the cumulative losses suffered by U.S. thrifts in the mid-1980s bankrupted not just individual companies, but the entire industry.

A close examination of these disasters serves two purposes. First, it underlines the importance of risk management. Second, it offers an insight into the prime tenets of a new, advanced approach to risk management—the approach called *enterprise risk management*, with which this book is primarily concerned. We'll develop these tenets in the next few chapters.

Let's take a deeper look now, going beyond the immediate headlines to assess the underlying causes and find some more durable truths. An entire

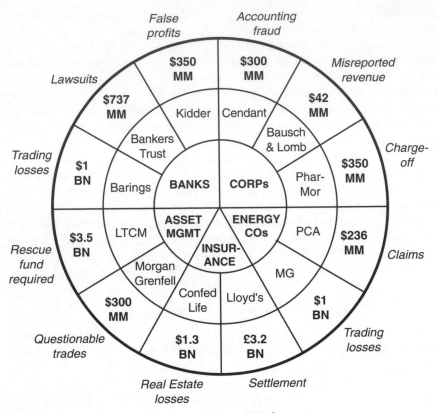

FIGURE 1.3 Wheel of misfortune. *Source:* ERisk.

book, if not several, could undoubtedly be written about notorious business disasters of the twentieth century, but we will review four illustrative cases from the mid-1990s here:

- Bausch & Lomb, a consumer products company
- Kidder, Peabody, an investment bank
- Metallgesellschaft, an energy company
- Morgan Grenfell, an asset management company

The Shortsightedness of Bausch & Lomb

In 1993, the optical manufacturer Bausch & Lomb (B&L) was a world leader in contact lenses and sunglasses. B&L was a company run very much according to the numbers, with failure to reach sales targets regarded as inexcusable. According to the *CPA Journal* (September 1, 1998), the company's contact lens division (CLD) had met or exceeded expectations for no less than 48 consecutive months, but in fall 1993 it was becoming apparent that it was not going to make its numbers.

The CLD regained some ground by offering distributors heavily discounted prices and extended payments. This promotion produced sales that surpassed third-quarter forecasts, but had the considerable drawback that the glut of contact lenses now in the market would depress fourth-quarter sales even more than they had been in the third quarter. If the CLD were to meet its fourth-quarter earnings expectations, it would have to resort to still more extreme measures.

It did. The CLD told its distributors that their relationships with B&L would only be maintained if between them they took on its remaining inventory. Most accepted, although this meant accepting ridiculously huge volumes of product—some ended up with as much as two years' worth of inventory. At the same time, the CLD also fell foul of its retail customers after *Business Week* alleged that it had been selling the same lenses as disposables (priced as low as $7.50) and as traditional lenses (priced at $70). More than 1.5 million buyers of the expensive lenses sued; the claim was ultimately settled in 1996 for a reported $68 million.

The CLD's actions—which, when uncovered, led to an SEC investigation and a $22 million charge against earnings—might have been considered an isolated aberration, had it not been for the fact that another B&L division was also employing dubious practices to shift product at around the same time. The Asian Pacific Division (APD) "sold" half a million pairs of sunglasses that were shipped to a warehouse in Hong Kong rather than to their putative buyers. This meant that the APD's accounts receivable balance rose rapidly; but rather than raise provisions against bad debts, it conducted exchange transactions so that the customers in question received credits to their accounts and then repurchased the goods.

The APD generated another $20 million of misreported revenue; together, the two rogue divisions led to a $17.6 million overstatement of net income. The company corrected its financial statements in 1996 and paid $42 million to settle a class-action suit brought by shareholders in 1997. The damage was done, however. B&L's share price grew only sluggishly as U.S. equity markets boomed during the 1990s, despite healthy revenues—perhaps the ultimate irony for a company that had valued performance above all else.

The Curtains Close on Kidder, Peabody

At the beginning of 1994, business at General Electric (GE) appeared to be going swimmingly. Under the direction of Jack Welch, considered by many to be one of the world's top CEOs, it had reported 51 consecutive quarters of earnings and was widely regarded as one of the few truly successful conglomerates. All that was about to change.

Trouble was brewing at Kidder, Peabody, the investment bank in which GE held an 80 percent stake. Kidder had already caused GE embarrassment in 1987—the year after it was acquired—when it was fined $25.3 million by the SEC for insider trading. This time the problem was much more complex and controversial. Kidder was about to take a $210 million charge after taxes against first-quarter earnings for 1994, resulting in a first-quarter loss of $140 million.

Kidder alleged that the loss was due to bogus profits recorded by Joseph Jett, the 36-year-old managing director of the government-trading desk. Jett's basic strategy was to enter into forward contracts that involved the exchange of "strips" (interest-only government paper) for bonds. His employer claimed, however, that when the date of the exchange came, Jett would roll the loss-making contracts forward and log fictitious profits (as reported in *The Wall Street Journal*, April 18, 1994).

Jett recorded $350 million in profits in 1993—enough to earn him a $9 million bonus. His $10 million compensation exceeded even that of Jack Welch. But according to Kidder, the profits were phony; Jett had allegedly concealed a $9.5 million loss in 1992, $45 million in 1993, and $29 million in the first few months of 1994. Jett claimed that he was made a scapegoat for Kidder's underperformance.

What really happened may never be known. Although the SEC subsequently found Jett guilty of books and records violations, no criminal charges were ever filed and the National Association of Securities Dealers cleared him of fraud. But the aftermath was nonetheless devastating. Jett was only the first to go, followed either through dismissal or resignation by at least five former colleagues including the CEO and the head of brokerage. Kidder itself was sold later that year to a rival brokerage, Paine Webber, for a knock-down price of just $90 million.

Although the Jett affair was more opaque than many later trading fiascoes, many of its root causes—inadequate oversight of traders and understanding of trading strategies—have been repeated. Most notable was Barings, the venerable U.K. merchant bank that collapsed in 1995 after more than $1 billion of trading losses were run up by "rogue trader" Nick Leeson. Kidder's tale, and the others like it, suggest that companies should not be so dazzled by the golden geese that they stop looking for the rotten eggs.

Meltdown at Metallgesellschaft

One of the most celebrated financial disasters of the 1990s was the massive loss racked up in crude oil trading by Metallgesellschaft Refining and Marketing (MGRM), an American subsidiary of the international trading, engineering, and chemicals conglomerate Metallgesellschaft (MG).

In 1992, MGRM implemented an apparently lucrative marketing strategy. The company agreed to sell specified amounts of petroleum products every month for up to 10 years, at pre-agreed prices above the current market price. The company then used a "stack" hedging strategy, under which it purchased a succession of short-term energy futures to hedge its long-term commitments. The assumption was that if oil prices dropped, the futures position would lose money, while the fixed-rate position would increase in value. If oil prices rose, on the other hand, the futures gains would offset the losses from the fixed-rate position.

This neat solution turned out to be badly flawed. Under MGRM's strategy, the company would gain over a long period of time if oil prices dropped, as it sold oil month by month at the prearranged higher rate. As margin calls came in, however, it would immediately be exposed to losses made on the energy futures. In addition, there was no stable relationship between the long-term forward commitments and the short-term energy futures— another major risk for the company. Thus, when oil prices actually dropped, the company faced a cash flow crisis and ultimately a funding crisis that reached all the way back to the parent company. In December 1993, MG was forced to bail out MGRM and cash in its positions, at a loss totaling more than $1 billion.

Academics have been arguing ever since about whether MG did the right thing. Theoreticians such as the Nobel prize–winning economist Merton Miller and his colleague Christopher Culp maintain that had MG been able to persevere, in the long term it would have made a profit, recouping the losses on the futures through profits on the sale of petroleum. Others have pointed out that this is irrelevant, given that the company could not have done so in practice, while some have cast doubt on the size of the potential long-term gains. An auditors' report, commissioned by MG shareholders, maintains that 59 million barrels' worth of the long-term contracts had a negative value of about $12 million, so the value of these contracts could never have offset the losses, even in the long term.

The MG episode illustrates a concept that can be referred to as "funding risk"—the risk that positions may be profitable in the long run, but bankrupt a company in the short run. This is a risk that arises if negative cash flows are mismatched with positive cash flows, with the emphasis jointly placed on "cash" and "flows." It is not enough just to think about how *much* money a strategy will bring in; risk managers must also think about *when* that money will come in.

Morgan Grenfell's Asset Mismanagement

Morgan Grenfell Asset Management (MGAM) was doing well in 1994. Pension assets managed by the company's Investment Services division had grown from $7.6 billion to $10 billion during 1994. The firm was fast developing a reputation for being knowledgeable and effective.

In 1995, however, one of its employees embarked on a course of action that would culminate in a media spectacle big enough to overshadow these recent successes. Sometime during that year, fund manager Peter Young began making covert purchases of large quantities of stock in companies that could charitably be described as little known. What Young saw in these companies was known only to himself; some of them were unlikely to have been endorsed by MGAM's investment guidelines.

One example was Solv-Ex, a company described by *Barron's* as having "a rather checkered past and nothing more tangible than ambitious plans for exploiting Canada's Athabasca tar sands for oil and minerals" (November 4, 1996). Young bought $30 million of stock in this gem—not at a discount, as might be expected for an extremely risky bulk purchase, but at a $2-a-share premium.

Young also managed to circumvent a Securities and Investment Board regulation forbidding a fund from owning more than 10 percent of any company. He did this by establishing a system of companies, apparently through a Swiss law firm. These companies were "paired," so that each owned some 90 to 95 percent of its partner company, while Young purchased the other 5 to 10 percent for the funds under his control.

In September 1996, the London regulators began investigating the valuation of assets in MGAM's three largest European funds. Trading on the funds shut down for three days and resumed only after Deutsche Bank, the parent company, replaced the questionable assets in the fund with $300 million in cash. Nonetheless, about 30 percent of investors left the funds within the next few weeks, taking $400 million with them.

The turmoil in the wake of this scandal was enormous. MGAM had to compensate more than 80,000 investors and was fined by the City of London regulators. Establishing the value of the compensation required two teams, each with 100 members, from two major accounting firms. Questions about how Young had been allowed to get away with his eccentric trading for so long—especially given reports that he had been cautioned about breaching investment guidelines months before the suspension—continued to haunt MGAM.

Young, meanwhile, briefly returned to the limelight a few months later, when he made his first court appearance wearing a dress and full make-up. Whatever the motivation behind this switch in gender polarity, it served as a suitably surreal coda to an affair that had been as perplexing as it had been expensive.

Bausch & Lomb, Kidder, Peabody, Metallgesellschaft, and MGAM: four very different companies. But it should already be apparent that there are common themes that can be drawn from these and other headline-grabbing incidents. We'll explore these in the next chapter.

Lessons Learned

A Chinese philosopher once said that a smart man learns from his own mistakes and a wise man from the mistakes of others, but a fool never learns. Most of us would rather be smart and wise than foolish. In order to avoid taking the fool's path to potential disaster, it is important for companies to develop organizational processes that allow them to learn from their mistakes. Ideally, the same processes would also allow them to learn from the mistakes, and the best practices, of other companies.

There is no shortage of learning opportunities. It seems as if a major business disaster happens every few months, reminding us of the dangers faced by all enterprises. Organizations fortunate enough to avoid a major crisis often experience lesser problems or "near misses" that highlight underlying exposures to risk.

Left unchecked, these exposures could lead to a major loss or incident in the future. If these disasters are to be averted, an organization must be open to the discussion of past mistakes, and must be able to learn from them. Moreover, the same process should promote organizational learning about the costly mistakes made by other companies as well as about the application of industry best practices.

When I started Fidelity Investments' enterprise risk management program in 1995, the concepts of "lessons learned" and "best practices" were central to initiatives to raise risk awareness. In the early stages of the program, my team (Global Risk Management) organized regular meetings of the company's top 200 executives, including corporate managers, business unit heads, and senior financial and risk management professionals. High on the agenda at these meetings was a discussion of the lessons learned from major disasters in the financial services industry, such as the troubles of Barings Bank and Kidder, Peabody. In each of these case studies, participants examined the sequence of events, the root causes of the problem and the financial and business impact that it went on to have. The focus of any such case analysis, however, was on how Fidelity Investments could avoid similar problems. These meetings were invaluable in building and maintaining awareness regarding risk management among the senior executives.

Another learning initiative for us was a series of visits to about a dozen financial institutions as part of an exercise in best-practice benchmarking. This initiative included visits to Brown Brothers, Chase, GE Capital, State Street Bank, and others. As a result of these visits, more than 100 best-practice applications were documented in a database that was part of the educational section of an intranet-based Global Risk MIS. This database allowed all Fidelity Investments' risk management professionals to benefit from the insights gained from these best-practice visits, while the intranet gave the user the capability to search for and identify best practices by risk, company, or application.

One of the most striking insights gained from these visits was the high value that other companies placed on their learning processes for risk management. For example, State Street Bank had a six-week "launch program" for new associates that trained them in business and risk management processes, while Brown Brothers had an "errors and omissions program" that educated employees about where problems usually occurred in their operations and how they could be avoided. Several of the companies we visited implemented systematic learning processes that reviewed important incidents, losses above a certain threshold, and other issues such as risk policy violations.

Following these visits, Fidelity Investments launched a number of initiatives at both the corporate and business unit levels. These initiatives included a "risk college," loss and incident review processes, and follow-up best-practice visits with our business partners and institutional clients. We also conducted an internal consulting project for a business unit. That business unit experienced an 85 percent reduction in annual losses after the introduction of a *risk event log*. Any loss above a certain threshold was recorded in this log and subsequently reviewed by the risk management committee—chaired by the business unit president—to ascertain the root cause of the problem and develop prevention procedures.

My experiences at Fidelity and elsewhere suggest that lessons learned from mistakes and from the best practices of other companies can be a valuable supplement to those learned from examination of a company's own operations.

Although a certain number of minor losses should be expected as a matter of routine in any business, management should nonetheless view every *significant* loss or incident as a learning opportunity. Without a systematic process for capturing and learning from such incidents and losses, a company is more likely to repeat old mistakes that could potentially develop into a real crisis.

The four cases described in the last chapter represent only a small sample of the risk management failures that have hit the headlines in recent years, or of the range of risk management problems that can cause financial losses. Collectively, these and other cases should serve as a loud wake-up call: improper risk management and control can have dangerous consequences. Lapses in risk management have resulted in significant losses for companies in different industries and countries around the world. A number of those companies—some once considered the pillars of their industries—no longer exist because they couldn't survive the financial and reputational losses they suffered.

The circumstances surrounding each story are unique, with the culprits ranging from a single rogue trader involved in unauthorized trading to groups of individuals involved in unsound business practices that were at one time accepted (or even encouraged) by management. Some events occurred over days or months, while others took a decade or more to unfold. Despite the many differences, there are some common themes. We can distill these into seven "key lessons":

- Know your business.
- Establish checks and balances.
- Set limits and boundaries.
- Keep your eye on the cash.
- Use the right yardstick.
- Pay for the performance that you want.
- Balance the yin and the yang.

We'll look at these in more detail in the section below.

LESSON #1: KNOW YOUR BUSINESS

Perhaps the most important lesson one can learn is that managers are obligated to "know the business." This responsibility should be shared by everyone involved in the business, ranging from the board of directors to front-line supervisors and employees, and is an integral component of risk management. In credit risk management, for example, "know the customer" is widely accepted as a tenet of a sound credit program, and has been adopted as a requirement by several regulatory agencies.

Although it is critical that managers with responsibility for oversight and approval know their businesses, it is also important that *all* employees understand how their individual accountabilities could affect the risks of the organization, and how their functions and responsibilities relate to others within the company. Business managers should be knowledgeable about all aspects of the business, including high-level business and operational processes, key drivers of revenue and cost, and the major risks and key exposures involved (i.e., "know the risks").

Failure to know the business was a contributing factor in both the Kidder,

Peabody and Metallgesellschaft fiascoes. Securities and Exchange Commission (SEC) enforcement chief Gary Lynch reported that Jett's supervisors "never understood [his] daily trading activity or the source of his apparent profitability," while GE's auditors "really didn't understand much about government [debt] trading." Overall, the Lynch Report was highly critical of management's failure to supervise, understand, and monitor the activities on the trading desk.

In Metallgesellschaft's case, had senior management better understood the cash flow implications of its New York arm's activities, the company might never have embarked on its disastrous hedging strategy—or at least, might have unwound it in a more orderly fashion, and thus avoided the liquidity squeeze and hedging loss. Metallgesellschaft, more than most, fell victim to an inappropriate, rather than intrinsically flawed, strategy.

LESSON #2: ESTABLISH CHECKS AND BALANCES

A prerequisite of effective risk management is that there should be a system of checks and balances to prevent any given individual, or group of individuals, from gaining excessive power to take risks on behalf of an organization.

This can be thought of as the application of portfolio diversification to the management of people and processes, rather than assets and liabilities. It is not desirable, from a risk management perspective, to have a concentration of market risk exposure to a specific segment (e.g., emerging markets) or a concentration of credit risk exposure to an individual counterparty. Likewise, it is not desirable to allow an individual or group of individuals to amass a concentration of the power, or authority, to commit the company's capital to a specific risk-taking activity. This might range from an individual trader with the power to make enormously leveraged bets on market prices to an executive whose orders go unquestioned by other managers or nonexecutive directors.

Reengineering efforts pose a potential problem in this respect. Checks and balances are often, by definition, redundant processes, and so may be reengineered out of a key operation or process altogether. It is important to realize that a system of checks and balances, along with the segregation of key duties, is not only a safeguard against errors made by people, processes, and systems, but it is also fundamental to sound business management. Real-life examples include appointing an independent board of directors, creating effective audit committees, and something as simple as having someone proofread an important document.

The collapse of Barings Bank is perhaps the best-known example of this principle. Both the trading and the accounting functions at Barings' Singapore branch reported to "rogue trader" Nick Leeson, enabling him to conceal mounting losses for over a year. The scandal that erupted when Barings ultimately collapsed under the weight of Leeson's billion-dollar losses led banking regulators and industry groups around the world to establish "segregation of duties" and "independent risk management" as core principles in risk management. In response, companies established risk management and back-office operations that were independent of the profit centers.

The case of Morgan Grenfell Asset Management also illustrates the need for effective checks and balances. Both Young's immediate boss and the company's compliance department were supposed to sign off on each of Young's purchases of unlisted shares, so they should have known exactly what was happening. However, it was not until Young's holdings of unlisted shares hit more than three times the legal limit that his boss first told him to reduce them.

LESSON #3: SET LIMITS AND BOUNDARIES

Just as business strategies and product plans tell a business "where to go," risk limits and boundaries tell a business "when to stop."

It is widely accepted that risk limits are an integral part of a sound risk management program. For market risk, these risk limits may include trading limits, product limits, duration, and other limits on a position's sensitivity to movements in market prices or rates (e.g., delta, gamma, vega, theta, also known as the "Greeks" of option pricing), value-at-risk limits, and stop-loss limits. For credit risk, they may include mark-to-market and risk-adjusted limits by counterparty, risk grade, industry, and country. For operational risks, the risk limits may include minimum quality standards (or conversely, maximum error rates) by operation, system, or process. They also may include firm deadlines to resolve outstanding audit items.

In addition to limits on financial and operational risks, boundaries should be established to control business risks, such as standards for sales practices and product disclosures. Boundaries also should be established to control organizational risks, such as the company's hiring policies vis-à-vis background checks on prospective employees, or its termination policies if an employee violates company policy. Without clear limits and boundaries, the management of a fast-growing company is in the position of the driver of a race car with no brakes.

In the Metallgesellschaft case, the company's failure to set appropriate limits on hedging activities compounded the problem. Forward and futures positions continued to grow larger even as oil prices fell: by the time the petroleum positions were liquidated, they were estimated to be 85 days' worth of Kuwait's entire output. In the Morgan Grenfell Asset Management case, the damage would likely have been contained if Young had been censured and his dealings investigated as soon as unlisted shares passed the legal limit.

LESSON #4: KEEP YOUR EYE ON THE CASH

A famous thief was once asked why he robbed banks. He replied: "Because that's where the cash is." This simple answer contains an important lesson for all financial institutions, as well as for the finance/treasury operations of any corporation. Crime—whether fraud, embezzlement, or straightforward theft—follows cash. And more innocent trading and operational errors are most immediately painful when they affect cash.

It's therefore important to make sure that there are appropriate safeguards for managing cash positions and cash flows. These include basic controls, such as authorized signatures to initiate, approve, and make cash transfers. They also include the development of internal processes to measure, monitor, reconcile, and document cash transactions and positions. Actual cash flows and positions also can provide management with valuable "reasonableness checks" against the company's trading systems and profitability models.

New and emerging technologies such as e-commerce, electronic banking, and smart cards will provide financial institutions with new challenges in this important area. Inadequate cash management and accounting systems represent opportunities for potential fraud to go undetected, as well as "blind spots" for trading and operational errors. In the Kidder case, Jett's trading operations recorded $350 million of profits on paper, but no one reconciled Kidder's cash positions with the reported profits over the course of three years. As the SEC's Lynch later said, "They were always unrealized profits." In the Enron case, the company reported $3.3 billion in net income over the five years ending 2000. Over the same period, it reported only $114 million of total cash generated—a mere 3 percent of reported income. A long time delay between reported earnings and actual cash flows should be a warning indicator for any company. To quote one analyst, "Cash is king. Accounting is opinion." The lesson here is to focus on the cash.

LESSON #5: USE THE RIGHT YARDSTICK

The "measures of success" used (or not used) by a company to track individual and group performance are a key driver of behavior, and by extension, of risk. Most companies establish performance goals in terms of sales, revenue, and profitability. Some have adopted the "balanced scorecard" approach, and augment their financial measures with performance measures pertaining to quality, customer satisfaction, and internal processes. If management is to gain a proper risk/return perspective, it is important that risk measures (similar to those alluded to in Lesson #3) are incorporated in the processes that generate management reports and measure performance. An integrated set of risk measures should provide management with timely information on all types of risks faced by the company, including actual (ex-post) and "early warning" (ex-ante) risk indicators.

Use of an inappropriate yardstick was clearly one of the factors leading to Bausch & Lomb's troubles. The focus on sales and earnings targets, plus an extremely demanding atmosphere, resulted in behavior that had adverse consequences at a variety of levels, from customer dissatisfaction to stock price. The disasters that befell the company were caused, at root, by an unyielding desire to succeed. Had the company not placed such emphasis on growth at all costs—or, to put it differently, on return regardless of risk—things would likely have turned out differently.

Other companies regularly set aggressive earnings growth targets in the range of 15 to 20 percent per year. These companies should ask themselves: are these targets realistic when the general economy is growing at 3 to 4 percent? What kind of pressures do these targets put on the business units? How will people behave if aggressive sales and earnings goals are not balanced with the appropriate controls and measures for risk? As has been said, the road to hell is paved with good intentions.

LESSON #6: PAY FOR THE PERFORMANCE YOU WANT

The other side of performance measurement is the issue of compensation and incentives. Organizations need to take a close and careful look at how compensation and incentives are designed and implemented, and whether or not they reinforce desired behavior and performance. The combination of performance measurement and incentive compensation is probably one of the most powerful drivers of human behavior and organizational change. This can either work in favor of the company's risk management objectives—or against them.

For example, the performance of managers and employees might be measured by, and rewarded for, sales- or revenue-based results alone, with no consideration given to risk exposures or losses. In that case, it should be expected that the company would be exposed to higher and higher levels of potential risk that may ultimately become inconsistent with its risk appetite and capitalization. Management should therefore pay careful attention to the signals that performance measurement and incentive compensation systems send out, to ensure that they are consistent with the company's business and risk management objectives.

As one of my professors at UCLA once said, "If you go into a company and see smart people doing stupid things, 9 times out of 10 they are being paid to do so." Improper incentive structure is a root cause of recent problems associated with the lack of independence of equity research (e.g., analysts recommending the stocks of investment banking clients while privately trashing the same stocks). In the Kidder case, did it make sense that in 1993 Jett earned a bonus of $9 million and his boss, Ed Cerrullo, earned $20 million—more than Jack Welch, the parent company's well-regarded chairman and chief executive officer?

LESSON #7: BALANCE THE YIN AND THE YANG

Much of the focus of risk management has to date been on building infrastructure: independent risk functions and oversight committees; risk assessments and audits; risk management policies and procedures; systems and models; measures and reports; and risk limits and exception processes. All of this makes up what might be called the "hard side" (the yin) of risk management.

However, it is equally (if not more) important that companies focus on the "soft" side (the yang) of risk management. "Soft" initiatives might include:

- Setting the tone from the top and building awareness through demonstration of senior management commitment
- Establishing the principles that will guide the company's risk culture and values
- Facilitating open communication for discussing risk issues, escalating exposures, and sharing lessons learned and best practices
- Providing training and development programs
- Reinforcing desired behavior and results through performance measurement and incentives

While the hard side focuses on processes, systems, and reporting, the soft side focuses on the people, skills, culture, values, and incentives. In many respects, the components of the soft side are the key *drivers* of risk-taking activities while the components of the hard side are *enablers*, which support risk management activities. As discussed in Chapter 1, there can be no reward without risk; but risk should not be taken recklessly or randomly. That means that both the soft and hard sides—the yin and the yang—of risk management are necessary; and managers should therefore take a balanced approach to managing risk at their companies.

As was suggested at the beginning of this chapter, learning is a critical part of any successful enterprise risk management program. An organization open to learning is less likely to repeat past mistakes, and more likely to benefit from new developments and innovations in the field of risk management—that is, to be smart and wise, and not to make a fool of itself.

Concepts and Processes

R isks come in all shapes and sizes; risk professionals generally recognize three major types. Market risk is the risk that prices will move in a way that has negative consequences for a company; credit risk is the risk that a customer, counterparty, or supplier will fail to meet its obligations; and operational risk is the risk that people, processes, or systems will fail, or that an external event (e.g., earthquake, fire) will negatively impact the company.

Other types of risk also have been suggested. Business risk is the risk that future operating results may not meet expectations; organizational risk is the risk that arises from a badly designed organizational structure or lack of sufficient human resources. In general, risk managers would consider market risk and credit risk as financial risk, and group all other risks as part of operational risk.

And each of these broad risk types encompasses a host of individual risks. Credit risk, for example, includes everything from a borrower default to a supplier missing deadlines because of credit problems. Although there are commonalities and interdependencies between these risks, each ultimately requires specialized attention.

How can a manager with responsibility for enterprise-wide risk hope to stay on top of all these various risks? It is impractical to simply hire an expert for every risk—since risk is a part of every business decision, this approach would require a risk manager for every business manager.

A more practical solution is to make risk a part of every employee's thinking and job responsibility. This has two advantages: first, no one is better placed to understand the risks of an activity better than those who specialize in that area; second, this approach means that risk is managed throughout the company.

However, this requires a substantial effort in training and education. Many staff, whether junior or senior, will not be familiar with risk management, and particularly not with quantitative forms of risk analysis. Although these quantitative analyses are often very important, they are not practical for every type of risk and fall under the remit of the corporate risk management function.

General employees therefore need to be taught to recognize and assess risks in ways that are relatively easy to understand. Fortunately, there are a number of key *risk concepts* that will apply to the risks of any kind of business and must be addressed by any effective risk management program.

RISK CONCEPTS

Not all of the risk concepts described in this section can be readily (or meaningfully) quantified, particularly if operational risks are involved. As we'll see, however, they are nonetheless important in understanding the nature of risk in any organization and should form the basis of the questions that a risk manager asks when assessing risk. Let's consider them in turn.

Exposure

What do I stand to lose? Generally speaking, the exposure is the maximum amount of damage that will be suffered if some event occurs. All other things being equal, the risk associated with that event will increase as the exposure increases. For example, a lender is exposed to the risk that a borrower will default. The more it lends to that borrower, the more exposed it is and the riskier its position with respect to that borrower. Exposure measurement is a hard science for some kinds of exposures—typically those that result in direct financial loss such as credit and market risk—but may be much more qualitative for others, such as reputational risk.

Volatility

How uncertain is the future? Volatility, loosely meaning the variability of potential outcomes, is a good proxy for risk in many applications. This is particularly true for those that are predominantly dependent on market factors, such as options pricing. Volatility also has broader applications for different types of risk.

Generally, the greater the volatility, the higher the risk. For example, the number of loans that turn bad is proportionately higher, on average, in the credit card business than in commercial real estate. Nonetheless, it is real estate lending that is widely considered to be riskier, because the loss rate is much more volatile. Companies can be much more certain about potential losses in the credit card business—and prepare for them better—than they can in the commercial real estate business.

Like exposure, volatility has a specific, quantifiable meaning in some areas of risk. In market risk, for example, it is synonymous with the standard deviation of returns and can be estimated in a number of ways. However, the general concept of uncertain outcomes also is useful in considering other types of risk: a spike in energy prices might increase a company's input prices, for example, or an increase in the turnover rate of computer programmers might negatively affect a company's technology initiatives.

Probability

How likely is it that some risky event will actually occur? The more likely the event is to occur—in other words, the higher the probability—the greater the risk. Certain events, such as interest rate movements or credit card defaults, are so likely that managers need to plan for them as a matter of course, and mitigation strategies should be an integral part of the business's regular operations. Others, such as a fire at a computer center, are highly improbable, but can have a devastating impact. A fitting preparation for these is the development of backup facilities and contingency plans that will likely be used infrequently, if ever, but must work effectively if they are.

Severity

How bad might it get? Whereas exposure is typically defined in terms of the worst that could *possibly* happen, severity is the amount of damage that is actually *likely* to be suffered. The greater the severity, the higher the risk. Severity is the partner to probability: if we know how likely an event is to happen, and how much we are likely to suffer as a consequence, we have a pretty good idea of the risk we are running.

Severity will often be a function of other risk factors, such as volatility. For example, consider a $100 equity position. The exposure is $100, since the stock price could theoretically drop all the way to zero and all the money tied up in the stock could be lost. In reality, however, it is not likely to fall that far, so the severity is less than $100. The more volatile the stock, the more likely it is to fall a long way. The severity associated with this position is therefore greater, and the position more risky.

As with our other risk factors, this way of thinking also can be applied to risks that are less easy to quantify. Consider, for example, the succession process after a key employee leaves or retires. Given that a change in management must occur at some point in time, and that the succession of new management will generally have a significant and potentially disruptive impact on the organization, it is alarming that companies don't plan more carefully for this risk.

Time Horizon

How long will I be exposed to the risk? The longer the duration of an exposure, the higher the risk. For example, extending a 10-year loan to the same borrower has a much greater probability of default than a 1-year loan. The time horizon also can be thought of as a measure of how long it takes (or, equivalently, how difficult it is) to reverse the effects of a decision or event.

The key issue for financial risk exposures is the liquidity of the positions affected by the decision or event. Positions in highly liquid instruments such as U.S. Treasury bonds can usually be reduced or eliminated in a short period of time, while positions in lightly traded securities or commodities such as unlisted equities, structured derivatives, or real estate take much longer to sell down. For operational risk exposures, the time horizon can be thought of as the time required for the company to *recover* from an event. A fire that burns a computer center to the ground will leave a company exposed during the time before backup facilities come online—a much greater risk if such backup procedures are not well tested.

Companies usually have little control over the level of market liquidity, or over many of the events that lead to operational risks. However, they do have some control over their effects. Problems arise when companies do not recognize that a risk event has occurred, are not aware of the time horizon associated with that risk, and/or have not developed a contingency plan.

Correlation

How are the risks in my business related to each other? If two risks behave similarly—they increase for the same reasons, for example, or by the same amount—they are considered highly correlated. The greater the correlation, the higher the risk. Correlation is a key concept in risk diversification. Highly correlated risk exposures, such as loans to the same industry, investments in the same asset class, or operations within the same building, increase the level of risk concentrations within a business. Thus, the degree of risk diversification in a business is inversely related to the level of correlations within that business. With financial risks, diversification can be achieved through risk limits and portfolio allocation targets, both of which are designed to reduce risk concentrations. With operational risk, diversification can be achieved through separation of operational units or redundant systems.

Capital

How much capital should I set aside to cover unexpected losses? Companies hold capital for two primary reasons. The first is to meet cash requirements, such as the costs of investments and expenses. The second is to cover unexpected losses arising from risk exposures. The level of capital that management wants to set aside for risk is often called *economic capital*.

The overall level of economic capital required by a company will depend on the institution's target financial strength (e.g., target credit rating). The more creditworthy the company wants to be, the more capital it will have to hold against a given level of risk. This is fairly intuitive: a credit rating (or the concept of creditworthiness in general) is an estimate of how likely a company is to fail. Clearly, it is less likely to fail if it has more capital to absorb any unexpected loss. So a company that wants a triple-A credit rating will have to hold far more capital against a certain set of risks than another company that has the same risks but is satisfied with a subinvestment-grade rating, such as double-B.

The concept of economic capital also applies to the individual business units *within* a company. Those business units that run greater risks (and therefore stand more chance of losing money) will have to be allocated more economic capital if they are to comply with the firm's overall target creditworthiness. The allocation of economic capital to business units has two important business benefits.

First, it links risk and return explicitly. Higher allocations of economic capital require business units that take more risks to compensate by generating greater profits. Second, economic capital allows the profitability of all business units to be compared on a consistent risk-adjusted basis. As a result, business activities that contribute to, or detract from, shareholder value can be identified easily, and so management has a powerful and objective tool to allocate economic capital to its most efficient users. In effect, this creates an "internal capital market" where good businesses will grow and bad businesses will die.

RISK PROCESSES

An appreciation of the risk concepts described above is the first step in a clearer understanding of risk. This understanding in turn supports the first step in any risk management process: risk awareness. The second step is to measure risk; the third, to control it. For all the quantitative sophistication that can be thrown at it, risk management is still ultimately carried out by people, and the three parts of a corporate risk management process can usefully be illustrated in terms of the ways that people manage risks in their everyday lives.

First, risk awareness. Most people think (at least a little!) about what they are currently doing and what they plan to do next; accidents happen when they misjudge an unfamiliar situation or fail to pay sufficient attention to a seemingly familiar one. People break legs when they first go skiing and cut their fingers when they drift off while chopping vegetables.

Companies obviously don't think in this way, but they do need to use the collective intelligence of their management and staff to think through the risks consequent upon the company's current and proposed activities. (Once again, we return to the need to anticipate and learn from mistakes). Promoting risk awareness should be the starting point for any risk management process. Half the battle is already won if people can be successfully encouraged to consider the risks involved in their activities, and to understand their roles and responsibilities in managing them. Mistakes can then be avoided or quickly corrected.

Awareness alone is not enough, however. It is one thing to know that a potential risk exists; it is another to know when it becomes a real threat and how serious it is. A person might see a distant threat (a car bearing down from a distance), or feel an immediate one (a tack in the foot). The scale and speed of his reaction will differ.

Similarly, a company must be able to recognize changes in its operating environment that signal potential risks and must also notice when a part of the company is unexpectedly afflicted by some event. That means effective transmission of information into and through the company, which in turn implies the need for efficient communications technology and clear, consistent reporting of risks (i.e., risk measurement).

Having identified and quantified the risk, a person must decide if anything should be done about it (i.e., risk control). A person might control his risks in a number of different ways. He might feel that a given risk is minor (the chance of being hit by a meteorite, for example) and continue about his business as usual. He might simply limit his potential risk—perhaps by capping the amount he is willing to bet on a spin of the roulette wheel. Alternatively, he might actually take action in order to reduce a risk—to move out of the way of an oncoming car or pull the tack out of his foot. He might even pay someone more skilled to carry out a risky activity—electrical rewiring, for example—on his behalf.

Similarly, a company might recognize a potential risk but be content to do nothing about it; establish and enforce risk policies and limits; change strategic direction; make a tactical alteration to one of its business units; or transfer a specific risk through insurance or hedging.

Ultimately, the function of risk management, whether for an individual or for a company, is to ensure that the level of risk remains within some acceptable range, while ensuring that life or business continues to be as enjoyable as possible. It's worth noting that different people have different appetites for risk—they are comfortable with different amounts of risk and with different types of risk. So are different companies, credit ratings and earnings volatility being key measures of these propensities.

It's also worth noting that people don't really think about a risk, then assess it and finally do something about it. In practice, people constantly reevaluate their situation in a way that involves continuous feedback between thoughts, senses, and actions. The same should be true for any company operating in the real world. A risk management process can only be effective to the extent that risk awareness, risk measurement, and risk control strategies are fully integrated. We'll discuss these three components in the next sections.

RISK AWARENESS

Risk awareness is the starting point of any risk management process. The objective of promoting risk awareness is to ensure that everyone within a business is:

- Proactively identifying the key risks for the company.
- Seriously thinking about the consequences of the risks for which he or she is responsible.
- Communicating up and down the organization those risks that warrant others' attention.

In a risk-aware environment, most risk management issues should be addressed before they become bigger problems.

There are many organizational processes and initiatives that can promote risk awareness within a company. Five of the most successful are to set the tone from the top; ask the right questions; establish a risk taxonomy; provide training and education; and link compensation to risk. Let's consider these in turn.

Set the Tone from the Top

In risk management, even more than other corporate initiatives, the involvement of senior management, and of the chief executive officer (CEO) in particular, is critical to success. The reason? Some aspects of risk management run counter to human nature. Although people are eager to talk about marketing or product successes, or even cost-saving opportunities, they are generally much less enthusiastic about discussing actual or potential losses, particularly those related to their businesses.

Overcoming this reluctance requires applied authority and power. The CEO must therefore be fully supportive of the risk management process, and "set the tone" not only through words, but also through actions. The CEO must first communicate that risk management is a top priority for the company at presentations, meetings, and in other forums. More importantly, the CEO must demonstrate his or her commitment through actions. Does the CEO actively participate in risk management meetings? Has the company allocated an appropriate budget to support risk management? Are senior risk executives involved in major corporate decisions? What happens when a top producer violates risk management policies? How the CEO and senior management respond to these questions will speak volumes on their true commitment to the risk management process.

Ask the Right Questions

It has been said that senior management may not always have the right answers, but it is their obligation to ask the right questions. So what are the key questions senior management should ask about risk? The acronym *RISK*—for *R*eturn, *I*mmunization, *S*ystems, and *K*nowledge—can help:

- *Return.* Are we achieving an acceptable return on the risks we take? What kinds of risk exposures are being created if a business unit is growing or making money at an exceptional rate?
- *Immunization.* What limits and controls do we have in place to minimize the downside?
- *Systems.* Do we have the appropriate systems to track and measure risks?
- *Knowledge.* Do we have the right people and skills for effective risk management?

Establish a Risk Taxonomy

We saw in the last section how efficient communication is a key requirement for the risk management process. One of the ways in which communication can be made efficient is by ensuring that people understand what each other mean—something that is not a given in the world of risk, where definitions are frequently poorly understood, open to interpretation, or extremely broad. That is, a company should strive to establish a common language for risk.

One important part of this effort should be to establish a taxonomy of risk—a common structure for describing the categories and subcategories of risks, as well as the tools, metrics, and strategies for risk management. A taxonomy is not only useful in talking about risks, but allows them to be both broken down into manageable components that can then be aggregated for exposure measurement and reporting purposes. This is not a one-off process; it should be iterative and reflect the dynamic and changing nature of the business.

Provide Training and Development

Executives involved in establishing risk management programs often cite training and development as one of their major accomplishments. In addition to promoting risk awareness, training and development equip employees with the skills and tools they need to manage the risks for which they are responsible.

Risk education should start at orientation, with new employees being introduced to risk management concepts and briefed on the various risk functions within the company just as they are introduced to its other management philosophies and operational functions. It should also include ongoing training programs that are tailored to the skills required for the individual's job responsibilities. These should tie the individual's responsibilities to the risk management policies of the company—and to the thinking behind them. To put it another way, employees should understand the spirit as well as the letter of the law.

Link Risk and Compensation

People naturally pay the most attention to what their job accountabilities are and how their financial incentives are tied to their performance. Clearly, risk awareness can be most powerfully cultivated by making sure that employees understand that risk management is part of their job, and that their incentive compensation is linked to the business and risk performance at both the business and individual levels. It is important that these facts should be seen to be true for *all* employees. If there is a perception that the same ground rules don't apply to all employees (particularly senior ones), others will soon stop paying attention or see the rules as something that can be circumvented in the pursuit of a career.

RISK MEASUREMENT

The axiom that you can't manage what you can't measure is largely true in risk management. Unfortunately risk measurement and reporting remain a major challenge for many companies today. Most struggle with the constraints associated with data, analytics, and systems resources. Frequently, there is no good historical data on losses and other risk metrics, and an unfulfilled need to establish the internal discipline to report and capture important risk information. At the other extreme, some companies drown their senior managers in data, much of it irrelevant and impenetrable.

Whether or not a company has too much or too little risk data and reports, senior management and the board need appropriate risk information to support business and policy decisions. What should be included in an executive risk report? That partly depends on the nature of the business. However, there are certain key elements that should be a part of any executive risk report—losses, incidents, management assessments, and risk indicators. Let's consider these in turn.

Losses

Losses arising from credit, market, and operational risks should be systematically captured in a loss database and summarized in the risk report. Although the loss database should account for losses at a detailed level, only overall levels of loss, and important trends, should be reported to senior management. The risk report should highlight specific losses above a threshold and total losses relative to revenue or volume. Businesses should also track actual losses against expected or budgeted levels.

Incidents

The risk report should report the major risk incidents for the period, regardless of whether these result in a financial loss or not. Risk incidents might include loss of a major customer account, policy violations, systems failures, frauds, lawsuits and so on. The potential impact, root causes, and business response to the major incidents should be reported. Any emerging trends or significant patterns in incidents also should be highlighted.

Management Assessments

While losses and incidents reflect risk performance after the fact, the risk report should also provide management's advance assessment of potential risks. The risk concepts discussed earlier should underpin this assessment. This portion of the risk report should address questions such as: What keeps you up at night? What are your top 10 risks? What uncertainties might prevent the achievement of business objectives? These are different questions that should lead management to the same answers. Key risks might include new business or product launches, the absence of key staff, new technologies, and more.

Risk Indicators

The risk report also should include a section on the risk indicators that quantify major trends and risk exposures for the business. For example, these indicators might include credit exposures compared with credit limits in lending, or mark-to-market profit and loss as well as value-at-risk for trading businesses. Operational risk indicators might include processing errors, customer complaints, systems availability, and unreconciled items. Risk/return metrics might include return on economic capital for businesses or the Shape ratio for investment portfolios.

It is important that the risk indicators include forward-looking measures that serve as "early warning signals." For example, widening credit spreads are usually an early warning of higher default rates and decreasing market liquidity. Higher employee turnover may be a leading indicator of increasing operational risks, such as higher error rates and lower customer satisfaction. Such early warning indicators allow management to take preemptive action to mitigate potential risks. Although businesses may track dozens or hundreds of risk indicators, they should report only the few that warrant senior management attention.

The prototype report in Figure 3.1 shows the key elements that should be included in a risk report. In addition, it contains a self-correcting feature that should be a design requirement. That feature works as follows: losses and incidents are items that can be captured easily on a regular basis. Over time, however, management may notice that losses and incidents originate from risks that are not qualitatively discussed in the management assessment or quantitatively tracked in the risk indicators. It then has at least one of two problems that need to be addressed. Either the business or operational unit needs to refocus its risk measurement efforts, or they are not escalating important risk issues to corporate management. Such a self-correcting feature should improve the quality and candor of risk measurement and reporting on continuous basis.

RISK CONTROL

The risk management process does not stop at promoting risk awareness or measuring risk exposures. The ultimate objective is to optimize the risk/return of the business; or, to put it slightly differently, to effect real change in the risk profile of the company. There are three fundamental ways in which this can be done. The first is to support selective growth of the business; the second, to support profitability; the third, to control downside risks.

Selective Growth of the Business

Risk management has a role to play as part of a cross-functional team that supports business growth. The risk team should work with line management, marketing, legal, operations, and technology representatives to establish and maintain a review process for vetting new business strategies[1] and ideas. This review process brings the right people together to discuss key issues at an early stage.

The review team should develop fair and objective criteria against which businesses and products will be evaluated, both at their outset and on an ongoing basis. This is not dissimilar to the way that many organizations handle individual risks. Banks, for example, compose lists of acceptable

---

[1]In this context, new business includes mergers and acquisitions.

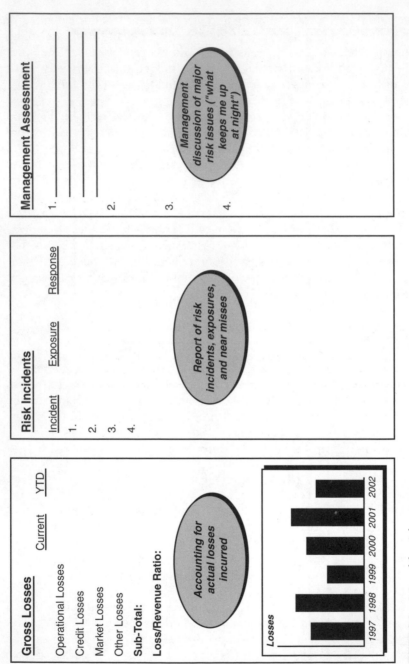

FIGURE 3.1 Monthly risk report.

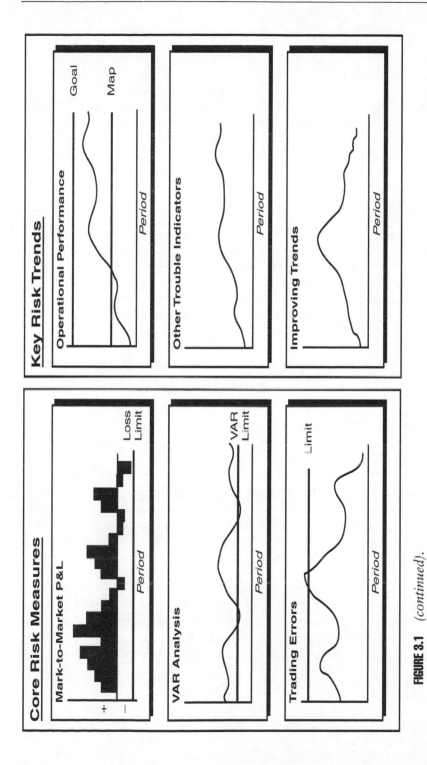

FIGURE 3.1 *(continued)*.

counterparties to speed up the approval process when a credit-sensitive transaction is proposed, and review outstanding transactions if the counterparty's status changes in well-defined ways, such as a decline in credit rating.

A key lever by which management can optimize risk/return is by allocating corporate resources to business activities with the highest risk-adjusted returns, subject to the risk limits discussed below. A risk/return matrix (as shown in Figure 3.2) can be a powerful strategic planning tool. This matrix shows the level of risk, expressed in economic capital and the return on that capital, for each business unit and risk type, and can be used to determine:

- Which business units are meeting or beating their hurdle rates of return on equity and thus contributing to shareholder value, and which business units are not?
- Are the credit, market, and operational risk levels at the businesses consistent with our expectations for their business plans?
- Do we have the right people and systems in place to manage these risk levels, both at corporate management and within the business units?
- How should we reallocate corporate resources in order to optimize risk/return and maximize shareholder value?

Support Profitability

Risk management can improve the control of business profitability, as well as growth, by influencing pricing decisions. Put simply, the idea is that the price for any product or transaction should reflect the cost of its underlying risks as well as more traditional costs. The cost of risk would obviously be higher for riskier transactions.

For example, the pricing on a loan should include the expected annual loss and the cost of capital[2] reserved against the loan, as well as funding and operational costs. In practice, commercial loans are often not fully priced, since banks frequently use lending to cement a customer relationship, not to generate profits as a standalone product. Risk-adjusted pricing can't change that fact of business life, but it does ensure that the bank knows how much it should be making from the customer overall to make up for the low-margin loan. Risk-adjusted pricing has been applied throughout the financial services industry. Nonfinancial corporations have been slower to adopt it, but

---

[2]See Chapter 9 for a more detailed discussion on expected loss, unexpected loss, and economic capital.

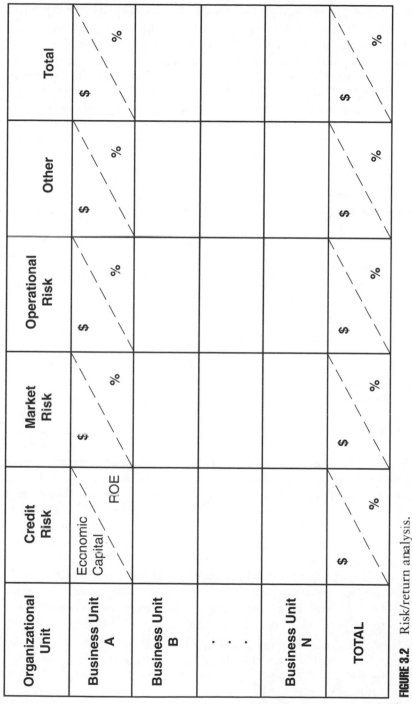

Organizational Unit	Credit Risk	Market Risk	Operational Risk	Other	Total
Business Unit A	Economic Capital / ROE	$	$	$	$ %
Business Unit B					
. . .					
Business Unit N					
TOTAL	$ %	$ %	$ %	$ %	$ %

FIGURE 3.2 Risk/return analysis.

also can benefit. Net present value (NPV) or economic value added (EVA) techniques for evaluating new investments and business performance do not usually incorporate the full cost of risk. This is because these tools are usually based on book capital, which typically doesn't fully capture expected loss, much less unexpected loss, and thus does not correspond to economic capital. The upshot is that NPV and EVA models are not sensitive to the underlying risks of the business. As such, they tend to overstate the profitability of high-risk businesses, and understate the profitability of low-risk ones. Adjustments to incorporate the full cost of risk, or the use of economic capital instead of book capital, should greatly enhance the usefulness of these models.

Control Downside Risks

While risk management supports business growth and profitability, its mandate is to control downside risks. It is important to remember that downside risks, including losses and failures, are an integral part of doing business.

A drug company faces the risk of a significant loss in research and marketing costs every time it introduces a new drug. A bank faces the risk of default with every loan. Any company developing a product or system faces the risk of cost overruns, schedule delays, and eventual underperformance.

The point here is that business is all about taking risks, and that risk management should not seek to eliminate downside risks, but to control them within an acceptable range. The acceptable range, as suggested earlier, will reflect the company's risk appetite, which is in turn determined by the human, financial, and technology resources available to manage the business and its associated risks. The risk appetite can be expressed in terms of the amount and likelihood of actual and potential loss; these are in turn controlled through stop-loss and sensitivity limits respectively.

Stop-loss limits control the amount of losses an institution can incur due to its risk positions. While stop-loss limits have been widely adopted in controlling market risk for trading houses, the same concept can be extended to other types of risk. For example, a stop-loss limit can be established for credit risk with actual credit losses being measured by the combination of charge-offs (i.e., realized losses) and "mark-to-market" losses based on credit spreads[3] (i.e., unrealized losses). For operational risks, management can control downside risk by setting limits on indicators such as error rates,

---

[3]For example, a loan or security that is downgraded (widening in credit spread) would incur a mark-to-market loss even though no defaults or charge-offs have occurred. Marking the credit portfolio to market using credit spreads provides an economic assessment of credit losses.

systems downtime, and outstanding audit items.

When actual loss or performance hit one of these limits, it should trigger some management decision or action, including management reviews, hedging strategies, contingency plans, or exit strategies. Some companies even establish "warning" limits below the stop-loss limits, acting like the yellow signal before the red at the traffic light.

Sensitivity limits ensure that potential economic losses do not exceed management's threshold levels. Sensitivity limits control the amount of capital an institution has at risk given various adverse economic scenarios and its risk positions. These sensitivity limits can be developed by taking extreme values of risk factors such as market volatility or by repeatedly simulating the evolution of the business and the environment over time.

The key use of sensitivity limits is in avoiding excessive concentrations of risk. If a risk position exceeds the sensitivity limit, management will know that the potential loss in that business may be greater than what they want to accept and they may cut back or otherwise mitigate that risk accordingly. The concepts of stop-loss and sensitivity limits are generally applied in market and credit risk management, but are closely analogous to the total quality management techniques used for operational risk management. Companies such as General Electric and AlliedSignal track actual and potential error rates against a "six-sigma" standard, and corrective actions are taken if performance falls below that threshold.

In addition to stop-loss and sensitivity limits, basic exposure limits (total credit exposure to emerging markets, say, or market exposure to technology stocks) can be established to control downside risks. However, setting risk limits is only part of the risk control process. If they are to be useful, information about limits (and particularly about violations of limits) must be reported efficiently to management, who must then act on this information decisively whenever necessary.

The appropriate frequency of reporting depends on both the nature of the business and on the audience. Companies trading in global capital markets or managing multi-site phone centers, for example, might need real-time risk monitoring for the business managers. Companies operating in less volatile conditions might need daily or weekly reporting. A monthly or quarterly interval should be appropriate for limit reports that go to senior management and the board.

Capital allocation, risk-adjusted pricing, and limit setting are three ex ante ways of controlling how much risk a company takes on. However, this is at best half the story: there are other techniques available for managing the risks that have already been taken on. One part of such management is to understand what those risks actually are, which implies a focus on better risk analysis and on the data and technology needed to perform and report on such analysis.

Another is to understand which risks offset or exacerbate each other. Duration matching is a common risk management technique under which a financial institution matches the interest rate sensitivities of its assets and liabilities to make sure that their values change in the same way when interest rates change. Active portfolio management, which grew increasingly popular at financial institutions in the 1990s, is another technique that seeks to establish if a new risk will disproportionately increase or decrease the overall risk of a portfolio.

These internal management techniques are usually preferred because they are typically longer term and more cost effective than transferring risk to an external party. However, they take time to implement and can only alter a company's risk profile up to a point. When time, resources, or flexibility are scarce, risk transfer, through either derivatives or insurance, can provide timely and effective solutions.

All of these techniques can be applied to single risks. However, their true power emerges when they are used to manage a collection of risks in an integrated manner. We'll see why that should be true in the next chapter.

The Enterprise Risk Management Framework

CHAPTER 4

What Is Enterprise Risk Management?

In the last chapter, we reviewed the concepts and processes applicable to all of the risks that a company will face. Certainly, it is a prerequisite that a company develop an effective process for each of its significant risks. But it is not enough to build a separate process for each risk in isolation.

Risks are by their very nature dynamic, fluid, and highly interdependent. As such, they cannot be broken into separate components and managed independently. Enterprises operating in today's volatile environment require a much more integrated approach to managing their portfolio of risks.

This has not always been recognized. Traditionally, companies managed risk in organizational "silos." Market, credit, and operational risks were treated separately and often addressed by different individuals within an institution. For example, credit experts evaluated the risk of default, mortgage specialists analyzed prepayment risk, traders were responsible for market risks, and actuaries handled liability, mortality, and other insurance risks. Corporate functions such as finance and audit handled other operational risks, and senior managers addressed business risks.

However, it has become increasingly apparent that such a fragmented approach simply doesn't work, because risks are highly interdependent and cannot be segmented and managed by entirely independent units. The risks associated with most businesses are not one-to-one matches for the "primary risks" (market, credit, operational, and insurance) implied by most traditional organizational structures. Attempting to manage them as if they are is likely to prove inefficient and potentially dangerous. Risks can "fall through the cracks," risk interdependencies and portfolio effects are not captured, and organizational gaps and redundancies result in suboptimal performance. For example, imagine that a company is about to launch a new product or business in a foreign country. Such an initiative would require:

- The business unit to establish the right pricing and market entry strategies.
- The treasury function to provide funding and protection against interest rate and foreign exchange (FX) risks.
- The information technology (IT) and operations function to support the new business.
- The legal and insurance functions to address regulatory and liability issues.

It is not difficult to see how an integrated approach could more effectively manage these risks. An enterprise risk management function would be responsible for direct management of certain risks, coordinate risk management activities for whichever other functions are ultimately responsible, and provide overall risk monitoring for senior management.

Nor is risk monitoring any more efficient under the silo approach. The problem is that individual risk functions measure and report their specific risks in different methodologies and formats. For example, the treasury function might report on interest rate and FX risk exposures, and use value-at-risk as its core risk measurement methodology. The credit function would report delinquencies and outstanding credit exposures, and measure such exposures in terms of outstanding balances. The audit function would report outstanding audit items and assign some sort of audit score. And so on.

Senior management and the board get pieces of the puzzle, but not the whole picture. In many companies, the risk functions produce literally hundreds of pages of risk reports month after month. Yet they still don't provide management and the board with useful risk information. A good acid test is to ask if the senior management knows the answers to the following basic questions:

- What are the company's top 10 risks?
- Do we have a concise report that shows the key exposures and trends for credit, market, and operational risks?
- Are we in compliance with internal policies, laws, and regulations?
- Were the majority of the company's actual losses and incidents identified by the risk reports?
- Are we managing businesses on a risk-adjusted profitability basis?

If a company is uncertain about the answers to any of these questions, then it is likely to benefit from a more integrated approach to handling all aspects of risk—enterprise risk management (ERM).[1] I would define ERM as fol-

---

[1]Other popular terms used to describe enterprise risk management include firm-wide risk management, global risk management, integrated risk management, and holistic risk management.

lows: A comprehensive and integrated framework for managing credit risk, market risk, operational risk, economic capital, and risk transfer in order to maximize firm value.

THE BENEFITS OF ERM

ERM is all about integration, in three ways. First, enterprise risk management requires an integrated risk organization. This most often means a centralized risk management unit reporting to the chief executive officer (CEO) and the board, with responsibility for broad policy setting across risk-taking activities. A growing number of companies now have a chief risk officer (CRO) who is responsible for overseeing all aspects of risk within the organization. We'll consider this development later.

Second, enterprise risk management requires the integration of risk transfer strategies. Under the silo approach, risk transfer strategies were executed at a transaction or individual risk level. For example, financial derivatives were used to hedge market risk and insurance to transfer out operational risk. However, this approach doesn't incorporate diversification within or across the risk types in a portfolio and thus tends to result in overhedging and excessive insurance coverage. An ERM approach, by contrast, takes a portfolio view of all types of risk within a company and rationalizes the use of derivatives, insurance, and alternative risk transfer products to hedge only the residual risk deemed undesirable by management.

Third, enterprise risk management requires the integration of risk management into the business processes of a company. Rather than the defensive or control-oriented approaches used to manage downside risk and earnings volatility, enterprise risk management optimizes business performance by supporting and influencing pricing, resource allocation, and other business decisions. It is during this stage that risk management becomes an offensive weapon for management.

All this integration is not easy. For most companies, the implementation of ERM implies a multiyear initiative that requires ongoing senior management sponsorship and sustained investments in human and technology resources. Ironically, the amount of time and resources dedicated to risk management may not be substantially different between leading and lagging organizations.

The difference is this: leading organizations make rational investments in risk management and are proactive, optimizing their risk profiles. Lagging organizations, on the other hand, make disconnected investments and are reactive, fighting one crisis after another. For the leading companies, their investments in risk management are more than offset by improved efficiency and reduced losses. There are three major benefits to ERM: increased organizational effectiveness, better risk reporting, and improved business performance.

Organizational Effectiveness

Most companies already have risk management and corporate oversight functions, such as finance/insurance, audit, and compliance. In addition, there may be specialist risk units; for example, investment banks usually have market risk management units, while energy companies have commodity risk managers.

The appointment of a CRO and the establishment of an enterprise risk function provide the top-down coordination necessary to make these various functions work efficiently. An integrated team can better address not only the individual risks facing the company, but also the interdependencies between these risks.

Risk Reporting

As previously noted, one of the key requirements of risk management is that it should produce timely and relevant risk reporting for the senior management and board of directors. As we also noted, however, this is frequently not the case. In a silo framework, either no one takes responsibility for overall risk reporting, or every risk-related unit supplies inconsistent and sometimes contradictory reports.

An enterprise risk function can prioritize the level and content of risk reporting that should go to senior management and the board: an enterprise-wide perspective on aggregate losses, policy exceptions, risk incidents, key exposures, and early warning indicators. This might take the form of a "risk dashboard" that includes timely and concise information on the company's key risks. And this goes beyond the senior management level; the objective of ERM reporting is by its nature to increase risk transparency throughout an organization.

Business Performance

Companies that adopt an ERM approach have experienced significant improvements in business performance. Figure 4.1 provides examples of reported benefits from a cross-section of companies (albeit mostly financial institutions given their early start). While the benefits experienced by individual companies will differ, a strong indication of realized benefits is that nearly every ERM program that has been launched has received continued support from their management. ERM supports key management decisions such as capital allocation, product development and pricing, and mergers and acquisitions. This leads to improvements such as reduced losses, lower earnings volatility, increased earnings, and improved shareholder value.

These improvements result from taking a portfolio view of all risks; managing the linkages between risk, capital, and profitability; and rational-

Benefit	Company	Actual Results
Market value improvement	Top money center bank	Outperformed S&P 500 banks by 58% in stock price performance
Early warning of risks	Large commercial bank	Assessment of top risks identified over 80% of future losses; global risk limits cut by one-third prior to Russian crisis
Loss reduction	Top asset management company	30% reduction in the loss ratio enterprise-wide; up to 80% reduction in losses at specific business units
Regulatory capital relief	Large international commercial and investment bank	$1 billion reduction of regulatory capital requirements, or about 8–10%
Risk transfer rationalization	Large P&C insurance company	$40 million in cost savings, or 13% of annual reinsurance premium
Insurance premium reduction	Large manufacturing company	20–25% reduction in annual insurance premium

FIGURE 4.1 Benefits of ERM.

izing the company's risk transfer strategies. The result is not just outright risk reduction: companies that understand the true risk/return economics of a business can take more of the profitable risks that make sense for the company and less of the ones that don't. We'll go into more detail on how these improvements are achieved in subsequent chapters.

Despite all these benefits, many companies would balk at the prospect of a full-blown ERM initiative were it not for pressures both internal and external. In the business world, managers are often galvanized into action after a near miss—either a disaster averted within their own organization or an actual crisis at a similar organization.

In response, the board and senior management are likely to question the effectiveness of the control environment and the adequacy of risk reporting within their company. To put it another way, they are questioning how well they really know the organization's major risk exposures.

Such incidents are also often followed by critical assessments from auditors and regulators, both groups constitutionally concerned with the effectiveness of risk management. Consequently, regulators are focusing on all aspects of risk during examinations, setting risk-based capital and compliance requirements, and reinforcing key roles for the board and senior management in the risk management process.

This introspection often leads to the emergence of a "risk champion" among the senior executives who will sponsor a major program to establish an enterprise risk management approach. As noted above, this "risk champion" is increasingly becoming a formalized senior management position: the CRO.

Aside from this, direct pressure also comes from influential stakeholders such as shareholders, employees, ratings agencies, and analysts. Not only do such stakeholders expect more earnings predictability, but management has fewer excuses today for not providing it. Over the past few years, volatility-based models such as value-at-risk and return on risk-adjusted capital have been applied to measure all types of market risk within an organization; their use is now spreading to credit risk and even to operational risk. The increasing availability and liquidity of "alternative" risk transfer products such as credit derivatives and catastrophe bonds also means companies are no longer stuck with many of the unpalatable risks they previously had no choice but to hold. Overall, the availability of such tools makes it more difficult and less acceptable for companies to carry on with more primitive and inefficient alternatives. Managing risk is management's job.

THE CHIEF RISK OFFICER

The role of a CRO has received a lot of attention within the risk management community, as well as from finance and general management audiences. Articles on CROs and ERM appear frequently in trade publications such as *Risk Magazine* and *Risk and Insurance,* but have also been covered in general publications such as *CFO* magazine, the *Wall Street Journal,* and even *USA Today.*

Before I discuss the role of the CRO, let me share with you how I came up with that title. In August 1993, Rick Price hired me to help him set up a new capital markets business within the Financial Guaranty Insurance Group at GE Capital. My job was to manage all aspects of risk, and I had direct management responsibilities for all functions outside of sales and trading, which included market and credit risk management, back-office operations, and business and financial planning.

Since this was a new business, Rick didn't have a title in mind for me and asked me to come up with an appropriate one. Around this time, GE and many other companies were appointing chief information officers (CIOs) whose jobs were to integrate IT resources and elevate the role of technology in the business. Today's CIOs are usually responsible for developing and implementing integrated technology strategies that include mainframes, personal computers, networks, and the Internet.

The CIO trend and my newly integrated responsibilities for market, credit, and operational risks gave me the idea for the role and title of "chief risk officer." The CRO would be responsible for developing and implementing an ERM strategy including all aspects of risk. I used the CRO title at GE Capital and subsequently at Fidelity Investments.

Today, the role of the CRO has been widely adopted in risk-intensive businesses such as financial institutions, energy firms, and nonfinancial corporations with significant investment activities or foreign operations. Today, I would estimate that there are more than 300 CROs[2] at financial institutions, energy firms, and nonfinancial corporations.

In many instances, the CRO reports to the CEO or chief financial officer (CFO); some CROs have a direct reporting line to the board of directors. Typical reports to the CRO are the heads of credit risk, market risk, operational risk, insurance, and portfolio management. The CRO is commonly also responsible for risk policy, capital management, risk analytics and reporting, and the heads of risk management at the business units. In general, the office of the CRO is directly responsible for:

- Providing the overall leadership, vision, and direction for enterprise risk management.
- Establishing an integrated risk management framework for all aspects of risks across the organization.

---

[2]Some people in a CRO role use other titles, such as head of ERM, principal risk officer, and executive vice-president of risk management. Nonetheless, these individuals are responsible for multiple risk functions and so fit the bill.

- Developing risk management policies, including the quantification of management's risk appetite through specific risk limits.
- Implementing a set of risk indicators and reports, including losses and incidents, key risk exposures, and early warning indicators.
- Allocating economic capital to business activities based on risk, and optimizing the company's risk portfolio through business activities and risk transfer strategies.
- Communicating the company's risk profile to key stakeholders such as the board of directors, regulators, stock analysts, rating agencies, and business partners.
- Developing the analytical, systems, and data management capabilities to support the risk management program.

I believe the role of the CRO has elevated the risk management profession in some important ways. First and foremost, the appointment of executive managers whose primary focus is risk management has improved the visibility and organizational effectiveness of that function at many companies. The successes of these appointments have only increased the recognition and acceptance for the CRO position.

Second, the CRO position provides an attractive career path for risk professionals who want to take a broader view of risk and business management. In the past, risk professionals could only aspire to becoming the head of a narrowly focused risk function such as credit or audit. Nearly 70 percent of the 175 participants in an ERisk online seminar that I gave on September 13, 2000, said they aspired to become CROs.

Finally, the value that companies attribute to CROs is reflected in the escalating salaries observed in the marketplace. Based on my discussions with CROs and executive recruiters, the high-end compensation packages for CROs have increased from the low to middle six figures in the beginning of the 1990s to over seven figures by the end of the decade. Today, those reporting to the CRO are sometimes commanding seven-figure packages.

Some argue that a company shouldn't have a CRO because risk management is ultimately the responsibility of the CEO or CFO. Supporting this argument is the fact that the CEO is always going to be ultimately responsible for the risk (and return) performance of the company, and that many risk departments are part of the CFO's organization. So why create another "C"-level position of CRO and detract from the CEO's or CFO's responsibilities?

The answer is the same reason that companies create roles for other C-level positions, such as CIOs or chief marketing officers. These roles are defined because they represent a core competency that is critical to the success for the company, and the CEO needs the experience and technical skills that these seasoned professionals bring. Perhaps not every company should have a full-time CRO, but the role should be an explicit one and not simply one implied for the CEO or CFO.

For companies operating in the financial or energy markets, or other industries where risk management represents a core competency, the CRO position should be given serious consideration. A CRO would also benefit companies in which the full breadth of risk management experience does not exist within the senior management team, or the build-up of required risk management infrastructure requires the full-time attention of an experienced risk professional.

What should a company look for in a CRO? An ideal CRO would have superb skills in five areas. The first would be the leadership skills to hire and retain talented risk professionals and establish the overall vision for ERM. The second would be the evangelical skills to convert skeptics into believers, particularly when it comes to overcoming natural resistance from the line units. Third would be the stewardship to safeguard the company's financial and reputational assets. Fourth would be to have the technical skills in credit, market, and operational risks. And fifth would be to have consulting skills in educating the board and senior management, as well as helping line managers implement risk management at their businesses. While it is unlikely that any single individual would possess all of these skills, it is important that these competencies exist either in the CRO or elsewhere within his or her organization.

COMPONENTS OF ERM

A successful ERM program can be broken down into seven key components (see Figure 4.2). Each of these components must be developed and linked to work as an integrated whole. The seven components include:

- Corporate governance to ensure that the board of directors and management have established the appropriate organizational processes and corporate controls to measure and manage risk across the company.
- Line management to integrate risk management into the revenue-generating activities of the company, including business development, product and relationship management, pricing, and so on.
- Portfolio management to aggregate risk exposures, incorporate diversification effects, and monitor risk concentrations against established risk limits.
- Risk transfer to mitigate risk exposures that are deemed too high, or are more cost-effective to transfer out to a third party than to hold in the company's risk portfolio.

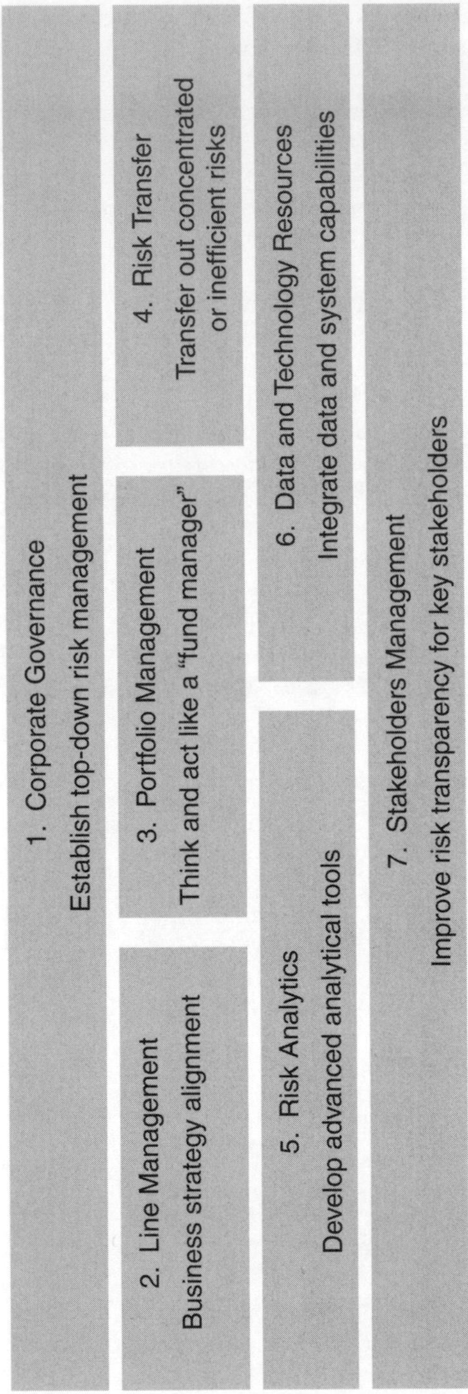

1. Corporate Governance
Establish top-down risk management

2. Line Management
Business strategy alignment

3. Portfolio Management
Think and act like a "fund manager"

4. Risk Transfer
Transfer out concentrated or inefficient risks

5. Risk Analytics
Develop advanced analytical tools

6. Data and Technology Resources
Integrate data and system capabilities

7. Stakeholders Management
Improve risk transparency for key stakeholders

FIGURE 4.2 ERM framework.

- Risk analytics to provide the risk measurement, analysis, and reporting tools to quantify the company's risk exposures as well as track external drivers.
- Data and technology resources to support the analytics and reporting processes.
- Stakeholder management to communicate and report the company's risk information to its key stakeholders.

Let's consider these in turn.

Corporate Governance

Corporate governance ensures that the board of directors and management have established the appropriate organizational processes and corporate controls to measure and manage risk across the company. The mandate for effective corporate governance has been brought to the forefront by regulatory and industry initiatives around the world. These initiatives include the Treadway Report from the United States, the Turnbull Report from the United Kingdom, and the Dey Report from Canada. All of these reports made recommendations for establishing corporate controls and emphasized the responsibilities of the board of directors and senior management. Additionally, the Sarbanes-Oxley Act provides both specific requirements and severe penalties for noncompliance with newly established governance and disclosure standards.

From an ERM perspective, the responsibilities for the board of directors and senior management include:

- Defining the organization's risk appetite in terms of risk policies, loss tolerance, risk-to-capital leverage, and target debt rating.
- Ensuring that the organization has the risk management skills and risk absorption capability to support its business strategy.
- Establishing the organizational structure and defining the roles and responsibilities for risk management, including the role of a CRO.
- Shaping the organization's risk culture by "setting the tone from the top"—not only through words, but through actions—and reinforcing that commitment through incentives.
- Providing appropriate opportunities for organizational learning, including lessons learned from previous problems and ongoing training and development.

Line Management

Perhaps the most important phase in the assessment and pricing of risk is at its inception. Line management must align business strategy with corporate risk policy when pursuing new business and growth opportunities. The risks of business transactions should be fully assessed and incorporated into pricing and profitability targets in the execution of business strategy.

Specifically, expected losses and the cost of risk capital should be included in the pricing of a loan or the required return of an investment project. In business development, risk acceptance criteria should be established to ensure that risk management issues are considered in new product and market opportunities. Transaction and business review processes should be developed to ensure the appropriate due diligence. Efficient and transparent review processes will allow line managers to develop a better understanding of those risks that they can accept independently and those that require corporate approval or management.

Portfolio Management

The overall risk portfolio of an organization should not "just happen"— that is, it should not just be the cumulative effect of business transactions conducted entirely independently. Rather, management should "act like a fund manager" and set portfolio targets and risk limits to ensure appropriate diversification and optimal portfolio returns.

The concept of active portfolio management can be applied to all the risks within an organization. Diversification effects from natural hedges can only be fully captured if an organization's risks are viewed as a portfolio. More importantly, the portfolio management function provides a direct link between risk management and shareholder value maximization.

For example, a key barrier for many insurance companies in implementing ERM is that each of the financial risks within the overall business portfolio is managed independently. The actuarial function is responsible for estimating liability risks arising for the company's insurance policies; the investment group invests the company's cash flows in fixed-income and equity investments. The interest rate risk function hedges mismatches between assets and liabilities. However, an insurance company that had implemented ERM would manage all of its liability, investment, interest rate, and other risks as an integrated whole in order to optimize overall risk/return.

Risk Transfer

Portfolio management objectives are supported by risk transfer strategies that lower the cost of transferring out undesirable risks, as well as increasing the organization's capacity to originate desirable but concentrated risks. To reduce undesirable risks, management should evaluate derivatives, insurance, and hybrid products on a consistent basis and select the most cost-effective alternative. For example, corporations such as Honeywell and Mead have used alternative risk transfer (ART) products that combine traditional insurance protection with financial risk protection. By bundling various risks, risk managers have achieved estimated savings of 20 to 30 percent in the cost of risk transfer.

A company can dramatically reduce its hedging and insurance costs even without third-party protection by incorporating the "natural hedges" that exist in any risk portfolio. In the course of doing business, companies naturally develop risk concentrations in their areas of specialization. The good news is that they should be very capable in analyzing, structuring, and pricing those risks. The bad news is that any risk concentration can be dangerous. By transferring undesirable risks to the secondary market (e.g., through credit derivatives or securitization), an organization can increase its risk origination capacity and revenue without accumulating highly concentrated risk positions.

Finally, management can purchase desirable risks that they cannot directly originate on a timely basis, or swap undesirable risk exposures for desirable risk exposures through a derivative contract.

Risk Analytics

The development of advanced risk analytics has supported the quantification and management of credit, market, and operational risks on a more consistent basis. The same techniques that allow quantification of risk exposures and risk-adjusted profitability can be used to evaluate risk transfer products such as derivatives, insurance, and hybrid products. For example, management can increase shareholder value through risk transfer if the cost of risk transfer is lower than the cost of risk retention for a given risk exposure (e.g., 12 percent all-in cost of risk transfer vs. 15 percent cost of risk capital).

Alternatively, if management wants to reduce its risk exposure, risk analytics can be used to determine the most cost-effective way to accomplish that objective. In addition to risk mitigation, advanced risk analytics also can be used to significantly improve net present value– or economic value-added–based decision tools by incorporating the cost of risk. The use of scenario analyses and dynamic simulations, for example, can support strategic planning by analyzing the probabilities and outcomes of different business strategies as well as the potential impact on shareholder value.

Data and Technology Resources

One of the greatest challenges for enterprise risk management is the aggregation of underlying portfolio and market data. Portfolio data include risk positions captured in different front- and back-office systems; market data include prices, volatilities, and correlations. In addition to data aggregation, standards and processes must be established to improve the quality of data that are fed into the risk systems.

As far as risk technology goes, there is no single vendor software package that provides a total solution for enterprise risk management. Organizations still have to build, buy, and customize, or outsource the required functionality. Despite the data and system challenges, companies should not wait for a perfect system solution to become available before establishing an ERM program. Rather, they should make the best use of what is available and at the same time apply rapid prototyping techniques to drive the systems development process. Additionally, companies should consider tapping into the power of the Internet/intranet in the design of an enterprise risk technology platform.

Stakeholder Management

Risk management is not just an internal management process. It also should be used to improve risk transparency to key stakeholders. The board of directors, for example, need periodic reports and updates on the major risks faced by the organization, as well as the review and approval of risk management policies for controlling those risks. Regulators need to be assured that sound business practices are in place, and that business operations are in compliance with regulatory requirements. Equity analysts and rating agencies need risk information to develop their investment and credit opinions.

An important objective for management in communicating and reporting to these key stakeholders is an assurance that appropriate risk management strategies are in effect. Otherwise, the company (and its stock price) will not get "full credit," since interested parties will see the risks but may not see the controls. The increasing emphasis of analyst presentations and annual reports on a company's risk management capabilities is evidence of the importance now placed on stakeholder communication.

In this chapter we provided an overview of what is ERM. In the following chapters we will discuss each of the seven components of ERM in greater detail.

CHAPTER 5

Corporate Governance

The 1990s were marked by a series of major risk management failures, some of them—including those that struck at Barings Bank, Metallgesellschaft, and Sumitomo—generating damages of more than *$1 billion*. The beginning of this decade saw even more dramatic corporate frauds and failures—Enron, WorldCom, Adelphia—that destroyed tens of billions of dollars in shareholder value and brought equity markets to their knees.

These disasters had devastating consequences for the stakeholders of the companies involved: investors, employees, customers, and business partners. Some even threatened the stability of entire markets. For example, the collapse of Barings threatened to seriously destabilize the futures markets in which rogue trader Nick Leeson racked up his colossal losses, while Sumitomo's Yasuo Hamanaka was notoriously the ultimate owner of 5 percent of the global copper market. More recently, the collapse of Enron has severely hurt the energy trading markets.

The examinations that followed each of these cases, and others, revealed a common theme behind the institutions' troubles: a lack of effective management and board oversight of corporate operations. That in turn prompted a renewed emphasis from regulators, stock exchanges, and institutional investors on compliance with codes of best practice for corporate governance. The passage of the Sarbanes-Oxley Act in 2002 established clear rules for corporate governance practices, such as requiring financial statement certification by the chief executive officer (CEO) and chief financial officer, and ensuring independence of auditors and audit committees. It is now essential that corporations put their houses in order.

Corporate governance is an essential component of enterprise risk management because it provides the top-down monitoring and management of risk. What is it? A good definition comes from CalPERS, a major institutional shareholder and enthusiastic proponent of shareholder activism:

The relationship among various participants in determining the direction and performance of corporations. The primary participants are (1) shareowners, (2) management (led by the chief executive officer), and (3) the board of directors.[1]

Senior management and the board of directors have a responsibility to ensure that effective risk management is in place—a responsibility to the shareholders and business partners who stand to lose money, to the employees who stand to lose their livelihoods, and to other stakeholders in the business—but are removed from the day-to-day risk-taking activities of the company. It is through corporate governance that they can manage the overall company risk profile.

The discipline of corporate governance begins at the top. The critical questions here are: How is a corporation's board of directors structured? Does it operate in a way that ensures their ability to fulfill their obligation to safeguard the resources of the company and the interests of corporate stakeholders?

Effective corporate governance requires the board to focus on general oversight and stewardship of the corporation, and to refrain from involvement in the day-to-day operations of the company. In this way, the board is able to maintain an integrated and relatively objective perspective on the company's operations, helping to steer it in the direction that will most benefit not only shareholders, but the corporation overall.

With the aid of a competent risk management function and an appropriate organizational structure, they can then direct and influence business and risk activities through policies and limits; ensure compliance with risk measurement and reporting, as well as audit processes; and create a strong culture that encourages desired business behavior by implementing compensation programs that reward risk-adjusted performance.

CODES OF CONDUCT

In recent years different bodies around the world have written a number of codes of best practice on corporate governance. Many of these were commissioned by various stock exchanges worldwide, others by industry or executive associations, some by institutional investors. One—the General Motors Board Guidelines—was actually commissioned by a corporation.

In the United Kingdom and in North America, as well as in many other

---

[1]Robert A.G. Monks and Nell Minow, *Corporate Governance* (United Kingdom: Blackwell Business, 1995).

countries around the world, codes of best practice on corporate governance are coming to have a strong impact on how companies govern themselves. It is extremely important to note, however, that compliance with these guidelines is typically voluntary, although disclosure of compliance or noncompliance may not be. Both the London and Toronto Stock Exchanges, for example, now require companies listed on those exchanges to report annually on whether or not they comply with the Cadbury/Hampel and Dey Reports, respectively. If a company does not comply, it must provide an explanation as to why not, but there is no requirement that a company change its practices to bring them in line with the guidelines.

Similarly, CalPERS' Core Principles and Governance Guidelines acknowledges that it describes only one way of doing things, and may not be universally accepted:

> *CalPERS believes the criteria contained in both the Principles and the Guidelines are important considerations for all companies within the U.S. market. However, CalPERS does not expect nor seek that each company will adopt or embrace every aspect of either the Principles or Guidelines. CalPERS recognizes that some of these may not be appropriate for every company, due to differing developmental stages, ownership structure, competitive environment, or a myriad of other distinctions. CalPERS also recognizes that other approaches may equally—or perhaps even better—achieve the desired goal of a fully accountable governance structure.*[2]

Nonetheless, the codes have had a significant impact on business practice. Stakeholders (particularly regulators and institutional investors) are increasingly reluctant to sanction companies that cannot demonstrate their proficiency in corporate governance. Compliance with a code is one easy way for a company to win approval.

For example, the Toronto Stock Exchange (TSE) Committee on Corporate Governance and the Institute of Corporate Directors recently conducted a survey of corporate practices five years after the adoption of the Dey Report guidelines, and found that "a number of the TSE guidelines are now broadly accepted business practices."[3] Although similar studies have yet to be done on the impact of the other codes, there is ample evidence that their recommendations are being adopted by leading companies.

---

[2]"CalPERS' Corporate Governance Core Principles and Guidelines," 1995, p. 3.
[3]Toronto Stock Exchange Committee on Corporate Governance and the Institute of Corporate Directors, "Report on Corporate Governance, 1999: Five Years to the Dey," 1999, co-chair's letter.

BEST PRACTICES

The various codes have a number of commonalities from which a number of best practices in corporate governance can be synthesized. Each has a slightly different focus, and therefore makes slightly different recommendations for the board. We'll consider some of the activities and issues most frequently cited below: stakeholder communication, board independence, performance assessment, and executive and director compensation.

Stakeholder Communication

Communication with company stakeholders[4] is one of the most important—and sensitive—responsibilities of the board of directors. While corporate governance codes of best practice concur that, in general, management should speak for the company, the board does have a key role in disclosing certain types of information.

One of the most important vehicles for disclosing key information to stakeholders is the corporate annual report. As discussed earlier in this chapter, the London Stock Exchange (LSE) and TSE have each adopted the recommendations of the Cadbury/Hampel and Dey Reports on corporate disclosure, and require that companies outline their corporate governance practices in each annual report.

This has significantly improved investors' access to information on the operations of the board of directors, which is considered a key benefit of improved corporate governance practices. The annual reports of both the Bank of Montreal and BP Amoco, for example, contain detailed disclosures about the companies' corporate governance practices. These disclosures make specific reference to the corporate governance requirements of the TSE and LSE, respectively, and rate the companies' performance relative to those guidelines. These disclosures also can be found on their corporate websites, significantly improving investors' access to information on corporate governance efforts.

There is no explicit requirement on the part of any U.S. stock exchange that corporations disclose corporate governance practices in their annual report. However, the Securities Exchange Act of 1934 was amended in 1978 to require the disclosure of "such additional details of corporate governance as structure, composition, and functioning of issuers' board of directors [and] resignation of directors" in proxy statements.[5] Thus, shareholders of Gen-

---

[4]The term *stakeholders* here refers not only to corporate shareholders, but also to employees, suppliers, and the general public wherever they have a direct interest in the affairs of the corporation.

[5]Charles J. Woelfel, *Encyclopedia of Banking and Finance,* 10th ed. (Chicago: Probus Publishing Company, 1994), p. 939.

eral Motors, General Electric (GE), Campbell Soup, and Compaq have access to detailed information on certain aspects of the corporate governance practices at each of these companies. Moreover, following the Sarbanes-Oxley Act, the New York Stock Exchange and Nasdaq have adopted more explicit corporate governance requirements for listed companies.

Board Independence

One of the most important changes in corporate governance practice in recent years concerns the issue of board independence. Most of the codes highlighted in this chapter specifically recommend the independence of the board of directors from the corporation and its management. England's Cadbury Report in 1992 provided one of the first recommendations that the board consist of a majority of independent directors:

Apart from their directors' fees and shareholdings, [directors] should be independent of management and free from any business or other relationship which could materially interfere with exercise of their independent judgement.[6]

This independence is considered critical to ensure that the board is objective enough to act in the best interests of the organization's stakeholders. Furthermore, independence is key in ensuring that the board is able to exercise its primary responsibility of oversight or stewardship of the company without being overly involved in its day-to-day management.

As a result of these guidelines, many organizations have taken steps to ensure that the majority of their directors are able to bring the objectivity and outside perspective considered crucial to good corporate governance. A majority of board members are independent at many companies known to have excellent corporate governance practices. For example, most of GE's board members are unrelated to the company. This is also true of Bank of Montreal, BP Amoco, and Campbell Soup. At Compaq, named as "Board of the Year" in 1997 by the Wharton School of the University of Pennsylvania, all board members except for the CEO are outside directors.

Conversely, a lack of board independence is apparent in a number of the disaster stories. All the directors of Metallgesellschaft's U.S. subsidiary, for example, were internal and related, resulting in a lack of independence and consequent allegations of conflict of interest in decision making.

There has been much debate in recent years as to whether it is appropriate for a company's CEO to also be the chair of its board of directors.

---

[6]"The Cadbury Report 4.12," 1992, p. 22.

The Combined Code of the UK's Committee on Corporate Governance summarizes the concern:

> *There are two key tasks at the top of every public company—the running of the board and the executive responsibility for the running of the company's business. There should be a clear division of responsibilities at the head of the company which will ensure a balance of power and authority, such that no one individual has unfettered powers of decision*[7]

Other codes concur. Most suggest that the decision to have one individual act as both CEO and board chair should be taken carefully and publicly justified. In recognition of the fact that it is extremely common to combine these positions in one individual, each of the codes suggests the appointment of a "lead director" as an option. The role of a lead director is to act in an independent capacity to coordinate board activities with the corporation's CEO, and to coordinate the other independent directors.[8] This lead director also has overall responsibility for ensuring that the board "discharges its responsibilities" in cases where the CEO is also the Chair.[9]

BP Amoco and Compaq both require the positions of Chairman of the Board and CEO to be held by different people. At the Bank of Montreal and Campbell Soup, where the CEOs serve as board chairs, the board's independence is strengthened by the existence of a lead director. Furthermore, each of these boards meets at least annually *without* the CEO being present to discuss issues where board independence is particularly important.

The issue of board independence also has implications for the board's governance structure. Each of the codes in question specifies that certain "key" committees should be composed "only" of independent directors, the compensation, audit, and "nominating or governance" committees being most frequently cited as those that should remain wholly independent.

In keeping with this sentiment, General Motors decreed in its Board Guidelines and in a corporate by-law that its Audit, Capital Stock, Director Affairs, Executive, Executive Compensation, and Public Policy committees would each consist of "only independent directors."[10] Much the same holds true for most committees at GE, the Bank of Montreal, BP Amoco, Campbell Soup, and Compaq.

One other key area where board independence comes into play is in selecting new board members. The Dey Report specifies that a committee of

---

[7]"The Combined Code," 2000, Principle A.2.
[8]"CalPERS' Corporate Governance Core Principles and Guidelines," 1995, p. 5.
[9]"The Dey Report," 1994, Guideline 12.
[10]"General Motors Board Guidelines," 1994, Guideline 22.

exclusively outside (independent) directors should perform this nomination and selection, and the National Association of Corporate Directors (NACD) Report concurs. "Creating an independent and inclusive process for nominating . . . directors . . . will ensure broad accountability to shareholders and reinforce perceptions of fairness and trust between and among management and board members."[11]

Board Performance Assessment

Another common recommendation is that boards of directors should periodically and formally evaluate their own performance against best-practice guidelines. Canada's Dey Report recommends that "every board of directors should implement a process . . . for assessing the effectiveness of the board as a whole, the committees of the board, and the contribution of individual directors."[12] The NACD Report goes into more detail of how the evaluation process should be made and specifying what criteria should be evaluated and how.[13]

The Dey recommendation proved one of the most challenging for companies in Canada to adopt. Five years later, fewer than 20 percent of Canadian-listed companies surveyed have in place "any formal process for assessing board effectiveness."[14] Many companies found themselves to be unsure of how to conduct such an evaluation in an unbiased and objective fashion.

Nonetheless, some companies with leading-edge governance practices do conduct regular board self-evaluations. The General Motors Guidelines, for example, specify that the Committee on Director Affairs "is responsible to report annually to the Board an assessment of the Board's performance."[15] Recognizing one of the sensitivities that has prevented some boards from adopting self-assessment processes, General Motors' Guideline 15 goes on to state that the purpose of the assessment "is to increase the effectiveness of the Board, not to target individual Board members."

The board of the Bank of Montreal assesses both the board as a whole and the individual directors annually. To do this, the Bank prepared a written statement of what was expected of its directors, using the recommendations of the NACD. Directors complete a detailed survey about the performance of their peers, based on this statement of expectations. The results

---

[11]"1996 NACD Report," p. 4.
[12]"The Dey Report," 1994, Guideline 5.
[13]"1996 NACD Report," p. 23.
[14]Toronto Stock Exchange Committee on Corporate Governance and the Institute of Corporate Directors, "Report on Corporate Governance, 1999: Five Years to the Dey," 1999, p. 19.
[15]"General Motors Board Guidelines," 1994, Guideline 15.

are compiled by an outside consultant, which produces a performance scorecard measuring effectiveness and activity.[16] According to the firm's Counsel, Blair MacAulay, "it wasn't easy to implement, but it has been highly successful."[17]

Executive and Board Compensation

The codes are more divided on the role that the Board should play in setting performance objectives and conducting a performance review of the CEO, although this has proved considerably easier for corporations to comply with. The U.K. codes make no recommendation in this respect, whereas the NACD Report recommends that boards "regularly and formally" evaluate the CEO, and specifies that independent directors should have control over this process.[18]

Here again, the General Motors Board Guidelines hold with best practice as identified by the other codes, and require all independent directors of their Board to review the CEO's performance annually, "based on objective criteria."[19] At BP Amoco, the board actively assesses its CEO's and executives' performance. At Campbell Soup, the board evaluates the performance of the CEO "at least annually in meetings of independent directors that are not attended by the CEO."[20]

Director compensation is, for obvious reasons, an issue of such importance that it is overtly mentioned by each code reviewed here, and has been the sole focus of numerous other studies and reports.[21] The United Kingdom's Combined Code recommends that "companies should avoid paying more than is necessary" to attract competent directors.[22] The Dey Report recognizes, however, that although directors should certainly not be overcompensated, the board of directors of each company should "ensure the compensation realistically reflects the responsibilities and risk involved in being an effective director."[23]

---

[16]"Non-US Firms Compete Through Good Governance," *Investor Relations Business*, March 6, 2000.
[17]"Non-US Firms Compete Through Good Governance," *Investor Relations Business*, March 6, 2000.
[18]"1996 NACD Report," p. 6.
[19]"General Motors Board Guidelines," 1994, Guideline 26.
[20]"Campbell Soup 1999 Proxy Statement," p. 11.
[21]For example, see the National Association of Corporate Directors' "1995 Report of the NACD Blue Ribbon Commission on Director Compensation" and the Conference Board of Canada's "Compensation of Boards of Directors," 1998 and every 2 years previously for approximately 20 years.
[22]"The Combined Code," 2000, Principle B.1.
[23]"The Dey Report," 1994, Guideline 8.

An important point agreed upon by all of the codes is that a significant portion of directors' compensation should be in the form of company stock, in order to ensure that the directors' objectives are aligned with those of shareholders. As General Motors Guideline 13 points out, "As part of a Director's total compensation and to create a direct linkage with corporate performance, the Board believes that a meaningful portion of a Director's compensation should be provided in common stock units."

At GE, outside directors each owned an average of $6.6 million in GE stock at the beginning of 2000, so their interests "are clearly aligned with the shareholders."[24] The Bank of Montreal's board reviews directors' compensation and benchmarks it against other Canadian and North American banks annually. Furthermore, the board has decreed that at least 50 percent of a director's annual retainer must be paid in Bank stock. Directors have an option to take 100 percent of their retainer and fees in stock, and in 1999, almost 90 percent of total director compensation was taken in this way.[25]

LINKING CORPORATE GOVERNANCE AND ERM

As mentioned above, the focus on corporate governance in general has provided a great deal of impetus for changes in corporate risk management practices. Some of the codes of best practice on corporate governance explicitly cite risk management as a key responsibility of the board.

Specifically, both the Dey Report and the Organisation for Economic Cooperation and Development (OECD) Principles of Corporate Governance overtly mention that the board has a responsibility for ensuring that appropriate systems and policies for risk management are in place.[26] The follow up to the Dey Report, "Five Years to the Dey," found that by 1999, 61 percent of Canadian-listed companies' boards had some formal process in place for managing risk.[27] A 1998 study of hundreds of Canadian companies (both listed and private) by the Conference Board of Canada found that directors' assumption of responsibility for risk management had increased 13 percent in the two years after the 1995 Dey Report went into effect.[28]

---

[24]John A. Byrne, "The Best & the Worst Boards," *Business Week*, January 24, 2000.

[25]"Bank of Montreal 1998 Annual Report," p. 101.

[26]"The Dey Report," Guideline 1(ii) and the "OECD Principles of Corporate Governance, 1999," Principles V.D.1 & V.D.5.

[27]Toronto Stock Exchange Committee on Corporate Governance and the Institute of Corporate Directors, "Report on Corporate Governance, 1999: Five Years to the Dey," 1999, p. 8.

[28]David Brown, Debra Brown, and Kimberley Birkbeck, *Canadian Directorship Practices 1997: A Quantum Leap in Governance* (Ottawa: The Conference Board of Canada, 1998).

Another important link between corporate governance and enterprise risk management is that both have similar focuses on strategic direction, corporate integration, and motivation from the top of the organization. The ultimate aim of both corporate governance and ERM is to prevent such debacles as Metallgesellschaft and Barings. Not only was poor risk management to blame for the scandals that threatened these two organizations, but so was ineffective corporate governance. Companies with poor corporate governance practices often have poor risk management skills, and vice versa.

Quite apart from anything else, good board practices and corporate governance are crucial for effective ERM. The development and success of ERM can be greatly enhanced with the commitment and involvement of the board of directors. In a strong company, the board is a single, independent body with an integrated perspective of the company's operations—the ideal entity to put weight behind an ERM initiative. A number of aspects of ERM are closely allied to the work of the board: setting risk appetite and policy; determining organizational structure; and establishing corporate culture and values. As discussed in the Export Development Corporation case study in Chapter 12, the involvement of the board was a key success factor in their ERM program.

Risk Appetite and Policy

An ERM initiative begins with a risk policy—a statement of the corporation's overall commitment to the effort. A risk policy is best formulated at the corporate management level with input from the business units, and approved by the board. Beyond a statement of commitment, the risk policy outlines the organization's risk appetite and clearly defines its risk tolerances in terms of limits. By codifying the commitment to risk management and the organization's risk appetite, a risk policy helps communicate the overall approach to risk management throughout the organization.

Risk policies naturally vary considerably from organization to organization. One excellent example is included in the Bank of Montreal's 1998 Annual Report:

> *Our objective is to earn competitive returns from our various business activities at acceptable risk levels. Risk management involves overseeing the risks associated with all our business activities in the environment in which we operate, ensuring that the risks taken are within prudent boundaries, and that the prices charged for products and services reflect these risks.*
>
> *Risk is calculated in terms of impact on income and asset values. We assess the potential effect on our business of changes in*

political, economic, market and operating conditions, and the cred-itworthiness of our clients, using four risk categories . . .

In the management of these risks we rely on the competence, experience and dedication of our professional staff operating with appropriate segregation of duties and utilizing sophisticated, quan-titatively based analytical tools and state of the art technology. This combination of prudence, analytical skills and technology, together with adherence to our operating procedures, is reflected in the strength and quality of earnings over time.[29]

Organizational Structure

No risk management effort can be truly successful until it is aligned effectively with the organizational structure.

Ideally, the day-to-day responsibility for implementing enterprise risk management should rest with an independent risk management function that reports directly to the CEO or board [through the chief risk officer (CRO), if one has been appointed]. This independence ensures that the risk management function is as unbiased and objective as possible, and the reporting relationship ensures that the risk management office has sufficient power within the organization to motivate good risk management practices.

The CRO, or nearest equivalent, should in turn report to a risk management committee of the board. As discussed above, the board's direct involvement will ensure that the risk management program is executed with an integrated, holistic view of the organization in mind.

We've previously discussed the importance of aligning employee incentives with good risk management practice. This alignment should begin at the executive level, which is where a risk-aware board comes into play. The compensation and incentives of the board, the CEO, and other executives should clearly be in line with the company's risk management policy and appetite.

Risk Culture and Corporate Values

One of the "softest," but most important, aspects of risk management is the integration of risk into a company's culture and values. Most obviously, risk needs be considered as an integral part of corporate strategy. Risk management targets should be included among corporate goals, and major

---

[29]"Bank of Montreal 1998 Annual Report," p. 37.

corporate initiatives should incorporate risk assessment and risk mitigation strategies.

Just as an organization's overall culture can be critical in determining how successful it will be, so its risk culture will determine how successful its ERM will be. A weak risk culture is one in which employees have little sense of the importance of risk management and their role in it. Such a culture will compromise efforts to manage risk, perhaps fatally. If, on the other hand, risk management is seen as a central part of day-to-day operations, it is likely that a strong risk culture is likely in place. Such an environment allows for truly effective risk management.

Like all cultural issues, a key factor is whether management "walks the walk" as well as "talks the talk." For example, how does senior management react when a high-revenue producer blatantly violates risk management policies? Do they take corrective action or simply turn their backs on the problem? The decisions and actions of senior management will do more to influence behavior than any written policy. It's critical that they act accordingly.

CHAPTER 6

Line Management

The key revenue-producing activities of a business enterprise are usually organized into strategic business units by geography, customer group, product, or some combination of all these in a matrix structure. These line units account for the vast majority of assets and employees in most organizations, and also can be the primary source of business, financial, and operational risks. Those responsible for these units, and their risks, are the *line management*.

Line managers face a wide variety of risks. Most common are those associated with day-to-day operations, such as defects in supplies of components or raw materials, or errors, failures, and wastage in production processes. In addition, line managers will face periodic risks associated with strategic business decisions, such as new product launches, potential mergers and acquisitions, or changes to incentive packages. Finally, they also face catastrophic risks from "once in a lifetime" disasters, such as fires or earthquakes, as well as extraordinary litigation.

Much has been written on the management of each of these kinds of risk, although sometimes under the rubrics of quality management, general business management, and continuity and crisis management rather than risk management.

In this chapter, we will concentrate on the interaction of the line managers and the enterprise risk management function.

As the origination point for many of the risks faced by a company, line management plays a key role in enterprise risk management. Because the line units have the closest contacts with customers and suppliers, their effectiveness in addressing risk issues will not only have a material effect on mitigating potential losses, but also on the reputation of the company as a whole. It is therefore critical that line managers pursuing new business and growth opportunities align their business strategies with the overall corporate risk policy.

That means the risks of business transactions should be fully assessed and incorporated into pricing and profitability targets. Specifically, expected losses and the cost of risk capital should be included in the pricing of a product or the required return on an investment project. In business development, risk acceptance criteria should be established to ensure that risk management issues are considered as part of the assessment of new product and market opportunities.

In this chapter, we'll discuss these and other risk issues in greater detail:

- The relationship between line units and risk management
- Key challenges for line risk management
- Best practices for line risk management

THE RELATIONSHIP BETWEEN LINE AND RISK FUNCTIONS

The relationship between line management and risk management is a key driver of the overall business and risk culture of a company. The challenge for any company is to establish an independent risk function without creating an adversary relationship between the line and risk units. A healthy relationship is required for any enterprise risk management program to be successful.

As Chief Risk Officer (CRO) of Fidelity Investments, I worked very hard to gain and maintain the trust and support of the business units.[1] My approach was to listen to their needs and requirements, provide them with regular updates on the enterprise risk management (ERM) plan, engage them to discuss best practices and lessons learned, and, most importantly, integrate risk practices into line management to help them achieve their business objectives. Other successful CROs also have built strong relationships with the business units in their companies. For example, the CRO at CIBC (see Chapter 16) helped business units understand their own risk/return trade-offs and subsequently make better business decisions.

The relationship between line management and risk management can be characterized in terms of three organizational models:

- *Offense versus defense:* In this model, business units are focused on revenue maximization and risk management is focused on loss minimization.

---

[1]James Lam, "Custom-Built for Success," *Risk Magazine*, Enterprise-Wide Risk Management Supplement, November 1997.

- *Policy and policing:* Business units can only operate within the risk policies established by risk management, and their activities are monitored by risk, audit, and compliance functions.
- *Partnership:* Business units and risk management jointly evaluate and resolve risk management issues and share common goals and objectives.

These organizational models are by no means mutually exclusive. For example, a company can adopt the partnership model for day-to-day business activities but use the policy and policing model for highly sensitive issues (e.g., information security, sexual harassment). However, it is useful to discuss the implications of these approaches to highlight how they may impact business behavior and shape the risk culture of a company.

Offense and Defense

During my early years in risk management, I often heard risk professionals—credit managers in particular—describe the line units as "offense" and risk management as "defense." I always found this description unproductive. In sports, where this analogy no doubt originated, one team wins while the other loses. The two teams have opposite goals, and in many respects are at war with each other. Some cynics might say this is a pretty accurate depiction of line management versus risk management. I would argue that it represents an unhealthy risk culture.

In the early 1990s, I worked as a consultant for one U.S. regional bank where the chief credit officer was fond of using the offense and defense analogy to describe the loan origination and credit departments. At that bank, the performances of the loan origination units were measured on the basis of number and size of loans funded, loan fee income, and total size of the loan portfolio. Meanwhile, the performance of the credit department was measured by loan defaults, losses, and the overall credit quality of the loan portfolio. Thus, the loan origination units were better off if a loan was approved and the credit department was better off if it was declined, regardless of the risk/return economics of the loan. Given that the credit department or credit committee had to approve all loans above a certain size, these opposing objectives created an unhealthy business environment.

The loan origination units would understate the credit risk of loans to get them approved, as a result of which many loans were downgraded or went into default shortly after origination. They would also present loan proposals at the last minute, hoping that they would be approved with little scrutiny. Meanwhile, the credit department was skeptical of the credit analysis performed by the origination units and would ask for more information and documentation. It would ask for a dozen or more signatures for large or complex loans in order to slow down the approval process and prevent last-minute proposals.

This cycle of behavior became increasingly vicious, and over time the risk culture of this bank became dysfunctional. The credit managers called the loan originators "cowboys"; the loan originators called the credit managers "Dr. No's." Performance deteriorated markedly and the bank ultimately lost its independence when it was acquired by another bank.

This example illustrates the potential pitfalls of an offense versus defense model. When line and risk functions are given opposing objectives, and particularly when they are given opposing incentives, the result is almost inevitable to be adverse, and ultimately very detrimental to the business performance of a company. This problem is not unique to risk management; it can occur in relationships between line management and *any* control-oriented functions such as audit, finance, quality, legal, compliance, and so on.

Policy and Policing

In the policy and policing model often used by large, decentralized companies, the risk management function establishes policies and limits within which the line units must operate. These serve as the "boundaries" for line operations and might consist of approved transactions, minimum credit standards, exposure limits, investment policies, and so on. Line operations within these policies and limits require no special approvals or reviews, whereas those outside them are approved or denied on a case-by-case basis. The risk management unit, along with the audit and compliance units, checks that these policies and limits are followed, and reports exceptions and excesses to senior management.

Unlike the offense versus defense model, where the relationship between line and risk functions is strictly adversarial, the relationship under the policy and policing model is more like one of government and citizenry. Risk management serves as a lawmaker (and sometimes as law enforcement): the line functions have full operating autonomy as long as they don't violate any risk management policies. New situations are judged individually, and their resolutions become part of the policy. This model is similar to the way that individuals and institutions are regulated in a common-law democratic society: they are free to act as they wish, so long as they remain within the law; punishments for law breaking are partially based on circumstances; and the detailed interpretation of the law is established by precedent.

There are a number of problems with this model, however. The risk management function is not engaged in the day-to-day operations of line management and as a result may lose touch with the changing business environment. Over time, existing risk management policies may become outdated and new policies may not be established in a timely manner. In addition, audit and compliance processes are episodic and may not fully identify critical issues. Significant risk events can occur between ex-amination periods no matter how good the audit and compliance functions may be.

The result is that there is likely to be a disconnect between the line and risk management. Typically, line units will complain that risk management doesn't understand the market or their business, and that they are sometimes blindsided by ill-conceived risk policies. In contrast, risk management might say that the line units don't fully understand the risk management policies, and that they get blindsided by the line units' actions and decisions.

What makes this situation worse is that line management is biased against communicating problems to the risk management unit. Consider the comparison with government and citizenry. Those who infringe the law, whether deliberately or inadvertently, do not usually seek out the police to make a confession. This is even truer if it is unclear that a law has actually been broken. Citizens are only likely to admit to breaking the law if they believe it is possible that the law will be changed in such a way that it benefits them—or if they have a guilty conscience, in which case it is likely that the damage is already done.

Similarly, line units do not have strong incentives to report out-and-out policy violations (whether deliberate or accidental) or to seek the advice of the risk management unit when it is not clear if a policy is being infringed. To put it another way, the line units may respect the letter of the law—although if they do not, the risk management unit may not find out in a prompt fashion—but they are unlikely to respect its spirit. Risk management will only hear about potential problems when the situation is too dire to be ignored or when the line management thinks the problem can be turned into an opportunity by a revision of policy.

Clearly, this is a caricatured picture of how the policy and policing model works. Arguments based on "the greater good" of the company carry some weight, as do incentives tied to policy compliance and well-judged punitive measures against violators. Although risk management is no longer in opposition to line management, it is still passive much of the time, acting mostly as a check on line activities. A better alternative is for risk management to take a proactive stance in helping the line units to make their businesses work. As we'll see in the next section, this partnership approach can be a powerful one in many respects.

Partnership Model

In the partnership model, risk management is fully integrated into the business, as opposed to being strictly a corporate oversight function. Line and risk management personnel work together to address risk/return issues not only when problems arise, but also in the front end of the business process when products are being developed and pricing or investment decisions are being made. The relationship between line and risk functions becomes more like that of a client and consultant, where the line units seek to use risk management expertise to improve business performance. In this environment, the line and risk functions have individual performance targets but also some important shared performance measures, such as risk-adjusted profitability and portfolio quality. Given their shared performance objectives, line and risk units have incentives to work together to address risk management issues in the front-end business processes, and to respond to problems when they emerge.

The keys to making this model work are cultural and organizational. First, line management must recognize the role that risk management plays in supporting long-term performance and stop obsessing over its role in constraining short-term profitability. Second, the risk management unit must recognize the need to understand and respond to the line units' business needs, not hand down academic, impractical, and inflexible policies.

The first item can be addressed by getting line management to recognize that risk and return are both inevitable parts of any business decision, so it is a good idea to have someone who understands risk on-hand to provide advice and guidance when undertaking a new activity. Rather than applying risk management tools because they have to, the line unit "clients" should apply them because they want to; they should see the risk management unit as a value-added business partner that can help them to understand the underlying risk/return economics of their business, keep them out of trouble, and help them to achieve their business and financial objectives.

The second item should be addressed by making sure that risk management sees itself as a consultant in a client–consultant relationship. That means it should be responsive to the needs of the business units and develop tools that can support business decisions, such as risk-based pricing models and scenario planning tools. As such, the risk management function cannot live in an "ivory tower," but must be decentralized in the business units. This can be accomplished by establishing risk management functions *within* the line units. Depending on the particular organization, this might be done by putting staff in each business unit in various geographic locations or by implementing other organizational structures that serve the operational needs of the business.

The main problem with the partnership model relates to the independence of the risk management function. As a business partner who participates in business decisions and problem resolutions, can risk management maintain its important role as a corporate oversight function? This is a similar challenge to the one faced by the "Final Four" accounting firms, whose independence as auditors has in recent years been brought into question by the growth and profitability of their consulting practices.

A likely resolution for the accounting firms is the divestment of the consulting practices into separate businesses. This is not really an option for a partnership risk management unit within a company. One answer is to mix up the models discussed in this section. As discussed earlier, the three models for line-risk relationship are not mutually exclusive. Many companies have blended the partnership and policy-and-policing models in order to maintain the independence of the risk management function. This hybrid approach establishes risk units with distinct but complementary mandates.

For example, many companies have established operational risk consulting units to serve as a business partner, but have maintained their audit function to preserve independence. Another example is the credit function at many commercial banks, where the origination versus credit approval model is replaced by a relationship management team that is fully responsible for sales and credit analysis, but a separate and independent credit review function is established to ensure compliance with credit policies.

KEY CHALLENGES

In aligning risk and line management, there are a number of key challenges that emerge from conversations with risk managers on both the line and risk sides of organizations:

- Conflict resolution between line and staff
- The role of line risk management
- Incentive alignment
- Nonfinancial risk measurement

Conflict Resolution

The issue most often cited in conversations with risk managers is the adversarial nature of the relationship between line business managers and staff risk managers. Although the three organizational models discussed above highlight ways to minimize potential conflict, there will inevitably be day-to-day issues that need to be addressed. Usually, there is a straightforward, more or less open, conflict between line business managers and staff risk managers. The form of the conflict most often concerns choices between business volume or revenue growth and risk control. At its most basic level, this is the conflict between perceptions of risk as "opportunity for profit" and risk as "opportunity for loss."

This is a classic problem in financial services businesses such as lending or insurance: as the business cycle picks up and perceptions of risk start to fall, the supply of capital for lending and insurance products starts to increase faster than the demand for those products. As a result, a provider's business growth will suffer. In most of these cases, line managers will argue for lower pricing or relaxed underwriting standards in order to increase volume, whereas staff managers will argue for maintaining the same standards and keeping losses within planned levels.

Similar conflicts occur outside financial services, however. Line units may on occasion be required by a staff department to add additional product features, for example, to minimize environmental damage and hence reduce catastrophic legal risk. More generally, salespeople will argue for marginal cost pricing to increase or maintain volume while finance will argue for full-cost pricing in order to increase or maintain profitability.

In these situations, there is the sense of an "arms race" between the staff functions and the line business units. In this process, the line seeks ways to avoid oversight by staff units, while the staff functions strive to unearth information on the line managers' activities so that they can be kept in check. Budgetary processes are often the focus of this game playing. This conflict tends to ebb and flow with the business cycle. In expansionary times, business development takes priority; in recessions, control is paramount. In the light of this apparently irreducible conflict, the issue is usually framed as constructive conflict management rather than reconciliation, with a focus on structures and processes.

Line Risk Management

One response to the perception of irreducible conflict has been for business units to increasingly install risk managers within their business units—a parallel development, in some ways, to the trend for appointing CROs at the corporate level.

The appointment of a line risk manager gives strength to the partnership model described above: he or she can help the business unit to understand its risks and to ensure compliance with the policies and standards established by the ERM function. It works: while at Fidelity, I noticed that the quality of risk management at each of the company's 40 business units was directly correlated with whether that business unit had a dedicated risk manager.

In early models, the line risk manager reported jointly to the CRO and to the business manager. Although this is perhaps the truest reflection of that person's role in the company, it is in practice highly ambiguous, and can be most uncomfortable. The rest of the line staff may perceive the line risk manager as part of "the enemy" while the ERM staff remains convinced that he is, at best, a double-agent working both sides to his own advantage! No wonder line risk managers often feel that they are walking a tightrope.

One solution is to have the line risk manager report to the head of the business unit and have a "dotted line" link to the CRO. Making the business manager the line risk manager's boss, while ensuring that he or she also must keep the CRO in the loop, reduces some of the ambiguity described above. For some companies, the reverse structure will make more sense. Either way, the CRO should always provide a meaningful input in the performance review and incentive compensation of line risk managers, especially in the early stages of an ERM program.

Another increasingly common industry practice is the creation of "communities of risk" that cut across hierarchical levels and business units. These have been created in response to the perception that risk expertise and know-how are usually scarce in any given organization, but similar problems and opportunities are common. Successful organizations have built on these new positions and communities, changing their processes so that the individuals involved can operate effectively.

Incentive Alignment

It is clear that in many cases the adversarial nature of the debate stems directly from misaligned incentives. One side is seeking growth; the other is seeking quality. One part of the equation is line manager incentive structures that reward them based on a combination of business metrics such as volume, revenue, profit, and return on equity. The other part of the equation is the structures in place for staff managers, which typically focus on minimization of losses, errors, or deviations from plan, with qualitative or subjective measures of performance (e.g., timely reporting, roll-out of a system, enhancements to methodologies) layered on top.

In theory, perfect incentive structures could be designed so that both parties are facing the same objective function and consequently will act synchronously. However, in practice, it is difficult to design and implement the metrics required given the difficulty in measuring—or even obtaining solid data about—certain aspects of performance. In this area, most effort is being put into balanced scorecard initiatives, with some additional emphasis on risk-adjusted performance measures. As such, the performance measurement and incentive systems are designed to incorporate corporate-wide performance metrics, as well as unit-specific metrics and nonquantitative criteria.

Nonfinancial Risk Measurement

A related emerging issue is how to assess and quantify nonfinancial risks (business, organizational, and operational risks) and how to incorporate these measures into performance measurement systems. As noted above, many techniques that are sometimes called risk management are also called other things. Part of the challenge is to establish agreement about what constitutes a risk—a risk taxonomy of the type proposed in Chapter 3 is important here.

For example, many types of operational risk in primary industries and manufacturing have been addressed through total quality management (TQM) initiatives and business continuity planning. Business continuity planning has been widely implemented in service and knowledge industries; meaningful TQM implementations are fewer, although GE Capital's Six-Sigma program is a notable exception.

There is still plenty of debate outside manufacturing about how to define, let alone measure and control, operational risks like a poor service experience, a power outage, or an inadequately specified contract. The topic of operational risk management has been the subject of increasing attention in the risk management community (see Chapter 14 for more discussion on operational risk management).

BEST PRACTICES

As noted above, the relationship between line management and risk management is a critical factor to the success of any ERM program. To establish a healthy relationship, a balance must be maintained between effective corporate oversight and efficient line decisions. In order to achieve and maintain such a balance, the ERM program should strive to integrate risk management into business management processes, including:

- Business strategy and planning
- New product and business development
- Product pricing
- Business performance measurement

Strategy and Planning

The business strategies and plans submitted by business units should include a full discussion of the risks involved, as well as the appropriate risk mitigation strategies. The business units should address five basic questions:

- Which risk factors could prevent us from achieving our key business objectives?
- How will we measure and track these risk factors?
- How will we mitigate these risks through internal processes or external risk transfer?

- What level or range of risk performance should corporate management expect?
- Who is responsible for measuring and managing the risks involved?

A company will obtain a number of benefits by ensuring that business unit strategies and plans address these questions. First, it focuses business units' attention on the key risk exposures in their operations, as well as on the necessary measurement and management strategies for containing these risks. A business unit that is unprepared to discuss its risks or its risk mitigation strategies should be an area for concern.

Second, it provides corporate management with timely (i.e., advance) information on the company's emerging risk exposures. For example, if many business units are planning to expand their businesses in Japan, then the treasury unit should plan on increasing its dollar/yen hedging program. Third, it facilitates early discussions between line management and risk management to ensure that business and risk issues are identified and resolved. Risk management can be more proactive in developing and implementing risk policies given business changes, and can use the experience gained to develop best practices across more business units. This way, useful approaches can be shared within the company and a mistake made by one business will not be repeated in another.

Product and Business Development

In addition to business planning, risk management should be a part of the development of new product and business opportunities. These opportunities should include new products, business and financial investments, market expansion plans, and mergers and acquisitions. When management pursues any of these business opportunities, it relies on a set of assumptions for the business, such as volume, price, costs, and technology. There are risks associated with each of these assumptions. For example, actual volumes might fall below expectations, losses might exceed forecasts, and technology might not meet user expectations. It is important, therefore, to address these risk issues not only when the business opportunity is first considered, but also during regular business review sessions.

One of the best practices for integrating risk management with new product and business development that I have seen first hand was a business review process called Policy 6.0 at GE Capital. When a new business or investment is considered, the business unit must address all of the key business and risk management assumptions underlying the business opportunity. The business unit must discuss its expectations for each of these key assumptions. One particularly useful exercise was to set "trigger points"— the level above and below expectations (e.g., plus or minus 10 percent) at which specific decisions or action plans are activated (or "triggered"). Individuals are then assigned to monitor and review business performance against these trigger points. If a business opportunity is not meeting expectations, the negative trigger points might initiate a plan to scale back the business, or even to exit altogether. If a business opportunity is above expectations, the positive trigger points might increase the company's investments and speed up the business development timetable.

Product Pricing

We discussed earlier how the pricing of a product or service should include the cost of the risks associated with that product or service. More generally, the pricing of products developed and sold at the line level need to reflect the group-wide costs of risk that will otherwise go unrecovered. A company can only recover the costs incurred in managing risk by incorporating those costs into its product pricing. Although many companies have established product pricing models that incorporate operating costs and profitability targets, they often fail to fully consider the cost of risk.

The cost of risk would include expected losses (from defects, errors, credit losses, etc.), the cost of economic capital (to absorb unexpected loss), and the cost of risk transfer (insurance premiums and hedging costs). Without incorporating the cost of risk, companies will underprice their products and not get compensated for the risk exposures taken. Moreover, if a company is not using risk-based pricing and its competitors are, then it is subject to "adverse selection," resulting in a money-losing portfolio. For example, if an auto insurance company is underpricing high-risk drivers and overpricing low-risk drivers, than it will systematically get a portfolio overweighted by high-risk drivers but without the higher premium income to absorb higher losses.

The lack of risk-adjusted product pricing also can motivate adverse business behavior. For example, a bank would motivate business units to take interest rate risk if it does not fully incorporate the full cost of matched funding in its product pricing. With an upward sloping yield curve (where long-term interest rates are higher than short-term interest rates), a business unit can show higher profitability by funding long-term assets (e.g., 30-year loans) with short-term liabilities (e.g., six-month deposits). However, such a strategy would expose the bank's earnings to rising rates and an inverted yield curve. This is what nearly bankrupted the U.S. thrift industry in the early 1980s.

Performance Measurement

The performance measurements and goals for business units should include risk. Ideally, risk measurement and reporting should be integrated into overall business reporting. Given that a company takes risks to generate growth and profits, it only makes sense to include risk in business performance measurement. Having separate risk and business reports is equivalent to having separate revenue and expense reports. Just as management can only assess profitability by combining revenues and expenses, it can only balance risk exposures and business opportunities by integrating risk and business reporting.

Many companies have adopted the "balanced scorecard" as a way to integrate business and financial reporting for senior management. The traditional balanced scorecard defines business performance in terms of four categories: financial, customer, internal, and learning and growth. A good case can be made that the balanced scorecard (or any other business reporting methodology) should include a risk assessment, either as a separate category or as a part of each of the four performance components. Only then will the balanced scorecard be truly "balanced" with respect to the information needed by both corporate and line management.

Portfolio Management

I t took seven years to persuade super-investor Warren Buffet to be the subject of *Nightline,* the ABC network's flagship news program. At that time, Buffet's Berkshire Hathaway investment vehicle had posted a succession of returns that put its competitors to shame; Buffet himself was known as "the sage of Omaha" and regarded by many as the world's shrewdest investor. To kick off the interview, the host, Ted Koppel, asked Buffet what he did for a living. Buffet reflected for a second and replied, "I allocate capital."

In that short answer from one of the greatest investors of our times lies an important lesson for all business managers. Capital allocation is a critical concept for *all* businesses: not just money managers but for other financial institutions, energy firms, and nonfinancial corporations. Capital is the link between risk and return, and so a sound capital allocation process is critical to business development and the creation of shareholder value.

Capital is typically allocated by evaluating a set of investment opportunities, then selecting those that meet a set of predetermined investment objectives. Over time, the investments aggregate into portfolios—a research and development portfolio, a plant portfolio, a securities portfolio, and so on. In essence, a company should be viewed as a portfolio of businesses, each with its own unique risk/return characteristics.

In most enterprises, the various business portfolios have historically been managed by separate entities, which rarely coordinate their investment objectives with one another. This fragmentation implies that the enterprise-wide portfolio is unlikely to be optimized. How, then, should we manage the sets of existing investments and investment opportunities in order to optimize the aggregation of portfolios across the entire enterprise?

Since the ultimate goal of management is to maximize shareholder value, the overarching principle for enterprise-wide portfolio management should be to manage the business portfolio in the same way that a fund manager manages a stock portfolio. In other words, business portfolio managers should strive to understand the links between risk origination (e.g., business lines and trading units) and risk transfer (hedging and insurance) and make those investment decisions that position the overall enterprise portfolio at the classic "efficient frontier" of risk/return—highest return for the same level of risk or lowest risk for the same level of return.

This process, as applied to money management, is widely known as "active portfolio management," or simply "active management." Generally, active managers implement a strategy or system designed to exploit mispricing or to manage risk. The alternative is to use a passive strategy, such as investing in a market index, or to make an alternative investment that requires no maintenance. Although both techniques have their merits when it comes to capital markets investments, only active portfolio management theory is particularly relevant in evaluating capital allocation decisions for a business.

THE THEORY OF ACTIVE PORTFOLIO MANAGEMENT

The theory of active portfolio management largely builds on the foundation established by Harry Markowitz[1] in the 1950s, revolving around the measurement and management of risk. As Markowitz himself said in a January 2000 interview, "Risk has been the same since the caveman. Modern portfolio theory has developed apparatus for risk evaluation and control. This apparatus, subject to further enhancement, will carry forward into the risk world of the future."[2]

The area in which the portfolio theory has been furthest enhanced is in money management, where there is now a large body of theoretical work. This is in part because return, volatility, and correlation information tends to be easier to quantify, and so it is easier to construct sophisticated, technical models for portfolio management.

It is not as easy to do the same for business enterprises, but the precepts of active portfolio management can nonetheless prove useful, and the interested reader should investigate further on the subject. We'll confine ourselves here to discussing how even a basic understanding of the theory can have marked benefits for businesses.

Let's begin by considering the fundamental concepts suggested by the portfolio theory of Markowitz and his successors: risk, reward, diversification, leverage, and hedging.

Risk, in this context, is typically equated with volatility, a statistical

---

[1] Harry Markowitz, "Portfolio Selection," *Journal of Finance* 7, no. 1, 1952, pp. 77–91.
[2] Steven Mintz, "The Gurus," CFO *Magazine (online edition)*, January 2000.

measure of the uncertainty associated with future events. Risk is therefore indeterminate by definition (since we do not know what will happen in the future), but we can estimate the *likely* future value of a business or investment and some range of variation around the value. In the stock market, this is done by looking at the standard deviation of past returns, or by extracting the market's current expectations of risk from the prices of stock options.

The opposite side of the coin to risk is reward, the gain that stands to be made from a risky investment. Like risk, the reward on an investment is indeterminate, but can be estimated in terms of its likely, or "expected," value. The reward for investing in equity is the expected return of the stock or index over a given interval. More generally, an enterprise's reward for a new business venture is the gain that an organization stands to make by taking on a particular risk. Clearly, it makes sense that the anticipated reward should be commensurate with the risk involved. This is not always the case in practice.

Diversification is the concept of lowering the total risk of an enterprise by spreading risk among many distinct projects: the total risk produced by a collection of diverse risks is *less* than the sum of those risks considered in isolation. Put this way, diversification may sound unintuitive, but it is in fact a very common-sense concept, as expressed by the adage that you should not put all of your eggs in one basket.

Put more technically, diversification is a result of the fact that not all opportunities are affected by risk-driven events in the same manner. For example, an increase in oil prices cuts into airline profits, but benefits oil companies. An investor who owned both an oil producer and an airline would be less affected in the event of a price rise than one who owned two airlines, or two oil producers.

Situations such as these allow diversification to reduce portfolio risk significantly when many different investments are combined. The more dissimilar the investments (the less the correlations between the investments), the greater the diversification. However, although these offsetting effects reduce risk at the enterprise level, the expected return on the enterprise portfolio remains a simple weighted average of the individual returns.

Leverage is the effect of borrowing to increase the risk profile of a venture. Money borrowed at a flat rate can be used to finance new investments. This has the effect of substantially increasing the risk in an investor's portfolio. Since the investor only needs to pay back the loan amount, any profits made with the borrowed capital are his to keep.

Thus, an investor might think he has spotted a sure thing and invest $200, comprising $100 of his own money and $100 borrowed from the bank. If he achieves a 25 percent return on the investment, he will make $50; since he only has to pay back $100 (ignoring interest in this simple example), he is left with $50, amounting to a 50 percent return on his own money. Of course, had he lost money, he would have lost twice as much. Simply put, leverage multiplies the risk/reward profile.

Finally, hedging is the process of offsetting risk by entering into a market position that is negatively correlated with an existing position. This is similar to diversification, but is motivated by the desire to reduce the risk associated with an existing investment, rather than to add new investments in a way that reduces overall risk. In this sense, hedging is much like insurance, and should be treated as such.

For example, say that a newly hired chief executive officer (CEO) is given shares of company stock valued at $50, but is not permitted to sell them for two years. Having done a sterling job, the stock has appreciated to $100 a share at the end of her first year, but the business climate is changing and so the CEO fears that the stock may drop again before she can sell her shares.

To hedge against this downside risk, she buys put options on the stock that allow her to sell the stock for $100 at the end of the two-year period. The options are not necessarily cheap, but this hedge guarantees that no matter what price the stock reaches, our CEO will be able to sell each of her shares for $100. The financial security allows her to stop worrying about college fees and enjoy life a little more.

Now let's look at how a consideration of these concepts can help in enterprise risk management (ERM).

BENEFITS OF ACTIVE PORTFOLIO MANAGEMENT

Instead of managing individual securities within an investment portfolio, the goal of ERM is to manage individual businesses within an overall business portfolio. Portfolio management supports ERM in four important ways, by:

- Unbundling risk origination, retention, and transfer
- Providing a risk aggregation function across the company
- Setting risk limits and asset allocation targets
- Influencing transfer pricing, capital allocation, and investment decisions

Unbundling

By definition, portfolio management goes beyond business management at the transactional level and manages the overall business as a whole. Ironically, one frequent result is the unbundling of the business in terms of risk organization, risk retention, and risk transfer. A company's management can consider its core competencies and risk/return economies, then decide which of these functions it wishes to compete in.

What does this mean in practice? This kind of disaggregation has been the norm in mortgage banking for more than 15 years, where the primary risks in question are consumer credit risk and mortgage prepayment risk. Companies can specialize in loan origination, loan funding and/or servicing, or loan securitization (packaging individual mortgages into pools for sale in the secondary markets as mortgage-backed securities).

In recent years, this portfolio management approach has extended into the credit card, auto loan, and more recently, commercial loan and junk bond markets. It is now becoming increasingly widespread among nonfinancial corporations; energy firms, for example, increasingly adopt it when addressing their interests in exploration, transportation and storage, product development and distribution, and trading. The key point here is that by understanding the risk/return economies of the overall business, a company can decide where within the value chain it should compete.

Risk Aggregation

The overall risk portfolio represents the aggregation of all types of risk within a company, across different business activities and risk types. Management needs information on aggregated risk exposures, as well as how these exposures correlate with each other; these should be the basis for setting risk limits and allocation targets, as discussed below.

For some companies, the aggregation of risks is performed for measurement and reporting purposes, and the risk profile of the company is managed through corporate management processes such as strategic planning, capital allocation, limits setting, and so forth. Some companies take a more dramatic approach to certain risks, in which all risk exposures are transferred directly or through a transfer pricing mechanism into a central function where portfolio management and hedging decisions are made.

For example, many large banks manage interest rate risk centrally, by providing each business unit with duration-matched fund transfer prices for all of their assets and liabilities. This serves two key purposes. First, the profitability of the loan origination and deposit gathering businesses can be measured without any earnings contribution from interest rate risk. Second, the interest rate risk of the bank can be aggregated into a central interest rate risk unit where hedging decisions can be made after considering the effects of portfolio diversification.

Nonfinancial corporations perform a similar function when they centralize treasury functions—funding and hedging—and charge hedging costs to business units by levying a transfer price for funds. These companies benefit from the aggregation of risks by tracking enterprise-wide risk exposures, incorporating the effects of diversification, and centralizing risk management decisions where appropriate.

Risk Limits and Asset Allocation

The portfolio manager of a stock portfolio can ensure a balance between diversification and performance by establishing risk concentration limits and asset allocation targets. For example, a stock portfolio's investment policy might indicate that the fund cannot own more than 5 percent of its assets in any company, or 20 percent of assets in any industry. These limits ensure appropriate diversification. Within these risk limits, the portfolio manager might set asset allocation targets that would overweight industries that are deemed undervalued, and vice versa. Such targets seek to maximize fund performance within the constraints established by the risk limits.

A business can set similar portfolio risk limits and allocation targets. For example, a global business operating in 10 countries might establish an upper limit of 20 percent for revenue contribution from any single country. On average, each country contributes 10 percent to total revenue. But given its positive outlook for, say, China, it might set a revenue contribution target at the maximum limit of 20 percent. In this case, the higher revenue target for China based on optimistic management projections is kept in check by the country limits. Risk limits and allocation targets provide complimentary controls for achieving optimal risk/return for the business.

Influencing Transfer Pricing, Capital Allocation, and Investment Decisions

Corporate management can influence the risk profile of the business portfolio in several ways. The global business in the above example can adjust its transfer prices for China by increasing income credits or lower transfer costs to that country, in an effort to motivate aggressive growth.

Management can also allocate more economic capital to businesses and products that are expected to produce superior risk-adjusted return on that capital. An efficient capital allocation process should function as an "internal capital market" where funding is provided only to businesses with the best prospects for earnings growth.

In addition to profitability and growth objectives, the capital allocation process should also be driven by diversification goals. For example, the investment decisions for research and development (R&D) at a drug company can be viewed as a portfolio of options. As with options, each new drug has an option premium (R&D investment costs), current price versus strike price (project status against plan milestones), implied volatility (project uncertainty), and time to maturity (time to launch product). For the drug company, its market value is determined not only by the success of its existing products (those that are "in the money" until patent expiration) but also by the pipeline of promising new drugs (options in its R&D portfolio). As such, the management of drug companies should pay close attention to managing the life cycles of existing products as well as those in its pipeline.

This dynamic approach to portfolio management can benefit all types of companies, especially those that deal with products that exhibit out-of-the-money option characteristics (e.g., venture capital firms, like drug companies, have many more failures than successes) or products with short life cycles (e.g., technology firms).

PRACTICAL APPLICATIONS OF PORTFOLIO MANAGEMENT

Although the theoretical arguments for active portfolio management in the capital markets seem sound, there is little indisputable evidence that active management of a pure equity (or pure debt) portfolio yields consistently higher risk-adjusted returns in practice. As a result, many proponents of index investing have argued that, given lower expenses, it makes more sense to invest passively in an equity index than to bet against the assumption that investors and markets are rational and efficient, or that a particular manager has extraordinary insight into potential investments.

Does this argue against extending those arguments to business enterprises, as we did in the last section? Actually, it doesn't, because the flaws in the theory don't necessarily apply in a business context. "Holding a market portfolio" means little for the managers of a company, so there is generally no passive strategy. On the contrary, competent managers should be expected to have superior "inside" information about the portfolio of businesses that make up their company, and to make rational decisions about them. Given this, a diligent active portfolio management approach can be highly effective for controlling return targets and risk limits.

Put another way, diversification can increase shareholder value, active management can keep risk within tolerable levels, and volatility can often be managed with existing financial instruments. It makes more sense to diversify and stay on the efficient frontier than to focus risk exposure in one arena and encounter more volatility than is necessary to achieve the same expected returns. If diversification through project selection is not an option, more advanced hedging techniques (such as options, futures, etc.) can be considered.

Let's put aside the theory, now, and instead consider two fictional case studies: an insurer concerned about a sharply increased chance of bankruptcy, and a manufacturer exposed to significant foreign exchange exposures.

Reinsurance

Although issuing insurance is the primary business activity of an insurance company, many insurance companies have publicly traded equity, and one of their primary management objectives is ensuring shareholder satisfaction. Thus, when the risk profile of outstanding contracts goes beyond a defined tolerable level, many insurance companies will purchase reinsurance (insurance for insurers) from other insurance companies.

Consider the case of WindGuard, a fictitious Florida insurance company that specializes in providing homeowners with insurance against damages caused by natural catastrophes such as hurricanes. WindGuard has historically performed very well, due to mild weather and well-priced contracts. The company has liquid assets, in the form of collected premiums, of $1 billion.

Insurance is, by its nature, a risky business. The value of an insurance company is in its ability to forecast risk and price its contracts appropriately: if the risk can be quantified accurately, the leftover cash from the premiums becomes the profit. In WindGuard's case, a typical year results in a payoff rate of around 0.7 percent. That would mean that the company would pay out some $700 million of the $1 billion in claims and book $300 million as gross profit.

However, as Hurricane Andrew demonstrated in 1992, the effects of even one severe storm can be so financially devastating that an unprepared insurance issuer could be put out of business. Several small insurance companies actually were bankrupted in 1992, stranding nearly a million policyholders.[3] And new proprietary studies indicate that the weather is becoming increasingly volatile, so there is a greater chance of a pay-off rate changing to anywhere between 0.2 percent and 1.2 percent of the face value of the contracts.

WindGuard's managers are concerned about this increase in loss volatility, and specifically about the $100 billion of disaster contracts it has already issued for the following year. They are afraid that if the next season is bad enough, there will not be enough money to pay the disaster victims. This could spell disaster for the insurance company as well as the unpaid victims.

From the portfolio management standpoint, the insurance company still has the same expected return, $300 million, but the risk has reached a level where the company cannot afford to be exposed to it. One way out is to purchase reinsurance; this would reduce the net expected return for the insurance company (since the reinsurance protection has a price), but it would

---

[3]David Jastrow, "Ikon Delivers in the Eye of the Storm," *Computer Reseller News*, September 27, 1999, p. 65.

also significantly reduce risk. A reinsurance policy transforms WindGuard's exposure from unpredictable hurricane risk to the more predictable, and presumably smaller, credit risk of its reinsurer.

The company decides that it should not take the chance of going out of business, and therefore finds a reinsurance contract from another firm that allows it to reduce its risk appropriately. The contract costs $150 million, but covers all payoffs beyond $700 million. That leaves it with only $850 million in liquid assets, but guarantees that it will keep a minimum of $150 million of the premiums it has earned.

Although this is not necessarily the most efficient risk/return profile, it makes good business sense if WindGuard believes that $150 million and lower chance of bankruptcy is preferable to a $300 million and 20 percent chance of bankruptcy. Provided that WindGuard's management explains the risks and its response effectively, the company's shareholders will likely come to the same conclusion.

Currency Hedging

Stable revenue streams are extremely important to any corporation striving to maximize shareholder value. Volatile revenue streams imply a risky business environment and an unclear picture of the future. Shareholders demand a higher rate of return for this sort of volatility, so they would rather put money in "safer" stocks that promise the same rate of return with less risk. As a result, the valuation of a volatile company is generally lower than that of its peers with more stable revenues.

Fortunately, a corporation often has more control than it realizes over this revenue generation risk. Consider the case of WidgetCo, a fictional U.S.-based company that has been manufacturing America's finest widgets for many years and impressed shareholders with steadily increasing revenue and earnings growth. This year, however, much of its sales are originating abroad for the first time. Specifically, a craze for all things widgety in Japan has significantly boosted its orders there, so its anticipated U.S. sales of $50 million are matched by an anticipated 5,000 million yen in Japanese sales, which are also worth $50 million, at an exchange rate of 100 yen to the dollar.

WidgetCo management has never worried about its negligible foreign exchange risk in the past, but is now afraid that these large foreign orders are adding considerable uncertainty to the firm's future revenue flows. The company manufactures custom widgets, whose complex nature means that most orders take a minimum of three months to complete. Payment arrangements are finalized before production starts, although payment is only made on delivery. To make matters worse, WidgetCo's powerful Japanese customers are unwilling to assume any foreign currency risk exposure and will only pay in Japanese yen. Moreover, WidgetCo's suppliers and manufacturing operations are U.S. based, so there is no "natural hedge" between its yen-based revenues and the U.S. dollar expenses.

WidgetCo is exposed to the risk that the value of the yen will change against the dollar between each order and its delivery, so its Japanese revenues will translate into more (or less) than the $50 million nominal value of the order. Should WidgetCo hedge this risk, and if so, how?

WidgetCo could decide to do absolutely nothing about the risk. The expected revenue is still $100 million, albeit the U.S. dollar value of the 5,000 million yen coming from Japan is at risk of fluctuations in the U.S. dollar/yen exchange rate. If nothing happens to the exchange rate during each of the three-month periods between orders and deliveries, Widget-Co will be able to exchange its yen for dollars at the 100:1 rate each time and achieve cumulative revenues of $100 million. This would make the shareholders happy and demonstrate that WidgetCo is still profitable and growing.

This is not very likely, however. If the exchange rate deviates at all over the three-month production periods (as is far more likely), the cash flows from Japan will become uncertain. WidgetCo doesn't take a view on the direction of the yen, so it assumes that the exchange rate is just as likely to rise as to fall. That means it is equally likely to realize more or less than the nominal U.S. value of the Japanese order. For example, if the exchange rate becomes 80:1, the 5,000 million yen will become worth significantly more than the anticipated $50 million. In fact, they will now be worth $62.5 million, and WidgetCo's cumulative revenues will be $112.5 million. However, if the exchange rate became 125:1, WidgetCo's Japanese revenue would only be worth $40 million.

If both of these possibilities are equally likely, what should WidgetCo do? The answer lies in the shareholder's view of the company. The shareholders expect the company to increase its revenues and profits steadily, and would likely lose much confidence if revenues came in lower than expected. In the case where the exchange rate becomes 125:1, the $40 million revenue would force WidgetCo to report a loss for the year, and shareholders would definitely lose confidence in its earning potential.

This uncertainty is best avoided. An upside surprise, though, would likely be unsustainable in the long term since fluctuations in a foreign exchange rate should be random through time. WidgetCo's shareholders will realize this, and will likely discount such extraordinary profits. They also may realize that the unexpected upside this time could give way to an unexpected downside next time.

Although WidgetCo might be lucky enough to report a short-term gain, it could not rely on a discernible increase in its longer-term expected returns. That makes it impossible to justify taking on greater risk, and so makes it apparent that management would be remiss if it did not hedge against this kind of foreign exchange risk. Portfolio management theory espouses that risk should be as low as possible for a specific rate of return, and it certainly makes sense in this example.

After some deliberation, WidgetCo decides that its new policy will be to enter into forward contracts at the same time as each sale to Japan is signed. The forward contracts are arrangements with a third party to exchange a fixed amount of currency at a predetermined exchange rate. And so WidgetCo's managers can rest assured that widget manufacturing will continue to be a solidly reliable business.

These two simplified examples illustrate how a business could decide whether to seek third-party protection against risk. In the next chapter, we'll look at the alternatives when it comes to actually carrying out a risk transfer strategy.

CHAPTER 8

Risk Transfer

Put simply, risk transfer is the act of moving risk from one entity to another. Put more precisely, it is the deliberate exchange of probabilistically different cash flows. Either way, it is most often taken to mean the movement of some of a company's risk to an external party, but it also can mean the shifting of a given risk to a different part of the same company, or the creation of a new subsidiary within that company for the specific purpose of managing the risk.

The most traditional way in which companies transfer risk is through the purchase of various kinds of insurance—workers' compensation, general liability, and property/casualty insurance being the three most common types. When a business buys an insurance policy, some or all of the risk associated with some event covered by that policy is effectively transferred from the business to the insurer. Insurance has been around for a long time: a form of marine insurance is mentioned in the Code of Hammurabi, written some 3,800 years ago.

The second common risk transfer mechanism is through derivative products such as futures, forwards, swaps, and options. Strictly speaking, a derivative transaction alters the characteristics of a company's cash flows through a financial obligation in a way that may alter the nature or amount of risk to the company. Unjustly maligned as dangerously volatile transactions for hardened speculators, largely due to their involvement in a number of disaster stories in the 1990s, derivatives actually have a pedigree comparable with insurance and have been safely used to manage risk at many corporations.

Risk transfer revolved around either insurance or derivatives for many years—in fact, for centuries. Since the late 1980s, however, there has been a proliferation of risk transfer products that combine the features of both insurance and derivatives. These products are known collectively as *alternative risk transfer* (ART) products. Although they have yet to realize their full

95

potential, they hold the promise of risk transfer rationalization that we cited as a major benefit of enterprise risk management (ERM) back in Chapter 4.

Insurance and derivatives may at first seem an unlikely pairing. People generally (inaccurately) associate insurance with risk reduction and derivatives with risk enhancement. The blending of elements from both categories into new financial instruments is therefore an uncomfortable idea for many. A more accurate perspective is to think of insurance as a source of capital that becomes available if some event occurs (*contingent capital*) and derivatives as a means of *risk manipulation*.

The combination of capital reserving and risk manipulation can allow companies to change their risk profiles in powerful ways. Modern corporations are coming to realize that by "outsourcing" risks that they had once regarded a normal part of business operations, they can reduce their risk management expenses, simplify their administration, and even increase shareholder value.

A BRIEF HISTORY OF ART

Alternative risk transfer has no formal definition, but is broadly understood as a range of nontraditional risk transfer products, vehicles, and techniques that have been developing since the early 1970s. Most of these can be placed into one of two categories: unconventional vehicles used to cover conventional risks, and vehicles based on instruments from the capital markets. A selection of these products is given in Table 8.1.

The ART market has its roots in a deeper trend: the convergence of the capital markets and banking industries. ART products cannot be created without a high degree of interaction between the insurance industry and the capital markets, which has traditionally been in short supply. Prior to the 1970s, insurance companies were banks' customers, and vice versa. Few firms offered any kind of integration of insurance and capital markets techniques.

This began to change during the early 1980s, as large companies began to seek alternatives to costly traditional insurance. An increasing number began practicing self-insurance through self-insured retentions, risk retention groups, captives, and rent-a-captives. It should be noted that self-insurance is not the same thing as no insurance. A self-insuring corporation explicitly assumes a given risk and establishes reserves for negative contingencies. Companies practicing self-insurance typically use it to cover well-defined, high-severity, and low-frequency events. Rather than pay premiums to an insurer over several years, they save the money in their captive, to be disbursed against the occasional catastrophe—saving themselves the insurer's margin. Technically speaking, this is risk financing rather than risk transfer, but it is often referred to as an ART practice because it is used as an alternative to conventional insurance.

TABLE 8.1   ART Products

Unconventional vehicles used to cover conventional risks:

Self-insured retentions (SIR): Retentions of capital set aside for use under negative contingencies.

Risk retention groups (RRGs): Self-insurance capital pooled by a number of small- to medium-sized companies.

Captives: Subsidiary companies set up solely to insure the parent company. These are often located offshore to exploit tax advantages.

Rent-a-captives: Captives shared among several medium-sized companies; funds are managed centrally.

Earnings protection: Policies triggered by a specified earnings shortfall within a given financial period.

Finite insurance: Insurance policies extended over a multiyear time period in order to smooth profit and loss. This kind of insurance often involves very little risk transfer, but has the effect of reducing capital requirements and/or taxes.

Integrated risk and multitrigger policies: Policies covering a basket of different risks, some of which are not conventional insurance risks; sometimes called "insuratization."

Multitrigger policies: Policies triggered only if a number of different specified events occur within a given timeframe.

Multiyear, multiline policies: Policies covering a basket of different risks, spread out over a specified number of years.

Vehicles based on instruments from the capital markets:

Insurance-linked bonds: Bonds whose interest and/or principal are wholly or partially forfeit if a specified event occurs. These are most popular as a way of transferring natural catastrophe risk from reinsurers to the capital markets.

Securitization: The process of packaging risks into debt or equity instruments that can be traded in financial markets.

Cat-E-Puts: Catastrophe equity put options; options allowing a company to issue and sell equity at a predetermined price in the event of a specified catastrophic event.

Contingent surplus notes: Notes providing access to capital to their holders in the event of a loss event.

Credit default swaps: Derivatives under which the buyer pays premiums to the seller, who makes a payment to the buyer in the event of a credit default.

Weather derivatives: Policies triggered by specified meteorologic events of predetermined magnitude.

The next step in the emergence of ART was largely the result of Hurricane Andrew, which caused a huge amount of damage to South Florida in August 1992. Even though it narrowly missed hitting Miami, this hurricane was the most expensive meteorologic event ever, causing an estimated $15.5 billion in overall losses. Insurers and reinsurers were not well prepared for this event. Several went bankrupt, while those that survived had to raise the premium they charged dramatically.

The aftermath of Hurricane Andrew brought the idea of securitization to the forefront of risk transfer thinking. It became clear that a company did not need to cover its risks through conventional insurance or even through self-insurance: it could instead package its risks and sell them on the open market. Mortgage-backed securities had been traded since the late 1970s, and items such as auto loans, home loans, and credit cards had been securitized almost as long. These instruments transferred financial risks—mostly retail credit risks—away from product providers and into the hands of capital market investors.

The possibility of doing the same with insurance risk was now a serious consideration. Although the claims associated with Hurricane Andrew were huge, they represented only a tiny fraction of the multi-trillion-dollar value of capital markets. Securitization also provided a way for large single risks (such as natural catastrophe risks) to be split up and spread among many investors, who could hold the individual pieces of the risk in a more diversified portfolio than a single insurer could.

A number of vehicles aimed at facilitating this transfer sprang up in the mid-1990s. In 1995, the Chicago Board of Trade, one of the world's largest derivatives exchanges, began to market futures on Property Claims Services' indexes of catastrophe insurance losses. The same year, the Catastrophe Risk Exchange, a "bulletin-board" enabling insurers and reinsurers to swap units of risk of different types and from different geographies under standardized contracts, opened for business. Two years later, the United Services Automobile Association (USAA) kick-started the market in catastrophe-linked bonds, whose repayments change in amount and/or timing if a catastrophic event occurs. The USAA obtained $400 million in coverage by issuing hurricane-linked bonds to investors.

The implied threat to the traditional insurance business went largely unheeded. The kinds of risk involved in early securitization deals—those associated with massive natural catastrophes—were risks that most insurers didn't have enough capital to take on. If anything, they presented a way for them to offer coverage in markets that hadn't previously been viable. Many insurers also assumed that securitization would be a passing fad, and thus not worth worrying about. Seven years later, though, a total of more than $3.5 billion worth of insurance risk had been sold in capital markets.

However, later ART deals offered protection for noncatastrophic risks that could conceivably have been covered by insurance. For example, weather is a major contributor to the volatility of earnings for companies in many varied industries, ranging from clothing to tourism to agriculture.

Until recently, it was a risk that companies typically just had to live with. From the mid-1990s onward, however, companies began to write insurance against weather based on average temperature (e.g., "average degree days") or other weather-related measures. One early success for the market was a substantial policy that Boston's Logan Airport bought as protection against snowfall of greater than 44 inches, an amount that would significantly impact airport revenues. That policy paid out to the tune of some $2 million following the winter of 1995–1996, when snowfall totaled 107 inches.

Although the Logan Airport case was not the first use of weather insurance, its outcome did much to increase demand for such coverage. Predictably, other companies hoped to benefit in the same way, and thus drove up demand for weather insurance for the winter of 1996–1997. This increased demand was countered by the insurance companies' newly raised premiums. That helped to spawn the popularity of capital markets alternatives—notably, weather derivatives—which also served to provide protection but did not rely on a single, capital-rich provider.

To the surprise of those who predicted a swift demise for the emerging ART market, groundbreaking deals continued to be struck over the course of the late 1990s. In July 1998, Honeywell purchased an unusually comprehensive "integrated risk" policy, covering substantial financial and insurance risks. In October of that year, British Aerospace purchased an innovative "earnings protection" policy, which effectively guarantees that there will be no shortfall in the company's expected $3.9 billion of leasing income over the next 15 years.

Since then, ART has continued to develop at considerable speed, and it is probably fair to say that the majority of industry executives today are of the opinion that more and more ART transactions are likely to occur in the near future. This further growth of ART will be supported by a convergence of banking and insurance that goes much farther than risk transfer instruments. Not only are the instruments converging, but so are the industries. During the 1980s, large insurance and reinsurance companies such as AIG and Swiss Re developed significant capital markets and derivatives businesses. More recently, the high-profile merger between Citicorp and Travelers highlighted the business potential for such combinations.

The integration of banking and insurance business, either through mergers and acquisitions or business expansions, will likely result in more supplier resources for the ART market. These companies possess the essential competencies required for ART transactions: the insurer's skill at quantifying the likelihood and magnitude of a risk, together with the bank's experience in packaging, underwriting, and placing securities. They also have the advantage of greater capitalization than most insurers, which enables them to retain more of the risk. This can prove key in getting complex deals off the ground.

ADVANTAGES OF ART

So what does ART have to offer, besides an alternative for companies that don't like insurance? The answer, as suggested earlier, is the rationalization of risk transfer across the organization—a fundamental benefit of ERM. The traditional management of risk in "silos," where different risks are managed by different organizational units, has resulted in risk transfer programs that have not been rationalized either from the point of view of corporate policy or of economics.

From a policy perspective, a typical company might have in place a conservative (and expensive) program for eliminating currency risks, but have no risk transfer strategies for other, potentially more significant, risks such as computer outages. Even within companies where these functions are part of the same department, these policy decisions are generally made independently. This is largely due to the decentralization of risk transfer, with little or no policy coordination from senior management.

The financial objectives of these risk transfer activities are also distinct from an economic perspective. For example, a company's treasurer may want to use financial derivatives to eliminate all exposures to currency movements and to minimize the cost of issuing debt. The credit risk manager may want to reduce the company's credit exposure to emerging markets, and the insurance risk manager may want to reduce premiums paid while maintaining the same coverage for general liability and property damage.

The key problem with this approach is that risk transfer activities will likely be inconsistent from a policy perspective, and may lead to insignificant risks being overhedged and critical exposures going unremarked. Enterprise risk management enables companies to measure, manage, and transfer risks on a much more integrated and rational basis. With specific reference to risk transfer, ERM is useful for:

- Establishing more consistent risk transfer policies, such as prioritizing risk exposures that have the greatest impact on the company's earnings volatility. This ensures that important risks receive the most immediate attention.
- Incorporating the full effects of diversification, so that only the company's *net* exposures are considered in risk transfer. A company that transfers out *gross* exposures without considering diversification is bound to overhedge.
- Establishing an economic framework in which the costs and benefits of various risk transfer strategies can be evaluated. As a rule, the company should only transfer out risks if the cost of risk transfer is lower than the cost of risk retention, unless it deems the retention of certain risks to be entirely unacceptable.

Table 8.2 provides a simple example of how enterprise risk management can rationalize a company's risk transfer strategies. In this example, the company's economic capital requirements for credit, market, and operational risks are $50, $30, and $40, respectively. Diversification benefits amount to $20, resulting in a total economic capital of $100. If the cost of capital is 15 percent, the total cost of risk retention is $15.

Now assume that the company is considering an ART strategy that can reduce its risk levels by half. That is, the ART strategy will reduce the economic capital required by half and reduce the cost of risk retention to $7.50. If the risk transfer costs only $5, there will be a reduction of $2.50 in the net cost of risk. That suggests the ART would be a good move.

Such a decision framework captures all of a company's sources of risk on a consistent basis, incorporates the effect of diversification, and evaluates the cost-benefit of risk transfer. The same framework can be used to evaluate risk transfer using traditional insurance and derivative products as well as ART, and so is useful for comparing and contrasting their various effects.

ART has other advantages, too: focus; customization; cost reduction and simplified administration; and earnings stability. Let's briefly consider these.

Focus

An emerging business paradigm is that a company should do what it knows how to do best, and outsource the rest. The average company, for example, does not manufacture its own computers or build its own office furniture, unless it happens to be a computer manufacturer or furniture maker. It follows that, since most companies are not in the business of managing certain risks, they would be wise to transfer risk to an outside party. This

TABLE 8.2 Cost-Benefit Analysis

	Economic Capital	
	Without ART	With ART
Credit risk	50	25
Market risk	30	15
Operational risk	40	20
Diversification effect	−20	−10
Total economic capital	100	50
Cost of risk @ 15%	15	7.5
Risk transfer cost	0	5
Net cost of risk	15	12.5

selective delegation of risk translates to more efficient use of capital for the business as a whole.

Customization

An ART policy is to a traditional insurance policy what an over-the-counter derivative is to an exchange-traded derivative. ART deals are company specific and made to order, unlike standard insurance policies. Thus, a company buying an ART product is not obliged to purchase coverage that it is unlikely to need, and can easily arrange for extra coverage in areas in which it has unusual levels of vulnerability.

This is particularly helpful for companies with unusual portfolios of risk that might not be adequately covered by traditional insurance. For example, a company that wishes to transfer some or all of its lending risk, counterparty risk, operational risk, or settlement risk can do so only through one form of ART or another. Given the recent focus on operational risk management, companies will likely identify more nontraditional risks that they want to transfer out.

Cost Reduction and Simplified Administration

If a company uses integrated risk policies or multiline insurance, it may be able to use the natural hedges created by noncorrelated risks to reduce the overall cost of the policy in comparison with the aggregate cost of the same kinds of insurance purchased separately. A multiline policy covering both currency and catastrophe risks will typically cost less than the combined prices of a standalone currency policy and a standalone catastrophe policy, because the occurrence of natural disasters is usually largely uncorrelated with fluctuations in exchange rates.

Another advantage of using an integrated risk policy or a multiline finite policy is the reduction in insurance-related administrative duties. If all coverage is purchased from the same company, there is less paperwork, fewer contacts to be addressed, and no need to compare multiple policies for overlaps.

Earnings Stability

We've already noted that shareholders and analysts have become increasingly sensitive to earnings volatility in recent years. Given the choice of two securities that perform similarly over the long term, investors will pick the one that exhibits less variation in periodic earnings. Earnings can be smoothed to some extent by more conventional hedging, but it would typically take a great many separate (and costly) hedges to achieve the same degree of homogenization as ART products can.

PITFALLS OF ART

Despite these many benefits, ART is not a panacea. In particular, ART cannot completely eliminate risk any more than any other form of risk transfer can. As noted in *Global Institutions, National Supervision and Systemic Risk*, the landmark 1997 report[1] produced by the Group of Thirty (G30), "Of course, there is no way to eliminate risk or failure completely. The business of market intermediation is to accept an appropriate amount of risk and manage it effectively. A financial system that attempts to eliminate risk rather than managing it well would be costly and inefficient."

This holds equally true for the companies working within that system: they cannot eradicate all risks without greatly hampering their operations and financial performance. There are limits to the utility of risk transfer, whatever form it may take. Even if a company *could* transfer out most of its credit, market, and operational risk does not mean that it should. The transfer itself would generate new risks—most obviously counterparty risk to the provider of the risk transfer service. The amount of risk that a business should transfer, and the means it should use to transfer that risk, are largely dependent on the specific needs and characteristics of that company.

Although most companies hold at least some conventional insurance, many have yet to use any ART vehicles. The usual rationale is inertia. If one's company has done fairly well with conventional insurance coverage, there is little incentive to try ART. Some executives have chosen not to consider use of ART on the grounds that it is new and therefore risky.

Certainly, there is a degree of truth to this. ART does not yet have a long history, so some of its methods inevitably need to be refined. Some risks are impossible to quantify with precision, so insurance-linked bonds may be needlessly expensive to issue, or provide insufficient coverage for a given event. There are also potential cost issues. An ART product may require a larger initial outlay than a conventional insurance policy, although this is not always the case. The complexity and customized nature of ART instruments also may make the deal-making and legal documentation processes somewhat lengthier than companies are used to.

The greatest barrier to ART adoption, however, is largely cultural:

---

[1]Group of Thirty, "Global Institutions, National Supervision and Systemic Risk," 1997, p. 9.

purchase and effective utilization of ART may require a company's employees to drastically alter the ways in which they define, measure, and manage risk. Although such a paradigm shift is ultimately in the best interests of the company as a whole, the adjustment process will take time.

If a company comes to the conclusion that ART would be a good solution, there is a certain amount of education that its executives would be wise to acquire before proceeding, including a basic understanding of the product, the seller, and the regulatory and legal environment.

Understand the Product

The nature of the ART market means that the majority of ART products are still much less standardized than conventional insurance policies. Although this can be a great advantage, in terms of customizing an instrument to the individual needs of the buyer, it also can make it difficult to determine fair prices and reasonable terms. Moreover, the insurance contract needs to be developed to facilitate the efficient processing of potential claims and settlements. To make sure that an appropriate product is purchased at an appropriate price, the following questions must be answered:

- How exactly does this product work? How are the triggers determined? What would the payoff be, given a range of contingencies?
- What is the net impact on the company's economic capital requirements with this product?
- Have similar deals been transacted in the past? If so, how were they priced? Have their purchasers been satisfied with the results?
- Would it be possible to obtain the same coverage through conventional insurance? Would it cost more or less? Would there be tax or regulatory advantages to choosing one over the other?

Know the Seller

Most ART practices were founded in the mid- to late 1990s, and have thus had relatively little time to establish expertise or reputations for themselves beyond those inherited from their parent companies. Even the older practices, however, are unlikely to have experience setting up all the available variations on ART, due to the great diversity of existing products. It is therefore prudent to make a careful assessment of the capabilities of any potential ART counterparty. Some illuminating questions include:

- Has this entity transacted any ART deals in the past? If so, were they similar to the one currently under consideration? How have these previous deals performed to date?

- Are there former or current customers of this practice who might be willing to offer informed assessments of the entity's skill in ART?
- If this company has not packaged ART deals in the past, does it possess the competencies necessary to put such a policy together? In particular, does it have the experience necessary to bridge both insurance and capital markets?
- How does this company measure and assess risk? What methodologies and models does it use? Does it outsource the risk measurement underpinning the protection it writes? If so, how reliable is the company to which the risk measurement is outsourced?
- Does this company possess sufficient capital and/or reinsurance to reimburse claims that may arise? Are its reinsurers, if any, also capable of sustaining potential losses?

There may be many additional questions to ask, depending on the circumstances of both the company and the risk transfer market. As a rule, the more that is learned about the prospective deal, the less chance there is of making a costly mistake.

Regulatory and Accounting Standards

One of the more salient problems with ART is the confusion regarding its regulation. Capital markets, banks, and insurance companies have traditionally been governed according to more or less separate, and frequently mutually exclusive, sets of rules and guidelines.

It was the breakdown of the barriers between these various markets and institutions in the 1990s that allowed ART vehicles, which exist at their intersection, to proliferate. A single ART transaction may be brokered by an insurance company, packaged by an investment bank, and placed with investors in the capital markets; this means it may be subject to scrutiny by three regulators and one accounting standards board.

In fact, the treatment of ART products is generally convoluted, with multiple regulatory, legal, and accounting standards coming into play for any novel product or application. Some ART techniques (such as self-retention or captives) are well established. Many others, such as earnings protection and catastrophe bonds, are still in their infancy, however, and it is likely that more new products will join them over time. Dealings in such products must be undertaken with an unusual level of expert legal advice.

A LOOK TO THE FUTURE

It is hard to tell what will happen to ART in the years ahead. Although a large number of major players, in both the insurance industry and the capital markets, are firmly convinced that ART is the wave of the future, there also remain many who believe that ART is a craze—an overly complex solution to a simple problem that will pass within the next few years. The key issue appears to be whether ART products can be executed more cost efficiently than conventional insurance.

Let us paint an optimistic picture. A harder insurance market than that of the 1990s increases the premiums charged for conventional coverage and makes ART look inexpensive by comparison. Companies adopting ERM programs turn to ART as the most efficient means for risk transfer. Their use of these products leads to impressive returns and earnings stability, encouraging other businesses to try out similar products. Increased demand encourages expansion of existing ART practices, and new banks and insurers enter the ART market, some in joint ventures between insurers and banks. Large corporations that own both banks and insurance companies realize that ART offers them much greater opportunity than simple cross-selling does.

The increased use of ART creates a need for standardized legal treatment, and both national and international governing bodies adopt guidelines for straightforward ART regulation. Even as the market for today's ART products grows, the older ART practices begin offering new vehicles, securitizing a greater variety of risks than ever before. Investors, made newly aware of the need for hedging created by increased capital markets volatility, become increasingly eager to purchase these products to diversify their portfolios. ART becomes standard practice for companies in virtually every industry.

This view is largely based on the impressive growth of the ART market in the 1990s, even in the midst of an unusually soft market for traditional insurance. The trend toward enterprise risk management should further support the development of integrated risk transfer products. It only makes sense that as companies take an enterprise-wide approach to managing risk, they will look for new integrated risk transfer solutions that will help them meet their risk management objectives.

Furthermore, it is likely that demand for ART will increase as the field of risk management matures. Companies will increasingly come to understand that managing risk does not necessarily mean eliminating risk. They will also learn to differentiate between risks that are at the core of their business competencies and risks that can be more efficiently transferred out. When they reach this point, businesses will finally be able to devote all of their attention to their true task: doing business.

CASE STUDY: HONEYWELL

In February 1997 Honeywell Inc. took an "intrepid step forward transferring its risks"[2] by blending its property and casualty exposures and foreign exchange translation risks in a single policy insured by American International Group and brokered by J&H Marsh & McLennan. "Our objective was to significantly reduce our overall cost of risk, as well as our administrative costs," said Larry Stranghoener, Honeywell's chief financial officer and vice president.[3] Mr. Stranghoener was looking for a policy that would limit the volatility of Honeywell's financial results under the assumption that, as was discussed earlier in this chapter, stock markets punish earnings volatility with sometimes significantly lower stock prices.

By taking an integrated view of their risk exposure and using alternative risk transfer methods, Tom Seuntjens, director of risk management at Honeywell, estimated that Honeywell was able to save more than 20 percent over its traditional risk management practices. It was able to cut the number of insurance carriers it used from 17 to 10, and noted real savings in staff time and overhead because of simplified transactions.[4]

Honeywell has been pleased with the policy's performance thus far, and is now considering adding a weather risk transfer element to help offset the risk of mild winters on sales of its thermostats. Honeywell is also considering adding interest rate risks and foreign exchange transaction risks to the mix.[5] Furthermore, it is considering moving in the direction of full enterprise risk management. "We believe it makes sense from a risk management standpoint to evaluate our total risk profile, not just hazard and financial risks, but also our operational and strategic risks. Once we do that, the next logical step is to find a comprehensive way of mitigating those risks. It's still too early to say if we will go this way, but I think we already have the reputation for being aggressive and innovative in this area."[6]

---

[2]John Conley, "Risk Coverage Coup," *Global Finance* 13, no. 4, April 1999.
[3]Russ Banham, "Kit and Caboodle," *CFO: The Magazine for Senior Financial Executives*, April 1999.
[4]Neil F. Carlson, "Global Risk Management," *Strategic Finance* 81, no. 2, August 1999.
[5]Russ Banham, "Kit and Caboodle," *CFO: The Magazine for Senior Financial Executives*, April 1999.
[6]Russ Banham, "Kit and Caboodle," *CFO: The Magazine for Senior Financial Executives*, April 1999.

CHAPTER 9

Risk Analytics

In risk management, as in many other business disciplines, you cannot manage what you cannot measure. As discussed in Chapter 3, risk measurement is one of three components of the basic risk management process, the other two being risk awareness and risk control.

Risk measurement analytics are therefore an invaluable part of the risk management process. Trying to manage risk without appropriate analytical tools is like trying to fly a plane without instrumentation: while the weather is good, everything is fine and the organization may not experience substantial losses. But in bad weather, the organization can be put in grave danger without any sense of where it lies.

Increased awareness of the challenges of enterprise risk management has therefore led to increased development of advanced analytical and reporting tools. Since the early 1990s, volatility-based models such as value-at-risk (VaR) have been applied to the measurement and management of all types of market risk within an organization. VaR can be defined as the maximum potential loss that a position or portfolio will experience within a specific confidence level over a specific period of time. In market risk management, the use of VaR models has become standard practice for estimating potential loss and establishing risk limits.

Similar models, along with models of corporate default, have more recently been applied to credit risk management. Some companies have even begun experimenting with the application of these techniques to operational risk management. This has supported the quantification and management of credit, market, and operational risks on a more consistent basis.

The same techniques also can be used to evaluate the merits of risk transfer products such as derivatives, insurance, and alternative risk transfer products, as well as in the quantification of risk exposures and risk-adjusted profitability. Take risk transfer. A company's management can increase shareholder value through risk transfer if the cost of transferring out a given exposure is lower than retaining it; for example, the all-in cost of risk transfer might be 12 percent and the cost of risk capital 15 percent. Alternatively, management might want to reduce the company's risk exposure from a VaR of $300 million to a VaR of $200 million. Risk analytics can be used to determine the most cost-effective way to do that.

Several different types of analytics are available for managing risk at the enterprise level. Each of these can be grouped into one of two categories. The first focuses on risk control. These are designed to ensure that the risks being taken by an enterprise conform to its overall risk appetite. The second category is oriented around risk/reward optimization. These analytics are intended to support the enterprise in determining which risks it should take (i.e., identifying those that offer a high return relative to their risks) and which it should avoid (i.e., low returns relative to risk).

RISK CONTROL ANALYTICS

There are three major forms of risk control analytics: scenario analysis, economic capital, and risk indicators (early warning systems). Let's review them in turn.

Scenario Analysis

The most basic form of risk control is scenario analysis. A scenario analysis is a top-down, "what-if" analysis that measures the impact that a certain event (or combination of events) will have on the enterprise. An example of a scenario analysis would be to assess the financial impact of a stock market crash similar to October 1997. A stress test is a form of scenario analysis focused on specific risk factors. Stress tests are meant to capture the impact on the enterprise given changes such as:

■ The effects of interest rate movements (e.g., what impact might a 100-basis point upward shift of the yield curve have on the enterprise?)
■ Changes in the default rates in a portfolio (e.g., what happens if credit card defaults increase by 20 percent?)

Scenario analysis and stress testing are not meant to capture the absolute worst that might happen (things can *always* get worse), but rather the most severe events that seem plausible in the minds of senior management. One of the shortcomings of stress testing is that it focuses on extreme adverse events and does not capture the impact of less extreme, but more probable, adverse events. One analytic approach that addresses this problem is the simulation of a range of scenarios for a particular risk factor or set of risk factors, such as interest rates.

A specific and common form of simulation is Monte Carlo simulation. A computer performing Monte Carlo simulation is basically a machine for generating "what-if" scenarios—random scenarios based on parameters specified by the user. For example, a Monte Carlo simulation of interest rate movements could be constructed by using the historical interest rate volatility to parameterize each scenario. Monte Carlo simulation has been used in the measurement of a variety of different types of risk, including credit, market, insurance, and operational risks.

Economic Capital

Another common risk control measurement is *economic capital*. At the enterprise level, economic capital represents the amount of financial resources that the institution must theoretically hold to ensure the solvency of the organization at a given confidence level and given the risks that it is expected to take. Economic capital is therefore a function of two quantities: the organization's so-called solvency standard and its risk.

The solvency standard is the desired creditworthiness of an organization and can be inferred from its (desired) debt rating. For example, an institution that has a target solvency standard of 99.9 percent would default, on average, only once every 1,000 years. This is roughly equivalent to an institution awarded an "A" rating by Standard & Poor's credit rating service.

A higher solvency standard implies that more economic capital is held for a given level of risk; put the other way, the greater the risk that an institution bears, the greater the financial resources it must have in order to maintain a given solvency standard. A widely accepted theoretical framework for relating the amount of capital a financial institution needs to hold against a given level of risk is based on Robert Merton's model of default,[1] which essentially says:

- A company's shareholders own the right to default on payments to debt-holders, and will do so if the value of the firm's equity ("net assets") drops to zero.

---

[1] Robert C. Merton, "On the Pricing of Corporate Debt: The Risk Structure of Interest Rates," *Journal of Finance* 29, 1994, pp. 449–470.

- Debt-holders charge shareholders for default risk by demanding a spread over the risk-free rate on the funds they provide.
- The probability of default is a function of the *current* level and potential *variability* (the probability distribution) of a firm's net asset value.

The calculation of an organization's economic capital is generally done "bottom up." That is, the economic capital is calculated separately for each type of risk, then aggregated, taking into account the effects of diversification, to come up with the overall economic capital for the entire enterprise. The basic process is:

- Generate standalone distributions of changes in the enterprise's value due to each source of risk.
- Combine the standalone distributions, incorporating diversification effects.
- Calculate the total economic capital for the combined distribution at the desired target solvency standard.
- Attribute economic capital to each activity based on the amount of risk generated by the activity.

Risk Indicators

A third form of risk control analytics is risk indicators, or "early warning systems." These are designed to give timely information about changes in risk conditions to allow management to take appropriate action to mitigate risk. Early warning systems use both external market data and internal data.

External systems make use of market and economic data to indicate changes in the amount of risk to which an institution is exposed. Data commonly used this way include interest rates, foreign exchange rates, credit spreads, unemployment rates, changes in gross domestic product, the volatilities of these factors, and so on. This information can be monitored with respect to their levels and trends, as well as translated into the economic impact on an organization, such as increases in funding costs.

Internal systems make use of institution-specific data to indicate changes in risk levels. The risks that are being measured may either be tied directly to the bottom line (e.g., credit card default rates) or associated less directly with an increase in risk levels (e.g., increased concentration in the lending book, or increased line utilization, indicates higher probability of customer default). In either case, the advance warning will allow management to establish policies and procedures to reduce exposure to the specific risks identified by the early warning systems.

RISK OPTIMIZATION ANALYTICS

The goal of risk management is not to reduce an institution's risk to zero, or even to minimize risk. Without risk, there is no return. Rather, it is to ensure that the enterprise is well compensated for the risk that it takes, subject to the constraint that the risks taken fall within the institution's overall risk appetite. The risk optimization analytics discussed below can be used to help maximize returns relative to risks.

Risk-Adjusted Return on Capital

Risk-adjusted return on capital (RAROC) can be calculated for an institution as a whole, or separately for each of its individual activities. Because the amount of economic capital that is required to support each of the enterprise's activities is proportional to the risk generated by that activity, economic capital can be used as a standard measurement of risk. Combining the economic capital required to support the risks of an activity with the activity's expected economic returns yields a ratio that represents the amount of return the institution expects per unit of risk it takes:

$$RAROC = \frac{Risk\text{-}adjusted\ Return}{Economic\ Capital}$$

The risk-adjusted return is based on net income or expected return. RAROC using net income provides an indication of actual profitability, whereas the use of expected return provides a measurement of normalized profitability. This is particularly relevant when applying RAROC to credit risk-related activities, because expected losses are often used in the calculation of return, rather than actual losses.

The primary use of RAROC is to compare the risk/return of different, and potentially quite diverse, business activities. This is particularly useful when capital is scarce and an institution needs a way to choose between investments.

Economic Income Created

One disadvantage of RAROC as a performance metric is that it does not capture the *quantity* of return that an activity generates. For example, suppose that a business unit currently has a RAROC of 25 percent, well above the parent institution's hurdle rate of 15 percent. If RAROC were the primary performance metric, the unit would not want to generate additional business that did not meet or exceed its current RAROC of 25 percent, because the additional business would move the average RAROC below its current level. This is obviously problematic, because the institution's management would like the subsidiary unit to pursue all opportunities that return the corporate hurdle rate of 15 percent or more.

It would therefore be desirable to use a metric that captures the quantity of return that a unit or activity generates in this case. Economic income created (EIC) is a risk optimization tool that can be used as just such a metric:

EIC = Risk-adjusted return − (Hurdle rate × economic capital)

Any business whose return on marginal economic capital is greater than the hurdle rate increases EIC. EIC is thus a better mechanism for setting performance targets, because it clearly encourages business unit managers to pursue all above-hurdle, marginal growth opportunities (whereas RAROC targets can have the adverse effect of discouraging growth in businesses with high historical RAROC performance).

Shareholder Value and Shareholder Value-Added

RAROC and EIC are measurements of performance in a given period of time. Although they give a sense of performance in the current period, they do not directly measure the economic value of businesses. Shareholder value modeling provides the translation from these point-in-time measurements to measurements of the *intrinsic* economic value of a business as an ongoing concern.

Shareholder value (SHV) models must capture the full economic value of a transaction or business activity, which is to say the *present* value of all future cash flows. Shareholder value-added (SVA) measures the degree to which shareholder value exceeds the value of the capital invested. Borrowing from the popular dividend discount model for equity analysis, formulas for these two measurements are shown below:

$$\text{SHV} = \text{Discounted Value of Cash Flows}$$

$$= \text{EC} * \left(\frac{\text{RAROC} - \text{g}}{\text{Hurdle} - \text{g}} \right)$$

$$\text{SVA} = \text{Discounted Value of EVAs}$$

$$= \text{EC} * \left(\frac{\text{RAROC} - \text{g}}{\text{Hurdle} - \text{g}} - 1 \right)$$

The new factor introduced by SVA analysis is the measurement of the future growth prospects of a business, g. This is inherently difficult to estimate, particularly for time horizons well into the future. Although it would be more useful, and accurate, to use detailed cash flow projections for each unit, most organizations employ a medium-term horizon of three to five years in determining the growth rate. Note that the ratio involving RAROC, hurdle, and growth (g) in the SHV equation is conceptually similar to a market-to-book ratio and can thus be benchmarked externally.

SVA is designed as a decision support metric. At the firm-wide level, SVA analyses are generally used to support decisions about internal resource allocation, as well as decisions on acquisitions, divestitures, and joint ventures. SVA employs many of the same conceptual factors that are used in the construction of the performance metrics described above, but differs from them in that it captures both tangible and intangible changes in value.

For example, changes in regulation or competition that may affect the long-term growth prospects of a business may not affect its contribution in a recent period (as measured by EIC). However, they will alter its value contribution to the firm over a longer time horizon (as measured by SVA).

So much for the models applicable at the enterprise level. Let's now review the models used in the evaluation of market, credit, operational, and insurance risks. Once again, volumes have been written about the technical details of these models. We will confine ourselves here to sketching out the properties of the various analytics, but the interested reader is strongly recommended to explore these subjects in more detail.

MARKET RISK ANALYTICS

Interest Rate Models

Broadly speaking, there are two uses for interest rate or "term structure" models: pricing interest rate–dependent instruments and interest rate risk management. In particular, such models are useful in predicting the dynamics of cash flows that are contingent on interest rates. Such cash flows are often path-dependent (i.e., they vary according to the behavior of interest rates, not just their level), a classic example being prepayment of mortgages.

Value-at-Risk Models

Value-at-risk (VaR) is one of the most common forms of market risk measurement. There are three broad approaches to calculating VaR, each with its own strengths and weaknesses. The *parametric* approach uses volatilities and correlations of risk factors; the *Monte Carlo simulation* method uses a simulation model to generate a large number of possible outcomes; and the *historical simulation* technique uses previously observed price and rate movements.

The primary advantage of parametric VaR is that it can be calculated quickly and is computationally simple, and is thus useful when analyzing portfolios with many different assets and risk factors. However, it assumes that asset returns are linearly related to risk factor returns, and that the risk factor returns are normally distributed. Thus, parametric VaR ignores non-linear price sensitivities, such as gamma for options and convexity for bonds. In addition, parametric VaR models (usually) assume that price movements are normal. Both of these factors cause underestimations of the potential future volatility of portfolios.

Monte Carlo VaR, on the other hand, does not make the assumption that asset returns are linearly dependent on price. In calculating portfolio profit and loss, Monte Carlo simulates normally distributed future scenarios, using the variances of risk factor returns as a parameter, and uses them to reevaluate the portfolio. More complex versions fully reprice the portfolio assets. As a result, Monte Carlo has some disadvantages. It is generally the form of VaR that takes longest to calculate, and it still assumes that risk factor returns are normally distributed.

Historical simulation VaR is the only method that removes the assumption of normally distributed risk factor returns, as well as the assumption that asset returns are linearly dependent on price. Under historical VaR, the daily fluctuations actually observed in risk factors in the past are used to simulate the impact on the valuation of a portfolio of assets. In so doing, historical VaR produces better estimates of the actual distribution of risk factor returns, using full repricing; however, it repeats the exact returns observed over some historical observation period. This means the model's predictions are based solely on market fluctuations that were actually observed and take no account of those that are possible (and potentially important) but have not actually happened. In addition, historical VaR is computationally expensive because full repricing is employed.

Asset/Liability Management Models

VaR models are suitable for portfolios that are composed of liquid instruments. However, illiquid portfolios and structural positions (such as a bank's "natural" asset/liability mismatch position) have some characteristics that make VaR models (particularly parametric VaR models) suboptimal for risk measurement. These characteristics include longer liquidation periods due to low liquidity, nonlinearity of customer behavior, and embedded options within the assets and liabilities.

Asset/liability management (A/LM) models represent an improvement over VaR for illiquid portfolios for several reasons. First, they allow more sophisticated interest rate and foreign exchange modeling. Monte Carlo and parametric VaR permit unusual yield curve movements that are unlikely to occur in reality. Historical simulation may or may not suffer from this problem, depending on how the simulation is constructed. A/LM models generally use more sophisticated mechanisms for capturing yield curve behavior, such as inversion between short-term and long-term rates, and are therefore more likely to yield accurate results.

A/LM models also offer better accounting than VaR for long holding periods. VaR models use a short holding period and volatility measurement period (generally either a 1- or 10-day holding period, with volatility measurement done daily). This approach makes sense for short-term trading exposures. However, there are long-term relationships between risk factors that may not manifest themselves in the short term. Issues such as the mean reversion of interest rates or "covered interest rate parity" for foreign exchange mean that the risk factors do not necessarily change in a purely random or independent manner. A/LM models are generally parameterized over a longer horizon and are therefore more likely to capture the effects of long-term relationships between risk factors.

A final advantage of A/LM models is better treatment of embedded options and path-dependent products. The bulk of traded products have relatively simple relationships with risk factors such as interest rates and foreign exchange rates. Illiquid portfolios, particularly the structural balance sheets of banks, may include asset and liability positions with complex relationships to risk factors. For example, assets such as U.S. residential mortgages effectively bundle prepayment options with debt, and as a result have a relatively complex relationship with interest rates. A/LM models are designed to capture this complex behavior, and appropriately value the change in assets and liabilities due to changes in risk factors.

CREDIT RISK ANALYTICS

A large variety of analytics are available for supporting credit risk measurement. Most of the available tools focus on estimating the components of expected loss for individual credit exposures. These analytics include:

- Credit-scoring models, which estimate the expected default frequency of a credit counterparty at a point in time.
- Credit migration models, which focus on how the credit quality of exposures changes over time.
- Credit exposure models, which estimate the loan equivalent exposure of credit transactions.
- Credit portfolio models, which assess the risk/return profile of a portfolio of credits and take the impact of diversification into account.

Credit-Scoring Models

One of the key inputs when measuring credit risk is the likelihood that a given credit exposure will default over a given period of time, often called the expected default frequency (EDF). The most common analytical tool used to perform this estimation is a credit-scoring model. There are three basic types of credit-scoring models: empirical models, expert models, and Merton-based models.

Empirical models are constructed by analyzing the historical default experience for similar credit exposures. For example, an empirical model might be based on an analysis that uses income, outstanding debt, and length of employment to predict the default frequency of a credit card customer. Fair Isaac's FICO score is an example of an empirical model applied to a consumer customer base.

Expert models attempt to capture the judgment of credit experts in the form of a model. In most cases, credit experts are senior individuals within the organization who are seen as having strong credit assessment skills. These models tend to be employed when the credit assessment process is considered to be complex and difficult, or when the analysis of a vast amount of data is required.

Finally, Merton-based models use finance theory and market information to develop implied default rates of companies. Credit Monitor, a product developed by the KMV Corporation, is an example of a credit-scoring tool that falls into this category. The basic finance theory used by such models is the Merton model of a firm's capital structure described above: a firm defaults when its asset value falls below the value of its liabilities. A company's default probability then depends on the amount by which assets exceed liabilities, and the volatility of those assets.

Market information (such as the volatility of a company's stock price) can be used to estimate the volatility of a company's assets. By making some assumption as to the shape of the distribution of changes in asset value (e.g., assuming that they are normally distributed), we can estimate the probability that the value of a company's assets will be lower than the value of its liabilities. This probability is then used as the basis for assessing the probability that the company will default.

Credit Migration Models

The credit-grading models described above are useful for developing a point-in-time estimate of the default frequency of a company or entity. However, credit quality can and does change over time. If an institution has long-term credit exposures, it is essential to understand how credit quality can change in the future.

The problem of estimating long-term default probabilities is complicated by the reality of credit migration, the fact that companies' fortunes and creditworthiness will likely change from one year to the next. Thus the EDF, per annum, of a long-term facility is not necessarily equal to the one-year EDF. It would only be the same if creditworthiness remained constant. Similarly, very short-term credits also may have different EDFs than one-year facilities.

The primary objective of credit migration models is to attach cumulative default probabilities over a number of years to internal grades. There are several ways of doing this, just as there are several ways to tackle the EDF-based calibration of a credit-grading scale. These methods can be classified into three categories according to the way that the relevant data are used or sourced: the cohort study approach, the migration matrix approach, and the benchmarking approach.

Under the cohort study approach, the credit portfolio is divided into cohorts based on origination year, geography, and risk grade. Then, multiyear EDFs are estimated by using the multiyear cumulative default rates actually observed historically for different grades of credit. This is similar to the historical method of calibrating the one-year EDF, and suffers from the similar problem: there are frequently not enough reliable data. This is particularly true for longer time periods, as many grading scales have not been used consistently for very long. Nonetheless, the cohort study approach is often used by credit card and mortgage lenders because the marketing programs and product features vary each year. These variations can have a material impact on the credit performance of each cohort.

Another way of estimating multiyear EDFs is through the use of migration matrices. The main idea is to avoid having to measure default rates directly by observing the rates at which grades change—the rates at which credits "migrate" between grades. Migration rates are much higher (and thus easier to measure accurately) than default rates, particularly for higher-quality credits. Together with the previously calibrated EDFs for each credit grade, a table of migration probabilities implies a complete series of long-term EDFs.

This process is most easily described by example. To find the two-year EDF for an A+ borrower, for instance, we would first measure the probability that, within a year (or some other period), an A+ company will remain an A+ company (e.g., 85 percent). In addition, we need the probability that it will become an A (10 percent), the probability that it will become an A- (4 percent), and so on. The probability of default in the first year will be the 2–basis point characteristic of an A+. The second-year default probability, however, will be the weighted average of the EDFs associated with each of the different grades to which the credit *might* migrate. The weights are assigned according to the probability that an A+ company will change to that grade in a year.

Counterparty Credit Exposure Models

The trading of financial instruments such as foreign exchange forwards, forward rate agreements, and swaps often generates *potential* credit risk exposure. The credit risk is generated when market conditions move in one party's favor, so the contracts in which it has engaged have a positive mark-to-market value, or replacement cost. If the other party to the trade (the counterparty) defaults and cannot honor its side of the contract, the first party is exposed to the current mark-to-market amount.

Because this exposure is contingent on the default of a counterparty, a credit risk framework is usually used to evaluate the risk. However, unlike the many forms of credit risk where the exposure is known (such as term loans), the exposure to a counterparty is in this case driven by *market* risk factors such as interest rates or foreign exchange rates. Analytical models are needed to estimate potential exposure to a counterparty.

The simplest approach is to use a percentage of the notional value of a contract as the expected exposure for calculating credit risk, potentially varying by type of contract and term of contract. This approach is generally too simplistic, and can substantially misestimate risk. An improvement is to use the present market value of the contract, although this does not take into consideration the potential for greater (or lesser) exposure in the future. Fortunately, potential credit exposures for most (but not all) instruments can be calculated using formulas that take as their inputs the volatility of the value of the contract and the maturity of the contract.

These formula-based approaches work well for single-payment contracts, such as foreign exchange forward contracts or forward rate agreements. However, they generally do not work well for multiple-payment contracts such as interest rate swaps. In these cases, a Monte Carlo simulation approach would be more accurate. In using a Monte Carlo approach, the expected and maximum credit exposures can be estimated given a large range of potential rate and price movements.

CREDIT PORTFOLIO MODELS

The credit risk analytic models we have described thus far in this chapter have focused on the assessment of individual credit risk exposures. Credit portfolio models are used to aggregate the credit risk of individual exposures, and to determine how losses behave at the portfolio level. There are three general approaches to modeling credit portfolios: financial models, econometric models, and actuarial models. We will discuss each of these, as well as how they can be reconciled.

Financial models such as The RiskMetrics Group's CreditMetrics and

KMV's Portfolio Manager rely on the Merton model of a firm's capital structure. As described above, this assumes that a firm defaults when its asset value falls below the value of its liabilities. A borrower's default probability then depends on the likelihood that the value of assets will drop below the value of liabilities, which in turn is a function of volatility of the value of those assets.

The asset value is usually modeled as log-normally distributed, which means that changes in asset value are normally distributed. The default probability can then be expressed as the probability of a standard normal variable falling below some critical value, representing the point at which the value of liabilities exceeds the value of assets. The distribution of possible losses on the portfolio is found through Monte Carlo simulation.

Econometric models such as McKinsey & Company's CreditPortfolioView attempt to model the default rate for a borrower (or group of similar borrowers) in terms of the behavior of macroeconomic variables. To put it simply, the default rate of each sector (representing a group of similar borrowers) is determined by changes in macroeconomic variables such as interest rates, gross national product, and so on. The portfolio loss distribution is again calculated by Monte Carlo simulation.

Actuarial Models

The CreditRisk+ model developed by Credit Suisse Financial Products makes use of mathematical techniques that are commonly used for loss distribution modeling in the actuarial (insurance) literature. CreditRisk+ is based on an analytical closed-form formula for default risk—in other words, a formula that takes average default rates and volatilities as inputs and provides a distribution of credit portfolio losses as the output. As such, it requires relatively little data and can be evaluated quickly compared with the computationally intensive and slow Monte Carlo simulations used by the financial and econometric models. The main problem with this approach is that it assumes that the bank already has useful default data, which is not always the case.

It has actually been shown (by Ugur Koyluoglu of Oliver, Wyman and Company and Andrew Hickman of ERisk) that these models are actually equivalent provided that their assumptions and input data are phrased in compatible ways. This might be expected: after all, the credit portfolio risk should be an absolute number, not dependent on the choice of model.

In practice, however, the models' incompatibility is not easy to overcome. A user might end up with quite different risk results when the same portfolio is analyzed using such dissimilar models—and this can, in fact, be a useful way to pin down the real risks of the situation.

OPERATIONAL RISK ANALYTICS

There are two basic approaches to estimating operational risk: top-down and bottom-up. The first is a top-down approach that generally applies to the entire enterprise. The second is a bottom-up approach that analyzes operational risks generated at the activity level, which are then aggregated to determine a measurement of operational risk for the enterprise.

Top-Down Approaches

There are two types of techniques that are employed in the top-down approach. The first is the use of "analogs." This technique first strips away all specific risks that can be identified, such as credit risk or market risk. Any remaining risk is classified as operational risk.

This is then estimated by benchmarking public companies whose operations are generally similar to that of the enterprise. Because these public companies are generally selected to be "pure play analogs" of the business operations of the enterprise, the amount of equity necessary to support operational risk (adjusted for credit quality and size differentials) can be based on these external benchmarks. For example, the equity required for the information technology (IT) function can be estimated by benchmarking the equity levels of pure IT companies.

The second technique uses historical loss data to provide an empirical distribution of operational risk losses. A "loss database" is used as the basis for parameterizing this loss distribution, and is then scaled to suit the size of the enterprise's operations.

Bottom-Up Approaches

One bottom-up technique for estimating operational risk is through "self-assessment." Basically, this technique is a credit assessment of a particular activity, as if the enterprise were "lending" money to finance the ongoing operations of an activity. The less the enterprise is willing to lend to an activity, the more equity the activity implicitly requires (and, consequently, the more risk it generates).

Another bottom-up technique is to build a model of the cash flows of an activity or operation. The inputs to the model are risk factors that affect the profitability of the activity, and Monte Carlo simulation could be used to generate a distribution of value for the activity. These types of models work well where business relationships can be explicitly tied to external market risk factors. An example of a business where this bottom-up approach works well is mortgage origination, where the amount of volume that is generated by the business unit can be directly tied to changes in interest rates.

CHAPTER 10

Data and Technology

As discussed in earlier chapters, organizations of all types—both financial and nonfinancial—have, in recent years, become much more appreciative of the importance of risk in all its various incarnations. Quite apart from the arguments for risk management as a good thing in its own right, it is becoming increasingly rare to find an organization of any size whose stakeholders are not demanding that its management exhibit risk awareness.

Faced with this pressure, but also with a discipline whose successes are frequently intangible and nonintuitive—for example, reduced probability of a significant loss—the management often turns to one of the few aspects of risk management that is easily measured in dollars and cents: investment in risk management technology. Chairpersons hailing the benefits of such investments have for some years been a staple feature of financial institutions' annual reports; the trend is now repeating in the nonfinancial sectors.

This heavy investment is at least partially justified. We noted in Chapter 2 that it is critical to balance the yin and yang—hard and soft issues—if risk management is to be truly effective, and the hard side of risk management is inextricably intertwined with technology: for carrying out the analytics described in the previous chapter, for gathering the data required as inputs to the analytics, and for reporting the data produced as their outputs.

But it is also easy for investment in technology to become an end in itself. Less emphasis has been paid to the value for money achieved in risk management technology projects—even though, in some cases, hundreds of millions of dollars have been spent with little to show for it. In this chapter, we'll consider the evolution and components of risk management systems and the keys to successful implementation.

EARLY SYSTEMS

The first implementations of risk management systems were, in many ways, steps into the unknown. The boom in trading during the 1980s and 1990s led to sharply increased demand for systems that could price instruments like bonds, equities, and derivatives quickly and accurately. The next stage was for systems that could carry out risk modeling of those individual instruments and trading portfolios—in other words, systems that implemented the stress test, simulation, and value-at-risk models described in Chapter 9.

Project managers were faced with the task of building these systems using huge amounts of data covering the terms and conditions of each of the instruments being analyzed, live market data, time series data for the construction of scenarios, and limits against which exposures might be compared. Most of these data were scattered, inconsistent, and error prone. The toughest to manage were the terms and conditions data: traded products are hugely variable and complex, especially when nonstandardized products such as swaps and structured products are considered. All of this complexity is reflected in the terms and conditions that describe these contracts.

Project managers typically had to choose between two main data sources when gathering terms and conditions data. The first source was the accounting system, in which all of the holdings of the bank could be found. However, this typically stored only a subset of the attributes required for risk calculations. The alternative source was in the front office trading systems. All the attributes for each deal could be found here, but the deals were typically split over a proliferation of position-keeping systems and spreadsheets.

In general, in the earliest projects, decisions were made to extend the data stored in accounting systems to include all the attributes required for risk management, and then to source risk data from the back-office system. Conceptually, this approach makes sense. Why rebuild multiple interfaces to trading systems when the majority of the data are already available in a single location?

Unfortunately, it hit two major problems. First, the process of extending the accounting system was often far more protracted than had been estimated, resulting in significant project overruns. Second, each time a new instrument type was traded, that instrument had to be implanted in the front-office system and mapped into the back-office system. Finally, the data model of the back-office system had to be extended and mapped into the risk management system—a lengthy process during which these new risks go unmeasured.

The basic problem was that project managers had tried to take advantage of the existing interfaces that had been built out of front-office systems.

These interfaces had been designed for accounting purposes rather than risk management purposes, so adapting them to risk management was a complex, extensive process. A new approach was required.

DATA MANAGEMENT

Data warehouses had achieved considerable success in the retail sector in the 1980s, where they had been used for a number of purposes, including the storage and management of customer information. The application of data warehouses to risk engine integration is conceptually appealing, a factor that helps to explain their significant, if short-lived, success.

The idea was as follows. Rather than extend the back-office system and all of the interfaces into the back office to transform risk data, why not simply build new interfaces into a custom-built database from which the risk engine could extract data for analysis? There were other clear advantages to this approach. By aggregating high-quality, clean, and comprehensive data into a single database, it would be possible to link other applications to the same database, such as performance measurement systems, customer relationship management systems, and even profit and loss engines.

However, the need to aggregate all risk data into a single location was partly driven by the technical inadequacy of the risk engines. The novel nature of risk management meant that risk engines were typically built by financial engineers whose understanding of mathematical finance was, in general, considerably greater than their understanding of technology.

As a result, the risk engines were often structured so that all of the data had to be mapped into them in a single batch and the risk analysis carried out in a single run. Such applications have been described as monolithic black boxes. A more logical approach would have been to recognize that a risk analysis could be split into multiple components, each analyzing a subset of the book using consistent assumptions, and with a final component aggregating the results.

Many financial organizations embarked on extremely ambitious warehousing projects, to the delight of software vendors and implementation consultants. The vast majority of these projects failed to live up to expectations; some of them just plain failed. There were three main reasons for this.

First, these projects were often technology driven, with business users providing little, if any, direction. In many cases the projects had no clear business objectives. As a result, they ran and ran without producing tangible results. A second problem was the time required to build and maintain the many interfaces with source systems. The third problem was the sheer ambition of the projects. Ultimately, the data types required for risk management are extremely complex and varied, and are not conducive to being stored in a single database.

The failure of data warehouse projects prompted some critics to liken the approach to "boiling the ocean." An obvious reaction to the cost and time overruns in many data warehouse projects was to change the scope of the warehouse project. Rather than having a single warehouse attempting to hold all of the risk data in an organization, teams realized that a more effective approach was to implement a series of data marts, each of which resembled a "mini-warehouse." Each data mart could then specialize in the data required for a single area of functionality.

Thus, rather than attempting to consolidate all data in a single location, a series of data marts would be set up containing subsets of data. One might hold market risk–relevant data from the trading room, for example, while another would hold credit risk information. A third would be set up to hold extracts from each of the two source marts to enable enterprise-level calculations. This approach reduced the scale of the database implementations to more manageable levels, although it magnified the scope of the reconciliation problem in many cases, due to extensive duplication of stored data.

Data marts effectively solved the problem of warehouse projects overrunning due to lack of specific, clearly defined business objectives. They did nothing, however, to deal with the time taken to develop interfaces and to reconcile the data stored in the marts. Nor did they solve one of the essential problems of any risk system implementation (or indeed, any technology implementation), namely, garbage in, garbage out.

Time series data, for example, typically contain a small amount of bad data. Corrupted data or an entry error can result in the price of a stock that typically hovers around $45 being recorded one day at $450. This kind of error can cause significant problems in risk calculations, so "data cleansing" algorithms must be implemented to search out and fix such errors. These algorithms work either by comparing price data from multiple sources or by comparing a given value against historical ranges within user-defined tolerances.

Another example of the need for data cleansing is found in counterparty data. Most financial institutions store information about counterparties using a huge variety of names and codes. Thus Chase Manhattan Bank might be recorded in systems as "Chase," "Chase Manhattan," "Chase Manhattan Bank," and a variety of other versions. In order to aggregate exposures to Chase Manhattan, the risk engine must understand that "Chase" and "Chase Manhattan Bank" are the same entity.

Several partial solutions have emerged to deal with data cleansing. The first class of solutions takes the form of clean data sources. These range from firms such as Interactive Data or Asset Control, who can provide cleaned and comprehensive databases of terms and conditions, through to vendors such as Olsen & Associates, Reuters, or Telekurs, who provide clean historical or live market data. The second class of solutions comprises algorithms or interfaces for cleaning specific data types, for example, FAME's Historical Market Data (HMD)/Risk.

INTERFACE BUILDING

The majority of the time and effort expended on a reasonably planned risk management system implementation project goes into interface construction. If the risk data are being extracted from front-office trading systems, it will be necessary to build interfaces from each of the trading systems to the risk engine. In many early implementations few tools or packaged interfaces were available to developers, so each had to be coded manually.

Each interface was made up of a number of distinct stages. First, a customized extraction program pulled the data out of the trading system. Many trading systems come with such extract interfaces, but these may need modification to provide all the data required for risk analysis. Second, the risk data must be transformed into the format required by the risk engine. While a coupon rate may be stored as "7% ANNU ACT/365" in a trading system, the same data might need to be reformatted to "0.07ANNACT-365" for a risk system. The rules for such a transformation have to be specified for every attribute of every piece of data going into the risk system.

Clearly, each interface is specific to a particular trading system and a particular risk system. If either is updated or replaced, the interface will have to be rebuilt. Similarly, if an organization starts trading instruments not previously coded into the interface, it will have to be extended. Problems arose because many early interfaces were poorly documented, so although they might have been well designed and understood by the original developer, they were in many cases completely incomprehensible to anyone else.

In situations where the original interface builder had left the organization, interface modifications became extremely time consuming. To solve these problems, vendors of risk management systems started to sell mapping tools alongside their principal offerings. Simultaneously, many integration consultants began offering experienced resources and similar tools to aid the process.

Mapping tools typically provide several features to their users. First, and most importantly, they make interfaces transparent, so that it is relatively simple for future developers to extend an interface. Each of the rules required to transform a given attribute of a given instrument from a given source system is stored in a database and clearly documented. It is simple to locate, understand, and modify all of the individual rules. Second, mapping tools can make interfaces reusable, since the transformation rules are specific to a trading system/risk system pair. Integration consultants have led the efforts to develop and resell such interfaces. Even with the support of mapping tools, risk management implementations still typically take many months, and sometimes years.

MIDDLEWARE

Another focus of efforts to reduce implementation time was a reduction in the total number of interfaces required. In a typical trading organization there are a number of front office trading systems and a number of systems that require extracts from the front office. These include the risk systems, the accounting systems, management information systems, performance measurement systems, and more. The number of interfaces that must be built between each of these systems is obviously a function of the number of systems that provide data and the number that consume data. Once there are two or more providers and two or more consumers, it becomes more efficient to implement messaging-oriented middleware (MOM) between the consumers and providers.

MOM, of which Tibco and MQ Series are prominent examples, uses a variety of models for interprocess communication and offers significant benefits for enterprise risk management, including guaranteed delivery and interface transparency and robustness due to rule-based routing, error logs, and audits.

Conceptually, it seems reasonable that implementing MOM will save time and effort when there are two or more consumers and providers of data, since fewer interfaces will need to be built. In many cases, however, MOM projects did not enhance risk management projects, since there is often only one consumer for any given type of risk data. Even looking at the broader picture, where there are many consumers of front-office data, the implementation of MOM is still not always the most practical move. This is because the consumers of data usually require different data from each other so, in essence, the implementation of MOM falls victim to the same factors that sank many warehouse implementation projects.

Given that MOM provides more reliable delivery than other channels, it does ensure that the data in a risk system are generally more consistent with the data in the source systems. Ultimately, however, this is not perfect, and reconciliation will still be required as long as duplicate data are stored, or functionality duplicated, in two locations. Eliminating the need to reconcile the two sets of data requires a further advance: distributed architecture.

DISTRIBUTED ARCHITECTURES

Advances in application design during the 1990s made it feasible to build distributed software applications. These shift the processing from centralized application servers (which require the relevant data to be extracted from the source and moved to the server) to an environment where processing is moved out to the source data. This is achieved by using enabling technologies that "hide" the location of distributed objects from the application servers, which in turn allows the implementation of much more modular and scalable solutions. The implementation of these frameworks usually delivers many network services (e.g., security), which overcome the additional overheads of working within the distributed environment.

Component-based software models are nothing new but the ability to deploy applications rapidly in a distributed environment using these technologies is. It allows the development process to concentrate on solving the business problem rather than the complexities of implementation. These software tools effectively allow source data to be encapsulated with their processing logic into distributed objects that exist throughout the enterprise. This results in a single transaction—an insurance policy, for example—having a single "point of persistence" throughout the enterprise, rather than multiple ones with all the associated reconciliation issues.

Leaving the data management in the source system and moving the functionality there removes the need for complex data reconciliation processes and changes the problem into one of synchronization: the need to ensure that data are viewed at the same time point and object version if the results are to be accurately aggregated.

An example of this would be a pricing component that produces a distribution of values for a set of transactions in a set of trading systems under a given set of scenarios. In order to aggregate these distributions correctly, one must ensure that the scenarios, the transactions included, and the pricing algorithm are consistent across all the pricing calculations. These challenges can be addressed with standard technology components, rather than the bespoke business logic required in the centralized approach.

With distributed object technology, the implementation of the data-specific functionality is hidden from the application server processes. This delivers great scalability to the architecture that can grow with the organization. Risk calculations, as we have learned, tend to be computationally intensive. The ability to distribute the additive components of a calculation across not only processors, but also machines, opens up whole new vistas of performance.

This architectural model implicitly requires the development of an enterprise-wide object model, but not an enterprise data model. From a data-centric view we are still left with the business object mapping tasks that are specific to each source system. This may sound like a return to the cumbersome point-to-point interfaces of ancient times, but the interfaces here are not between applications but between source data and business object. These are usually less complex to implement and do not need to be forced into a single representation that meets all requirements.

KEY FACTORS FOR A SUCCESSFUL IMPLEMENTATION

The development and implementation of risk management systems to analyze enterprise-wide risks require substantial resources, yet they are a requirement for any enterprise risk management program. A successful effort can provide management with important information to help them control risks and make better business decisions. A failed effort can result in not only wasted money but also wasted time and organizational resources. There are key success factors that can increase the probability of success:

- Appointing a seasoned risk professional as the project leader, as opposed to leaving it to the technical staff
- Clearly defining the user requirements, including a prototype report that lays out the functionality and reporting specifications
- Establishing consistent standards for data and programs so that the risk management systems can communicate with other systems both inside and outside the company
- Using structured and modular programming techniques so that the risk management systems are scalable with new products and new methodologies
- Developing a clear project plan with specific responsibilities, milestones, timing, and expected performance
- Applying "chunking" methodologies where the project is broken into individual components that can be developed and tested
- Making the appropriate changes in personnel, vendors, and approach based on how the project is executed relative to expectations

One clear reason for the failure of many risk management projects is where they attempted to modify systems to address business problems that fall outside their intended core functionality. Examples include the misguided data warehouse projects and attempts to extend back-office systems to be a single repository of all risk data.

In many cases, this occurs because vendors have oversold the systems. Apart from the clear economic incentive, vendors often underestimate the tasks associated with extending their systems beyond their core competencies. The overselling process often takes the form of promised functionality that is "in development." Potential buyers of such systems should pin down the core functionality offered by each system and discount future development. If the core competency of a system is market risk management for a trading room, then it should not be applied for enterprise-level risk management, and vice versa.

Also, many businesses have chosen and attempted to implement systems that are inappropriate for their size, sophistication, and resources. Most risk management systems are designed for a specific group of target organizations—insurance risk management systems, for example, are different from trading risk management systems.

Similarly, the systems designed for the large, multinational finance powerhouses who can dedicate a team of dozens to the implementation project are different from the systems and ASPs dedicated to smaller players with more modest budgets. Early on, the choice was between buying an off-the-shelf system from a vendor or building one in-house. Typically the largest institutions built in-house while the majority bought vended systems. That choice has now evolved into a "buy and build" versus ASP choice. The largest players have the budgets to buy sophisticated risk engines, which come equipped with toolkits that allow limited amounts of extra development. The majority of financial and nonfinancial institutions may attain superior service in a fraction of the time by leveraging the implementations already carried out by ASPs.

Another critical factor is that a risk management system is unlikely to succeed unless it has the backing of senior management. Risk management systems by their very nature touch on a large number of businesses. Such systems are politically sensitive, as in many institutions performance measurement and remuneration are linked to parameters set in the system. As such, it is essential to secure the support of senior management.

Fortunately, this is relatively simple. It is fairly straightforward to provide approximate risk results from relatively little work—the first 20 percent of the implementation effort can sometimes yield enough information for senior managers to make informed strategic decisions. That opens the way for further, more detailed work.

CHAPTER 11

Stakeholder Management

In order to appreciate the significance of good stakeholder management, we need only reflect on the high turnover rate of customers, employees, investors, and other stakeholders at a company. On average, U.S. companies lose half of their customers over five years, half their employees over four years, and half their investors in less than *one* year.[1] These high turnover rates have an enormous impact on a company's profitability.

When people think about a company's stakeholders, they often think only about those who hold its equity and perhaps those who hold its debt. However, a truer picture is that the stakeholders include any group or individual that supports and participates in the survival and success of a company. The obvious stakeholders are employees, customers, suppliers, business partners, investors, stock analysts, credit analysts, and special interest groups. Regulators also should be included if permits or licenses are required or there are regulations that need to be observed.

Stakeholder management also should involve providing key risk information to these stakeholders. The board of directors and regulators need to be assured that the company is in compliance with internal policies and external laws and regulations. Stock analysts and rating agencies are increasingly asking for risk management information on a company's investment and derivatives activities. For financial institutions, they may even request line-of-business information with respect to profitability and risk. Institutional and individual investors need financial and risk information to make the appropriate investment decisions. The informational needs of key stakeholders are becoming more complex, and management must respond to improve risk transparency to these groups.

In stakeholder communication, it is important to bear in mind the needs

---

[1]Frederick F. Reichheld, *The Loyalty Effect* (Boston: Harvard Business School Press, 1996), p. 4.

of individual groups in the development of risk management presentations and reports. For example, boards of directors need summary information that highlights key risk information and the company's compliance with regulations and board-approved policies. Stock analysts are more concerned about return on equity capital, so they need risk-adjusted profitability information, ideally by line of business so they can make comparisons with their own models. Rating agencies are focused on the relationship between risk and capitalization, so they need information about capital plans and underlying risk exposures, especially any risk concentrations. Regulators are focused on the safety and soundness of regulated entities, as well as the overall industry, and need information about economic capital, internal controls, and proper disclosure.

Each of these groups is essential to the success of the company, so the company must communicate relevant information to each group and ensure that it is taking steps to make sure that each group's particular needs are being met. Indeed, a 1998 survey of chief executive officers (CEOs) (summarized in Table 11.1) revealed that, along with unions, individual shareholders were the only group rated by a plurality of executives as likely to be *less* important 10 years from now than they currently are. By contrast, customers, suppliers, outside board directors, institutional investors, and communities—all stakeholders often neglected in risk management—were rated as likely to be *more* important 10 years from now.

The needs of boards of directors and investors are discussed in more detail in Chapter 5 on corporate governance. In the rest of this chapter we will discuss the risk management requirements of three key groups of stakeholders: employees, customers, and business partners.

EMPLOYEES

Employees should be viewed as major assets of a company, especially in companies that depend heavily on intellectual or human capital. A company seeking to extract the maximum value from its employees must carefully manage both upside and downside risks throughout the duration of an employee's tenure with the firm, beginning with recruiting and ending with the employee's retirement, termination, or resignation.

Companies stand to gain more than warm feelings if they get it right. In 1999, *Fortune* magazine found that firms listed in its "100 Best Companies to Work for in America" outperformed their peers by around 9 percent.[2] Effective employee management not only saves unnecessary cost due

---

[2]Shelly Branch, "The 100 Best Companies to Work for in America," *Fortune,* January 11, 1999, p. 119.

TABLE 11.1   CEOs' View of Stakeholders' Importance in 10 Years

Stakeholders	More Important	No Difference	Less Important	Don't Know
International customers	90%	6%	2%	2%
Consumers	76%	22%	1%	1%
Employees	75%	20%	4%	1%
Suppliers	67%	28%	5%	1%
Outside board directors	63%	27%	7%	3%
Institutional shareholders	61%	30%	8%	2%
Communities (where companies are based)	48%	31%	19%	1%
Public (public opinion)	44%	47%	7%	2%
Media	31%	56%	13%	1%
Government (federal, state, local)	23%	48%	28%	2%
Individual shareholders	21%	32%	46%	2%
Unions	4%	23%	70%	3%

Source: Foundation for the Malcolm Baldrige National Quality Award, and Louis Harris & Associates, "The Nation's CEOs Look to the Future," July 1998.

to employee turnover, but also generates value for the company and its shareholders.

Employee turnover is no longer just a question of hiring and firing. Companies today have to manage an increasing number of "free agents"— individuals who see themselves less as employees and more as hired guns. These free agents may or may not be on the payroll; what is important is that their incentives are not automatically aligned with those of the company. These individuals are having an increasing impact on today's working world. In mid-1999, about 16 percent of the American workforce—at least 25 million people—consisted of free agents, defined as those who work for themselves, or could if they wished.[3]

Finally, companies operating in unionized industries have to face additional risks specific to unions: strikes, wage contracts, and morale issues. Union strikes upon contract renewal have become more prevalent in recent years, particularly in the airline and auto-manufacturing sectors. Such incidents are both disruptive and costly. Strikes not only disrupt a firm's operations, but are also likely to destroy workers' morale and damage the company's image. For example, the 54-day strike of General Motors workers in 1998 caused plants to shut down and halted production. The strike cost General Motors $2.2 billion in lost sales, and may have taken

[3]Jeff Mangum, "Free Agents to Play Bigger Role in Working World," *Gannett News Service*, August 6, 1999.

an even greater toll over the long term, due to losses in market share and reputation.[4]

It is important to acknowledge that employees' needs and employers' desires do not necessarily match. Because employees have a high impact on business profitability, it is important to manage them effectively. This might seem self-evidently important, but as Peter Drucker has said:

> *All organizations now say routinely, "People are our greatest asset." Yet few practice what they preach, let alone truly believe it. Most still believe, though perhaps not consciously, what nineteenth-century employers believed: people need us more than we need them. But, in fact, organizations have to market membership as much as they market products and services—and perhaps more. They have to attract people, hold people, recognize and reward people, motivate people, and serve and satisfy people.[5]*

We can consider employment as a series of stages:

- Recruiting and screening
- Training and development
- Retention and promotion
- Firing and resignation

There are different needs at each of these stages, and different employee management strategies are therefore required.

Recruiting and Screening

First, companies face the challenge of hiring the right employees. Employees' skills, experience, attitude, and potential determine their performance and productivity, and thence their contribution to the profitability of the firm. The risk of not hiring the right employees is tremendous. In an extreme case, such as that of a rogue trader, one mistake in hiring can bring down an entire company. A growing number of companies, including Fidelity Investments and Disney, have instituted background checks as part of their preemployment screening process.

Many companies would benefit from putting more resources and emphasis into recruiting. As the job market has become more competitive, companies have had to take more time and effort in hiring the right employ-

---

[4]Aaron Bernstein, "What Price Peace?" *Business Week*, August 10, 1998, pp. 24–25.
[5]Peter F. Drucker, "The New Society of Organizations," *Harvard Business Review*, September–October 1992, p. 100.

ees, who spend less and less time at any given company. The logical conclusion of this is the increase of the free agent, who may be integral to a company's operations, but may work for a number of different employers in quick succession, or even simultaneously. Not surprisingly, compensation is often cited as the top incentive for employees; however, other incentives and benefits should be considered as appropriate, and can make a real difference in hiring where cash alone cannot.

Training and Development

If hiring the right employees is important, keeping them is crucial. Employee turnover is costly. Not only may valuable people, skills, and information be lost, but they may be lost to competitors. Then, of course, there is the cost of recruiting and training new employees. According to one study, the cost of replacing a worker is somewhere between 1 and 2.5 times the salary of the open position; the more sophisticated the position, the higher the cost.[6]

Training offers value to both employees and employers. In addition to on-the-job training, Andersen Consulting (now Accenture), the world's largest consulting firm, spent more than $430 million (i.e., 7 percent of net revenue) on formal continual learning programs for its consultants in 1997. The brokerage firm Edward Jones offers its new brokers 17 weeks of classes and study sessions at a cost of $50,000 to $70,000 per head. The firm considers this an investment rather than an expense.[7] Career development is also important. It provides a direction that an employee can follow and a goal for which he or she is motivated. Upon proper implementation, this can improve retention, productivity, and morale.

Retention and Promotion

According to *Fortune* magazine, "swimming pools and surging pay may give employees a lift, but continual training and humane treatment get the best ones to stick around."[8] In addition to the training and career development discussed above, companies have to value and recognize their employees. This may include a culture of professionalism among co-workers and subordinates, appropriate delegation of responsibilities and project ownership, and awards and public announcements.

---

[6]"Don't Let the Talent Crunch Hurt Your Company's Chance for Success," *PR Newswire*, June 8, 1999.
[7]Shelly Branch, "The 100 Best Companies to Work for in America," *Fortune*, January 11, 1999, p. 119.
[8]Shelly Branch, "The 100 Best Companies to Work for in America," *Fortune*, January 11, 1999, p. 119.

In the words of former General Electric (GE) boss Jack Welch, "you have to get rewarded in the soul and the wallet."[9] Promotion has to be based on meritocracy and not bureaucracy. The talent pool at GE is constantly refined by promoting the best performers and weeding out the worst. Talented executives are also nurtured in a rigorous meritocracy, where performance is lavishly rewarded and failure mercilessly punished.

Firing and Resignation

Massive layoffs reduce company morale and increase employee resignation. Managed firing, on the other hand, can increase employee motivation and improve company performance. At GE, for example, the company gets rid of the least effective 10 percent of its workers each year.[10] Leading consulting firms have always adopted an "up or out" practice. If employees do resign, companies should find out why, by use of tools such as exit interviews. Although negotiating with departing employees in order to retain them is a highly desirable goal, a number of studies have suggested that the use of counteroffers often does not yield the expected benefits. Therefore, companies should leverage information gathered in exit interviews so they can identify and fix the root causes of employee discontent.

CUSTOMERS

People may be a company's biggest asset, but not many managers in business would claim that their prime focus was on anything but their customers. After all, a company cannot survive without customers, and hence there is obviously a great need for customer management.

Nevertheless, customer turnover is extremely high in most industries: on average, U.S. corporations lose half of their customers every five years. At least part of the reason for this is that many corporations do not really embrace customer management as a central concern, and many CEOs still take a primarily sales- or product-driven perspective on their businesses. This may not continue to be a viable approach as customer power increases, a trend that many pundits expect to be an inevitable consequence of e-commerce.

There are numerous aspects and strategies of customer management. We will discuss some of the major ones relevant to risk management here:

---

[9]Carol Hymowitz and Matt Murray, "How GE's Chief Rates and Spurs His Employees," *Wall Street Journal,* June 21, 1999, p. B1.
[10]Carol Hymowitz and Matt Murray, "How GE's Chief Rates and Spurs His Employees," *Wall Street Journal,* June 21, 1999, p. B1.

- Attrition and acquisition
- Loyalty and satisfaction
- Knowing the customer
- Handling crisis

Attrition and Acquisition

It is essential that a business attract new customers and even more crucial that it keep them. Even small differences in customer retention can translate into large shifts in a company's competitive position—particularly when it can cost five times as much to acquire a new customer as to retain an existing one.[11]

Long-term customers are profitable for other reasons, as well. They buy more, are less price sensitive, and bring in more new customers than recently acquired customers do. In some industries, reducing customer turnover by as little as 5 percent can increase profitability by more than 50 percent.[12]

Good customer management does not mean that a company should attempt to obtain *all* possible customers, in an effort to maximize revenues. Rather, companies need to identify and retain the *right* customers, where the right customers are the ones who will help the company to increase its overall profitability, not necessarily total revenues.

Consider a supermarket chain—at first sight a volume business, if ever there was one, and thus one where winning customers might seem all-important. However, not every customer is profitable to the store. In fact, even customers who buy a great deal are not profitable if they "cherry-pick"— seek out deeply discounted items. The supermarket doesn't particularly want to retain these customers' business and so it might, for example, increase its range of luxury goods to attract shoppers who do not mind paying a premium, and scale back discounting campaigns.

Loyalty and Satisfaction

Customer retention is one result of effective customer relationship management—or, to put it another way, of customer satisfaction. Not only does a company lose the business of dissatisfied customers (normally to competitors) but it also may lose the business of the potential and existing customers that the dissatisfied customers warn off.

---

[11]Helena Frenz, "Don: Need to Ensure that Customers Are Fully Satisfied," *Business Times*, February 8, 1999, p. 3.
[12]Frederick F. Reichheld, *The Loyalty Effect* (Boston: Harvard Business School Press, 1996), pp. 33–37; Victor L. Hunter, *Business to Business Marketing: Creating a Community of Customers* (Lincolnwood, IL: NTC Business Books, 1997).

More than a third of the nation's households switched long-distance carriers at least once between 1996 and 1998. Although this is partially attributable to aggressive marketing by competing carriers, it was also partly due to customer dissatisfaction. Internet users were even more dissatisfied. About 40 percent of customers who have changed Internet service providers say that they did so because of because of poor service.[13]

Ensuring customer satisfaction is not just a question of protecting against negative consequences. On the contrary, customer satisfaction positively creates shareholder value. In 1999, researchers at the Wharton School found, using data from the American Customer Satisfaction Index, that a 1 percent rise or fall in customer satisfaction ratings translates into a $250 million rise or fall in stock market value.[14]

Unfortunately, customer satisfaction does *not* correlate well with customer loyalty: a customer may be satisfied but still leave. As many as 85 percent of customers who defect have nonetheless been satisfied by the prior relationship.[15] Clearly, it is not sufficient just to attain high levels of customer satisfaction. What's also important is whether customers feel they have received enough value to keep them loyal.

Consider the American car industry: it has a customer satisfaction index of about 80 percent, but only about 40 percent of customers repurchase.[16] Loyalty is better measured in terms of customer retention and rate of repeat purchasing. Delivering zero-defect products is not enough in today's business: understanding customers' needs and satisfying them are prerequisites for success.

Know Your Customer

"Know your customer" is a variant on "know your business," the first lesson learned in Chapter 2. Companies that know their customers and act strategically on that knowledge can improve customer satisfaction and retention. Listening to customer opinions through a consumer hotline or sur-

---

[13]David Larcker and Pamela Cohen, "The Return of the Shrimp or Listening to Your Customers and Hearing Their Silence," *Wharton Alumni Magazine,* summer 1999, p. 24.
[14]David Larcker and Pamela Cohen, "The Return of the Shrimp or Listening to Your Customers and Hearing Their Silence," *Wharton Alumni Magazine,* summer 1999, p. 24.
[15]Graham Foster and Karin Newman, "What Is Service Quality When Service Equals Regulations?" *Service Industries Journal* 18, no. 4, October 1998, pp. 51–65.
[16]Helena Frenz, "Don: Need to Ensure that Customers Are Fully Satisfied," *Business Times,* February 8, 1999, p. 3.

veys is one way to ensure that customers' voices are heard. "Data mining" is another.

Amazon.com, for example, collects customers' purchasing behavior, stores it in a giant data warehouse, and analyzes it to provide more personalized service to each customer. Comparison of multiple purchasers' orders allows it to recommend other books that customers may be interested in after only their *first* purchase at the website.

Just as with other business issues, it is important to know how far to go. Privacy is becoming an increasingly significant issue; if information is used improperly or left unprotected, knowing customers *too* well may introduce the risk of unnecessary losses and lawsuits.

Handling Crisis

Crises can occur no matter how efficient a firm's risk management. That should not be a cause for despair. Every crisis contains within itself the seeds of success as well as the roots of failure.

Consider Johnson & Johnson's Tylenol poisonings in 1982 and 1986. Each of these incidents cost the company more than $100 million directly, and could have cost it much more in reputational damage. However, Johnson & Johnson's swift responses allowed the company to turn these tragedies into opportunities, including setting industry standards for safety features in customer goods packaging. Customers and the general public regarded Johnson & Johnson more highly *after* the incidents.

The keys to crisis management are to make contingency plans in advance and to avoid compounding the problem by trying to cover it up or deny responsibility. If a crisis occurs, the company must act fast, be honest, and keep customers and the general public informed. Today, it is no longer realistic to believe that the truth will never come out or that financial damage can be postponed indefinitely, so attempting to cover up a debacle may result in greater reputational damage to the company than openly admitting any mistakes that have been made. The company's response should focus on its long-term good, rather than on minimizing immediate losses.

BUSINESS PARTNERS

Strategic alliances have become a critical tool for almost any company operating in today's fast-moving, networked economy. An alliance can help a company to speed up product cycles, obtain access to a new market, share the financial risks of developing a new technology, or profit from economies of scale.

Many companies have jumped eagerly onto the bandwagon, with

the number of strategic alliances growing by 25 percent per year in recent years.[17] However, there are abundant risks inherent in striking alliances. More than 60 percent of alliances ultimately fail to achieve their goals,[18] and 80 percent of joint ventures end in the sale by one of the partners.[19] Failed ventures waste a company's resources, can cause them to fall behind competitors, and sometimes lead to reputational damage. There are other perils to the alliance approach, too, including the risks of loss of intellectual capital, conflicts of interest, and legal disputes over intellectual property rights.

How can the potential pitfalls of strategic alliances best be avoided? Careful attention must be directed to risk management at each stage of the alliance process:

- Weighing up the pros and cons of an alliance
- Finding the right partner
- Monitoring progress as time goes on

Weighing Up an Alliance

All alliances should be formed with a specific, value-creating goal in mind. They should never be born of desperation. Some alliances are executed in the hope that a stronger company can be used as a crutch. This is likely to lead to the weaker company being bought out by the stronger at an unfavorable price. Others link one weak company with another weak company in the hope of magically becoming more competitive. This is like the blind leading the blind.

Of course, all of these goals can be achieved by means other than strategic alliances, including internal development, market-based transactions, or vertical or horizontal integration. So not only must the goal be achievable through a strategic alliance, but it must be *best* achieved through a strategic alliance.

In general, an alliance is suitable in cases where a considerable amount of control is needed (which could not be achieved through market transactions), but internal development would be expensive or difficult. Alliances, for example, allow potentially incompatible partners to work together without the integration risks of a full-blown merger.

They also carry the potential for loss of intellectual capital. Alliance

---

[17]Joel Bleeke and David Ernst, "Is Your Strategic Alliance Really a Sale?" *Harvard Business Review,* January–February 1995, pp. 97–105.
[18]Joel Bleeke and David Ernst, *Collaborating to Compete: Using Strategic Alliances and Acquisitions in the Global Marketplace* (New York: Wiley, 1993).
[19]Joel Bleeke and David Ernst, "Is Your Strategic Alliance Really a Sale?" *Harvard Business Review,* 73, no. 1, 1995, pp. 97–105.

partners may be very close in one area of their business, but this may be a temporary or narrow arrangement. Before entering any alliance, a company should assess the degree of risk involved in sharing information with its prospective partner, which will vary depending on the nature of the intellectual capital, the capabilities of the alliance partner, and the nature of the alliance.[20]

An example of an instance where an alliance would likely be the best solution is the case of an auto manufacturer determining how it can best obtain the 15,000-plus parts needed to assemble a car. Building the parts internally, buying them in the open market, or buying up the parts manufacturers would all be impossibly unwieldy, uneconomic, and impractical solutions. An alliance, however, allows the car and parts manufacturers to share information where advantageous and establish a reliable stream of transactions, while leaving the management of individual processes to the teams that understand them best.

Finding the Right Partner

Choosing an inappropriate alliance partner is a virtually certain route to a failed alliance. Since an alliance partner must be compatible in a large number of ways (from cultural fit to competitive position to legal status), it is crucial that the evaluation at *all* steps of the selection process be carried out by people who can appropriately screen potential partners on all of these dimensions. All members of the decision-making team need to agree on what the goals of the alliance are in order to make a coherent decision.

The first step is to determine a concrete set of criteria for evaluating potential partners, to ensure that important factors are not overlooked, provide support for the eventual decision, and screen out unsuitable candidates. Questions to ask in setting the criteria include:

- Do the two firms have similar interests and goals?
- Do they have complementary resources and skills?
- Are both dealing from positions of strength, or could one be exploiting the other?
- Do they have similar work styles, cultures, and business practices?
- Can they trust each other?

The criteria should then be weighted to indicate those that are most important. The next step is to develop a ranked list of potential partners to

---

[20]For a more in-depth treatment of these issues, see C. Christopher Baughn, Johannes G. Denekamp, John H. Stevens, and Richard N. Osborn, "Protecting Intellectual Capital in International Alliances," *Journal of World Business* 32, no. 2, 1997, pp. 103–115.

meet with. Not all the criteria can be evaluated in advance (e.g., work style), but those that can be should be, while plans should be developed for evaluating the others as soon as possible after contact is made.

After meeting with each company, *all* members of the selection committee should grade the potential partner for each criterion. This should be done immediately after each meeting, while it is still fresh in people's minds, not after an entire round of meetings. Although it can be argued that the latter approach allows a better perspective on the relative strengths of candidates, in practice any delay is likely to reduce the quality of the assessment.

Monitoring Progress

The importance of regular status checks cannot be overemphasized, although it is surprisingly often forgotten. Indeed, in many alliances it seems to be the case that more attention is given to selection of an alliance partner than to maintenance of the subsequent relationship.

Realistically, however, there will be routine differences of opinion or reorientation of work efforts. It is also likely that major reassessments of alliances may be called for, since partners' goals and needs often change over the multiyear lifespan of most alliances.

Evaluating the success of the alliance is necessarily a difficult task since the needs and goals of the alliance may sometimes conflict with the needs of either or both parent firms. Although it is important to regularly evaluate the alliance and take corrective steps as soon as possible, one should not be overzealous. Like any relationship, alliances often go through "growing pains," particularly once the "honeymoon phase" at the beginning of the alliance wears off.

What's more, alliance projects are often breaking new territory, meaning that standard financial measures of success are usually not appropriate at the outset. Indeed, early on, evaluation of the alliance should focus on the quality of the relationship, rather than the results. Quality of the collaboration, equality in the relationship, productivity, and knowledge acquired should all be evaluated. If these are found to be lacking, concrete steps for improving them should be put in place.

Sometimes a company makes the mistake of viewing work on an alliance as a project of secondary importance and assumes that if something more pressing comes up a member of the alliance team can simply be staffed on the new project. This is a dangerous view since the intellectual capital and harmonious working conditions upon which an alliance depends are easily destroyed by the removal of the members who have created them. The alliance manager and the alliance team should be individuals who are committed to staying at the firm and with the alliance. High turnover among the alliance staff is almost always a recipe for disaster, just as it can be disastrous for a company.

While the key stakeholders for each company will differ, and this chapter discussed the requirements of three major groups, management should explicitly address the risk management and reporting requirements for all key stakeholders.

Stakeholder management, more than perhaps any other aspect of enterprise risk management, requires cooperation at many levels and in many departments of the organization. Top executives, business managers, risk managers, human resources, investor relations, marketing, and public relations must all be involved in ensuring that the company maintains good relationships with its stakeholders.

Risk Management Applications

CHAPTER 12

Credit Risk Management

The effective management of credit risk is a challenge faced by all companies, and a critical success factor for financial institutions and energy firms faced with significant credit exposures. Most obviously, banking institutions face the risk that institutional and individual borrowers may default on loans. Banks must therefore underwrite and price each loan according to its credit risk and ensure that the overall portfolio of loans is well diversified.

However, both financial and nonfinancial institutions also face credit risk exposures besides the default risk associated with lending activities. For example, the sellers of goods and services face credit risk embedded in their accounts receivable. Investors may see significant decreases in the value of debt instruments held in their portfolios as a result of default or credit deterioration. Sellers and buyers of capital markets products will only get paid on any profitable transaction if their counterparties fulfill their obligations to them. And the increasing mutual dependence involved under arrangements such as outsourcing and strategic alliances exposes companies to the credit condition of their business partners.

Given this multiplicity of phenomena, there is obviously a need for a clear definition of credit risk. Credit risk can be defined as the economic loss suffered due to the default of a borrower or counterparty. Default does not necessarily mean the legal bankruptcy of the other party, but merely failure to fulfill its contractual obligations in a timely manner, due to inability or unwillingness.

A consultative paper issued recently by the Basel Committee on Banking Supervision recognized that "the major cause of serious banking problems continues to be directly related to lax credit standards for borrowers and counterparties, poor portfolio risk management, or a lack of attention to changes in economic or other circumstances that can lead to a deterioration in the credit standing of a bank's counterparties."[1] While this quote focuses specifically on the banking industry, the need to establish sound credit risk management practices for customer receivables, investment activities, and counterparty and business partner exposures is relevant to any industry.

Credit risk management deals with the identification, quantification, monitoring, controlling, and management of credit risk at both the transaction and portfolio levels. Although the level and volatility of future losses are inherently uncertain, statistical analyses and models can help the risk manager quantify potential losses as input to underwriting, pricing, and portfolio decisions. Before we can do this, however, we will need to define some key concepts in credit risk management.

KEY CREDIT RISK CONCEPTS

Exposure, Severity, and Default

The credit loss on any transaction, whether a straightforward loan or complex swap, can always be described as the product of three terms:

$$\text{Loss} = \text{Exposure} \times \text{Default} \times \text{Severity}$$

Loss is the actual economic loss to the organization, as a result of the default or downgrade of a borrower or counterparty—that is, as a result of a *credit event*. *Exposure* is the loan amount, or the market value of securities that the organization is due to receive from the counterparty at the time of the credit event.[2] It is the amount at risk. *Default* is a random variable that is either one (if the transaction is in default) or zero in the context of a single borrower or counterparty, but it may represent the overall default rate of a portfolio. *Severity* is the fraction of the total exposure that is actually lost. The severity of loss can be reduced by debt covenants, netting and collateral arrangements, and downgrade provisions.

Expected Loss

Another key concept is *expected loss* (EL), which represents the anticipated *average* rate of loss that an organization should expect to suffer on its credit risk portfolio over time. This is effectively a cost of doing business,

---

[1]Basel Committee on Banking Supervision, "Principles for the Management of Credit Risk," consultative paper, July 1999.
[2]We always assume that the exposure is at best zero but never negative; if the firm represents an exposure to the counterparty, it is highly unlikely that the firm will benefit from the counterparty's default: either a successor entity or a court appointed administrator will eventually collect.

and should thus be reflected directly in transaction pricing. The expected value of credit losses is equal to the product of the expected values of each of its components:

$$EL = \text{Expected Loss} = E(\text{Loss})$$

$$= E(\text{Exposure}) \cdot E(\text{Default}) \cdot E(\text{Severity})$$

E(Exposure) is the expected exposure at the time of the credit event. It depends strongly on the type of transaction and on the occurrence of future random events. For loans, exposure is usually just the amount of the loan. Where a trading exposure to a counterparty is involved, the expected exposure must usually be modeled. For example, it is usually necessary to use a simulation model in order to find the expected exposures of long-dated transactions such as swaps or forwards.

E(Default) is the expected default frequency and reflects the underlying credit risks of the particular borrower or counterparty. It can either be estimated from the borrower's or counterparty's public debt rating, or by calibrating the organization's own credit grading scale. While each individual transaction is obviously either performing or in default—there is no middle ground between the two states—there is an expected frequency of default *within* an overall portfolio.

E(Severity) is the net loss in the event of default. It is a function of facility type, seniority, and collateral. The severity is equal to the lost principal and interest, together with the cost of administering the impaired facility; it is expressed as a percentage of the exposure at the point of default. Because there are few public data on recovery rates, and these tend to vary with the type of transaction, they must usually be estimated from the organization's own recovery data. Recovery rates for publicly traded bonds can be obtained from the major rating agencies.

The EL for a portfolio is simply the sum of the ELs of the individual transactions:

$$EL_{Portfolio} = \sum EL_{Transaction}$$

Unexpected Loss

Unexpected loss (UL) is a more important measure of risk than EL. EL is, as the name suggests, a reasonably predictable average rate of loss. Organizations do not have to hold capital against EL, assuming that they have priced it into the relevant transactions correctly. UL represents the volatility of *actual* losses that will occur around the expected level. It is the existence of UL that creates the need for a capital "cushion" to safeguard the viability of the organization if losses turn out to be unexpectedly high.

Statistically speaking, UL is defined as the standard deviation of credit losses. It is derived, mathematically speaking, from the components of EL:

$$UL = \sigma \ (Credit \ Losses) = Var^{1/2} \ (Credit \ Losses)$$

If all transactions were to default at the same time, we would simply add up the UL of individual transactions to determine the overall UL of a portfolio. However, this is obviously extremely unlikely to happen unless there are common factors driving the credit performance of all the transactions in the portfolio.

It is unlikely, for example, that a number of individual borrowers from different geographic locations would all default on their credit card debts at exactly the same time, although the changes in the national levels of interest rates would likely be an important common factor. Similarly, a shared geographic location or industrial sector is likely to be an important common factor for corporate borrowers.

The degree to which individual default behaviors are related is known as the *default correlation*. Broadly speaking, the more diverse (less correlated) the transactions in the portfolio are, the less likely it is that many of them will suffer a credit event simultaneously. Hence, the UL on a portfolio is dependent on its level of diversification as well as on the ULs associated with individual transactions. This is measured in terms of the default correlations *among* transactions. Thanks to diversification, the UL on a portfolio will be less than the sum of the ULs of its component transactions. In fact, it is:

$$UL_{portfolio} = \sqrt{\sum_{i=1}^{N} \sum_{j=1}^{N} \ (UL)_i (UL)_j \rho_{ij}}$$

where $(UL)_i$ is the UL on the ith transaction in the portfolio and ρ_{ij} is the default correlation between the ith and j^{th} transactions in the portfolio. The higher the correlation between a new transaction and the portfolio, the more risk it adds to the portfolio. One of the key objectives for a risk manager is, therefore, to ensure that portfolios are sufficiently diversified—thus reducing the UL on the portfolio—by ensuring that credit exposures are not overly concentrated in any obligor, industry, country, or economic sector.

Reserves and Economic Capital

A credit loss *reserve* represents the amount set aside for ELs from the firm's total portfolio of credit exposures. For example, bad debt provisions might be made to cover anticipated losses over the life of a loan portfolio. A reserve is a specific element of the balance sheet, whereas provisions and actual losses are treated as income statement items.

A firm also must earmark some capital to guard against large ULs. This capital is known as *economic capital*, the amount that is required to support the risk of large ULs. The amount of economic capital[3] required is determined from the *credit loss distribution*, which we will describe below.

Economic capital is an important concept for equity-holders as well as debt-holders. For equity-holders, economic capital can be used as a yardstick against which returns from different risk-taking activities can be consistently measured. For debt-holders, the economic capital can be viewed as the capital cushion against UL that is required to maintain a certain debt rating. It is determined in a similar way to the solvency tests applied by agencies such as Standard & Poor's (S&P) or Moody's Investors Service when assigning credit ratings.

For example, firms rated double-A by S&P default with a 0.03% frequency over a one-year horizon. If a firm has a double-A target solvency standard, its economic capital can then be determined as the level of capital required to keep the firm solvent over a one-year period with 99.97% confidence. Because this is a probabilistic quantity, it will depend on the distribution of credit losses (see Figure 12.1).

Credit loss distributions are skewed because credit losses can never be less than zero. That would imply that borrowers pay back more than they owe when conditions are better than expected, which clearly does not happen.[4] However, when times are worse than expected, losses can be much higher than average. In most economic environments, one would expect relatively low levels of losses (at any competent institution, anyway). Occasionally, however, a recession will cause a high level of losses, and thus generate a longer, skewed tail. The distribution is *leptokurtic*, that is, the probability of large losses occurring is greater for a given mean and standard deviation than would be the case if the distribution were normal.

The loss distribution can be estimated by:

■ Assuming that it conforms to one of the standard textbook distributions, such as the beta or gamma distribution, and parameterizing the distribution to match the portfolio's mean and standard deviation.

■ Analyzing publicly available information for peer firms, that is, their capital relative to their historical loss volatility (this requires some simplifying assumptions).

---

[3]Economic capital is defined as the level of capital that is needed to cover unexpected losses, whereas book capital is the actual capital on the balance sheet and regulatory capital is based on capital requirements from the regulators.

[4]Some lending institutions incorporate warrants or other equity-like features into their lending programs in order to capture some "upside."

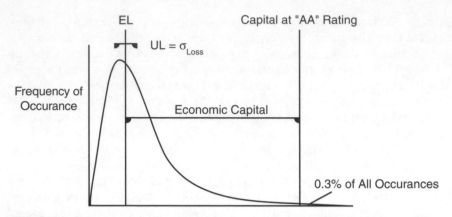

FIGURE 12.1   Illustration of *EL*, *UL*, and *CM* on the loss distribution.

■   Using numerical techniques or simulation to estimate and aggregate the yearly loss level of the portfolio over many business cycles.

Once the UL has been calculated and the loss distribution estimated, the desired debt rating has to be factored into the economic capital calculation. This is done by introducing a *capital multiplier* (CM), which represents the number of multiples of UL required to create a capital cushion sufficient to absorb a loss at the confidence level implied by the institution's credit rating. It is determined from the loss distribution. As mentioned above, an institution that is seeking a double-A rating must hold enough economic capital to protect against all losses except those so large that they have less than a 0.03% chance of occurring in any given year.

$$Credit\ Risk\ Economic\ Capital = CM \times \$UL_{Portfolio}$$

Off–Balance Sheet Credit Risk

When one thinks about credit risk, it is large loan losses that come most immediately to mind. The dramatic and highly publicized credit crises of the past two decades include those associated with commercial real estate, less developed contries debt, leveraged buy-out debt, Russian bonds, long-term capital management, energy trading counterparties, and the consumer debt problems that have plagued retail lenders (major mortgage write-offs in the early 1990s and sporadic credit card problems).

However, as discussed in the beginning of this chapter, credit risk is not limited to banking or financial institutions. In every market and every business, transactions with counterparties inevitably lead to credit exposures, which can result in economic loss or business interruptions. The most significant credit exposures faced by an organization may not even appear on the balance sheet. Nowadays, organizations frequently assume credit risk from various off–balance sheet financial instruments such as foreign exchange transactions, forwards transactions, swaps, bonds, options, special-purpose entities, and financial guarantees. Two examples of off–balance sheet credit exposures are provided below to illustrate how off–balance sheet items can create credit risk exposures.

Credit Risk of Options   A basic call option provides its holder with the right, but not the obligation, to purchase an asset at a predetermined price. Once the buyer pays the option premium, the seller of an option never has any credit risk exposure, because the buyer has no obligations to fulfill and there is therefore nothing to default on. The best-case scenario for the seller is that the option expires worthless and thus no future payment needs to be made.

However, the buyer of the option can have a credit risk exposure, because the seller is obliged to pay up if the option becomes profitable for the buyer and is therefore exercised. So the buyer's credit risk exposure at any given time is the value of the option at that time, because that is the economic loss (or replacement value) that would be incurred if the seller option writer were to default. Options always have positive value until expiry (since there is always a chance that they will become profitable before the expiry date), so the buyer of a basic option is always exposed to some credit risk until the option expires. The Black-Scholes option pricing formula allows one to calculate option values, and hence the credit exposure.

Credit Risk of Swaps   A swap is a financial agreement under which two counterparties exchange cash flows, based on one or more price indices. Let's use an interest rate swap to illustrate the challenges associated with the estimation of credit risk of derivative products.

There are two principal difficulties in estimating credit risk for interest rate swaps:

- There is little information about severity in the event of default by a swap counterparty. This is due to the paucity of defaults involving swap transactions. It appears that under U.S. bankruptcy law, swap counterparties would have the lowest claim on the defaulted party's assets. However, the lower claim status of swap transactions is often mitigated by other credit protections, such as downgrade triggers and collateral requirements.
- The crucial element in the assessment of credit risk is the exposure amount, or the mark-to-market value of a swap (which is usually close to zero at inception). Any exposure is generated later by the effect of price movements. The credit exposures of swaps and most other derivative transactions are indeterminate in that they can be an asset *or* a liability depending on movements in the underlying price or rate. For example, if interest rates fall, the party receiving

a fixed rate in an interest rate swap has essentially acquired an asset. They will then have credit exposure to the counterparty. If rates were to rise, however, the situation could easily reverse.

A number of different approaches have been taken to the estimation of swap exposures. The most straightforward is the addition of a fixed percentage (add-on) of the swap's nominal amount to the current mark-to-market value. There are two difficulties with this approach. First, how should the add-on percentage be estimated? Second, the relevant exposure is not that of one particular swap but rather the total (net) exposure over all transactions with any given counterparty.

Sophisticated derivative dealers and users apply a simulation-based approach to the quantification of swap exposures. The basic concept behind simulation is that if we knew what the yield curve would be at the time of the counterparty default, we could value the swap and hence estimate the exact exposure amount.

Of course we have no idea when a counterparty might default or what the yield curve might look like at that point in time. However, if we can model the possible evolution of the yield curve, we can generate lots of potential paths for interest rates over the remaining life of the swap and estimate the exposure for each separate path. We can then come up with an estimate of the most likely exposure and the potential variation in the exposure.

The success of this procedure clearly depends on the quality of the model used for the evolution of the yield curve. The basic procedure is indicated schematically below (see Figure 12.2):

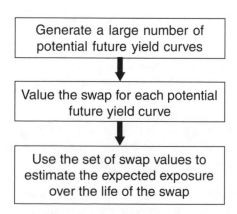

FIGURE 12.2   Basic procedure.

Consider for example a plain vanilla swap with a notional principal value of $1 million, a maturity of 5 years, and a fixed rate coupon of 6 percent. The short-term interest rate, which is also the floating coupon of the swap, starts out at 5 percent.[5] The results of the simulation procedure are illustrated in Figure 12.3, in which are displayed the expected exposure and the 97.5 percent confidence bound on the exposure (the maximum likely exposure, or MLE).

Notice that the expected exposure rises until approximately the midpoint of the swap's term and then falls back toward zero. On the final day of the swap the exposure will, in fact, be zero. A similar approach can be used for foreign exchange and commodity derivatives. In addition to the yield curve, a simulation model would estimate the price movements of the underlying price indices.

THE CREDIT RISK MANAGEMENT PROCESS

Figure 12.4 provides an overview of the credit risk management process. There are five stages: policy and infrastructure; credit granting; monitoring and exposure management; and portfolio management and credit review. Let's examine each of these in turn.

---

[5]The short-term interest rate has a long-term reversion to a mean of 6 percent; its adjusted volatility is 7.5 percent.

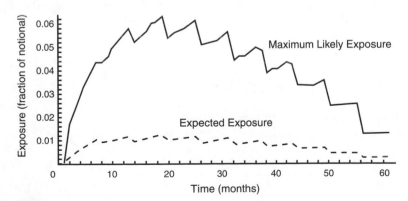

FIGURE 12.3 Exposure simulation for a plain vanilla swap.

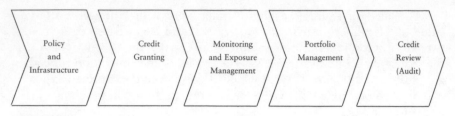

FIGURE 12.4   The credit risk process at a glance.

Policy and Infrastructure

This stage relates to the establishment of an appropriate credit risk environment; the adoption and implementation of credit risk policies and procedures; the development of methodologies and models, supported by appropriate systems; and the definition of data standards and conventions. It is the foundation on which management will build to ensure adequate controls are in place for managing credit risk.

An organization should have documented credit policies, methodologies, and procedures to ensure that credit risks are identified, measured, monitored, controlled, and regularly reported to senior management and the board of directors. These documents should reflect the firm's perspective on the prudent management of credit risks and take into account the nature and complexity of its activities, its business objectives, its competitive and regulatory environment, and its staff and technology capabilities.

Regulatory bodies take such policies very seriously. For example, the U.S. Federal Reserve System Trading Manual says:

> *Credit risk management should begin at the highest levels of the organization, with credit risk policies approved by the board of directors, some form of credit risk policy committee of senior management, a credit approval process, and a credit risk management staff which measures and monitors credit exposures throughout the organization.*[6]

There is no one-size-fits-all in credit risk management, but generally credit policies should address such topics as:

■ Credit risk philosophy and principles.
■ Credit analysis and approval processes.

---

[6]Federal Reserve System, "Trading Activities Manual—Part 1," March 1994, pp. 1–74.

- Credit rating systems and linkage to reserve and economic capital requirements.
- Underwriting standards and risk-adjusted pricing guidelines.
- Measurement of exposure of on– and off–balance sheet items.
- Delegation of lending authority and exposure limits.
- Target portfolio mix and use of risk transfer strategies.
- Credit monitoring and auditing processes.
- Exception and problem credit management.
- Risk measurement and reporting activities.

The policies adopted by senior management and the board need to be communicated to all employees involved in the credit process, implemented in a timely and consistent manner, and monitored to ensure compliance. They should be revised at least annually to take into account internal and external changes, such as new financial products, new markets and customers, and change in regulatory environment.

Credit Granting

The second stage refers to the extension of credit to customers or counterparties. It encompasses credit analysis/rating of counterparties; credit approval by appropriate authorities; pricing and terms and conditions of transactions; and proper documentation.

An accurate, consistent system of risk rating is the essential underpinning of sophisticated credit risk management. A credit rating represents a firm's overall assessment of a given credit risk. It is the foundation for a set of critical activities: assigning loss provisions and risk capital, developing risk-adjusted profitability and pricing models, setting exposure limits, and managing the firm's risk/reward trade-off.

Just as publicly available debt ratings are assigned by rating agencies such as Moody's and S&P on the basis of data about the creditworthiness of a corporation, internal risk ratings summarize a firm's assessment of the probability of economic loss resulting from a credit-sensitive transaction. In developing the rating process, a firm should decide whether to rate the counterparty/issuer or to rate the specific transaction. The former would result in the same rating for all transactions related to one counterparty; the latter, in a rating that incorporates the characteristics of the transaction, such as collateral or guarantee. The latter approach has the advantage that it is more refined, but the disadvantage that it is more difficult to evaluate accurately. Some firms assign both counterparty and transaction ratings.

Risk rating systems should be designed so that it is possible to strike a balance between effectiveness (accuracy, consistency, and timeliness of ratings) and efficiency (cost of assigning the ratings with a given frequency). Risk rating can be carried out on the basis of anything from pure judgment to deterministic modeling. In general, it will be a combination of both, including:

- Analysis of company financials, industry trends, and credit outlook.
- Use of a vendor-supplied or internal credit rating model.
- Use of external rating agencies' credit ratings.[7]

A credit rating should be assigned to each on– and off–balance sheet credit exposure of the firm at origination. In addition, the system should be responsive to changes in credit risk characteristics of a counterparty/issuer/ transaction. Exposures with deteriorating credit characteristics should be put on a "credit watch-list" that is reviewed regularly by senior management and the board of directors.

A consultative paper issued by the Basel Committee on Banking Supervision in July 1999 outlines the factors to be considered in a bank credit approval process.[8] These elements can be generalized to credit granting in general and would include an assessment of:

- The nature of the credit.
- The current risk profile of the borrower or counterparty and its sensitivity to economic and market developments.
- The borrower's repayment history and current capacity to pay its obligations, based on historical financial trends and cash flow projections.
- A forward-looking analysis of its capacity to pay obligations based on various scenarios.
- The reputation of the issuer or counterparty.
- The legal capacity of the counterparty to assume the liability.
- The proposed terms and conditions of the credit, including collateral and covenants designed to limit changes in the future risk profile of the counterparty (however, these should not be used to compensate for a lack of analysis, or for poor information).
- Where applicable, the adequacy and enforceability of collateral or guarantees.

The credit granting criteria listed above are obviously closely linked to the risk rating system, since they represent the basis for rating assessment.

---

[7]Today, commercial rating agencies rate more than 2,000 U.S. companies and corporate issues, but only around 250 European companies.
[8]Basel Committee on Banking Supervision, "Principles for the Management of Credit Risk," consultative paper, July 1999.

Granting credit involves accepting risks in order to produce profits or transfer some risks to another party (e.g., transferring market risk by entering into a swap agreement). With respect to loans, many banks have found that they can significantly improve their return on assets simply by setting pricing floors by risk rating.

The delegation of credit granting authority should be designed to ensure an appropriate balance between the efficiency of credit operations and the effectiveness of credit review and approval. Lending authority is normally expressed in terms of notional transaction size, risk rating, and economic capital usage.

Monitoring and Exposure Management

Both individual and portfolio exposures should be monitored on a regular basis. Single-entity credit exposures should be monitored against established limits to prevent undue exposure to an individual counterparty. Moreover, aggregate exposures by industry, country, and economic sector should be monitored against limits to ensure appropriate portfolio diversification. Indicators such as credit spreads and stock price volatilities should be tracked for early warning signals of potential adverse credit events. Large individual and aggregate credit risk exposures should be reported to senior management and to the board of directors.

A basic requirement of effective credit risk management is updated credit exposure information. For example, a firm might have different transactions with a single counterparty, conducted by more than one of its business units. In order for management to measure the current exposure to the counterparty, the individual transactional exposures must be aggregated. Exposure measurement is important for a number of purposes, such as risk reporting, comparison with policy limits, and determination of required level of credit reserves and economic capital.

There are two types of credit exposure: current exposure and potential exposure. Current exposure is defined as the amount at risk today. It's the loss that would be suffered here and now if all the credit transactions were to be settled and all the credit assets were to be sold immediately. It is obvious from this definition that current exposure takes no account of any future changes in market prices.

Potential exposure, on the other hand, depends on the *type* of transaction and on the occurrence of future random events. For loans or receivables where there is no line of credit, potential exposure and current exposure are the same absent any loan amortization or principal payment. For other transactions, such as swaps or credit lines, potential exposure needs to be modeled or estimated, since it is a function both of time to maturity and of the volatility of the underlying instrument. Furthermore, credit enhancements such as collateral and third-party guarantees, downgrade triggers,[9] and netting agreements[10] can be used to reduce a firm's counterparty credit risk. The calculated exposures should reflect these risk-reducing features if they are legally enforceable in the relevant jurisdictions.

Different approaches can be taken to exposure calculations. The calculation might be based on current exposure; maximum potential exposure; average expected exposure; or some rule of thumb, such as an add-on as a percentage of notional value. In addition, the exposure can be measured in terms of notional amounts or in terms of economic capital requirements, the latter being more representative of the risk involved in the transaction. Economic capital exposure is such that each dollar of economic capital represents an equal exposure to credit loss volatility. The selection of the appropriate exposure calculations for a business depends on the level and complexity of credit risk, as well as the business applications for the exposure calculations.

The important concept to remember in exposure measurement is consistency. One challenge that a firm faces is the development of consistent measurements for credit exposure throughout its portfolio. Because the exposures need to be aggregated in order to obtain a meaningful view of the total portfolio and in order to compare exposures against approved limits, all transactional exposures must be measured in a consistent manner.

A concentration of credit risk is the single most important cause of major problems. One senior credit officer I met in the early days of my career put it succinctly when he said, "Concentration kills." Concentrations arise in a credit portfolio as a direct consequence of business specialization. It is this specialization that allows a firm to achieve market leadership and gain competitive advantage, and concentration cannot be eliminated entirely. However, it *can* be controlled through the use of exposure limits.

The establishment of exposure limits is an important element of credit risk management that ensures appropriate diversification of a firm's credit portfolio. Limits should be defined for single counterparties, groups of connected counterparties, products, industries, and even for countries or geographic regions in which the firm currently holds or could potentially hold credit exposures.

Credit limits are useful in all areas of the firm's activities that involve credit risk. They should reflect management's appetite for a credit risk, and be meaningful constraints on business activities in order to mitigate risk. They should not, therefore, be so high that they are never breached or so

---

[9] A downgrade trigger would allow any of the counterparties to terminate a transaction if the other's credit rating falls below a certain level.

[10] A netting agreement would allow two counterparties to net their payment obligations.

low that they are breached too often. Actual credit exposures should be regularly compared with the established limits, and procedures should be in place for taking appropriate action within a defined period when limits are approached or exceeded.

Risk limits serve four main interrelated credit processes:

- *Risk control:* The presence of limits prevents the firm from engaging in business activities that are too risky, such as extending too much credit to a single counterparty or industry. It ensures that the firm enters into new products and markets only once the proper risk management prerequisites are in place. Limits are also set to control activities in areas where the firm does not think it should be taking positions because it is likely to be competitively disadvantaged. As such, the limits reflect not only a business judgment that the risk/reward trade-off is inadequate, but also serve to manage operational risks. For example, smaller credit limits might be allocated in countries where business and contract laws are questionable.

- *Allocation of risk-bearing capacity:* Like any other scarce financial resource, credit limits must be rationalized across products and business activities. Limits should be set to reflect management's determination of the risk/reward trade-offs made by potentially placing bets in a concentrated manner. A good example of the dangers of risk concentration is the case of the 1998 default of Power Company of America (PCA, a power-trading company). On June 24, 1998, a freak combination of factors led to power prices in the Midwest skyrocketing from their typical level of $30/MWh to the astounding level of $7,500/MWh. One of PCA's suppliers, Federal Energy Sales, failed to deliver. PCA was forced to default, too, and was subsequently forced into bankruptcy by $236 million of outstanding claims. Had credit concerns stopped PCA from doing business with Federal earlier in 1998, as other companies had, its exposure to the company might not have been as lethal. An effective limit management process might have made for a very different story.

- *Delegation of authority:* The credit limit system ensures that credit decisions are made by people with the requisite skills and appropriate authority. The delegation of credit authority is usually granted from the board of directors through the credit policy. From that point the firm's senior management may further delegate credit authority to the business units. This process may extend further still, with delegation to the individual personnel within business units. The delegation of credit authority through explicit credit limits ensures that central management retains control over credit risks, while providing business and risk-taking flexibility on a day-to-day basis.

■ *Regulatory compliance:* Regulators across all industries are increasingly focused on the corporate governance and audit procedures of the companies they monitor. For companies with significant financial risk exposures, the application of value-at-risk measures has become an accepted standard. For companies that are credit risk intensive, such as banks and brokerage firms, regulatory authorities can be expected to maintain close scrutiny of credit risk controls, including exposure limit management processes.

A credit risk–reporting process provides relevant information to senior management and the board of directors so they can effectively perform their oversight and fiduciary function. Effective and timely reporting of the firm's key credit exposures helps to ensure that risk management objectives are met, and facilitates appropriate management decisions and actions.

Credit risk reporting should be prepared by the risk management function and should typically include information on portfolio trends, risk-adjusted profitability, large and complex transactions, aggregate credit exposures against policy limits, and key exceptions. In practice, the effectiveness of the firm's credit risk–reporting process will be highly dependent on the quality of data resources and management information systems. In fact, the greatest challenge faced by most institutions will be the integration of various databases and systems to obtain a comprehensive credit portfolio perspective.

In July 1999, the Basel Committee on Banking Supervision published a paper, "Best Practices for Credit Risk Disclosure." According to this report, credit risk information should be:

■ *Relevant and timely:* Information should be provided with sufficient frequency and timeliness to give a meaningful picture of the institution's financial position and prospects. To be relevant, information should also keep pace with financial innovation and developments in credit risk management techniques such as credit risk modeling.

■ *Reliable:* Information should be reliable. Typically, it is more difficult to obtain precise measurements of credit risk than of market risk. This is because the estimation of default probabilities and recovery rates is usually less precise than the measurement of price movements in liquid markets. Moreover, credit ratings assigned to a counterparty usually include an element of judgment, which in turn depends on the quality of the credit staff.

■ *Comparable:* Market participants and other users need information that can be compared across institutions and countries, and over time. As such, it is useful to apply industry standards for credit exposure measurement, as well as map internal credit ratings to those established by the rating agencies.

- *Material:* Disclosures should be adapted to the size and nature of an institution's activities, in accordance with the concept of materiality. Information is material if its omission or mis-statement could change or influence an assessment or decision made by a user relying on that information.

Portfolio Management

Until recently, credit risk would typically stay on a firm's balance sheet until settlement of transactions or maturity/sale of financial assets. The introduction of active portfolio management, loan securitization, and risk transfer strategies has advanced the concept of credit portfolio management. With these tools, a "target" portfolio with optimized risk and return characteristics can be defined. The actual credit portfolio can then be steered toward this target by the use of portfolio management strategies. Such strategies may include the outright purchase or sale of assets; alternatively, part of the portfolio might be securitized or hedged through credit derivatives. Credit portfolio management can be used not only to optimize the risk/return of the credit portfolio, but also to free up scarce capital and credit limits in order to grow origination activities.

A portfolio management function should be responsible for optimizing the risk/return characteristics of the overall credit portfolio. The risk profile of a credit portfolio can be optimized through the use of origination targets, pricing, and risk transfer strategies. Origination targets determine which kinds of credit exposure the organization can safely take on, given the existing portfolio; pricing can be used to ensure that it is adequately rewarded for taking on such exposures. Risk transfer strategies allow it to reduce or eliminate risks that are deemed undesirable or inefficient within the firm's portfolio. Alternatively, they can allow it to take on, or increase, desirable risks. The credit policy should document the financial vehicles that can be used— for example, securitization, derivatives, insurance products, sales of assets, and alternative risk transfer products. It should also specify the permitted transactions and applications of portfolio management and risk transfer techniques.

An innovative trend in wholesale banking has been the disaggregation of origination, portfolio management, and servicing activities. The rationale for this transformation in wholesale banking is nearly identical to the rationale underlying the same trend in mortgage banking a decade earlier. One part of this rationale is that corporate lending is generally a low-margin activity, and generally unprofitable unless it is bundled with noncredit transactions. The combination of poor economics, high capital consumption, and unfavorable tax treatment[11] conspires to suggest that these loans, if they are to be made at all, should be sold to investors. The packaging of loans into collateralized loan obligations and commercial mortgage–backed securities also provides market discipline on three key components of a company's credit risk management process: underwriting, pricing, and documentation. First, the company's credit underwriting is confirmed as rating agencies review the creditworthiness of individual loans when they rate the various tranches of the deal. Second, investors will provide market feedback on appropriateness of the initial loan pricing when they bid on the supported securities. Finally, legal review will establish a check on the quality of loan documentation and collateral protection embedded in the loan contracts.

Credit Review

In order to ensure compliance with the established credit policies and processes, a formal credit review should be implemented as a separate credit risk process or as part of the overall audit process. This involves a thorough review of a sample of transactions and documentation, testing of systems and data integrity, the enforcement of underwriting standards, and compliance with specific policies and procedures. The credit review group must be independent from the origination group; it may even be independent from the risk management function.

It is essential to define a disciplined process which ensures that transactions are monitored and that individual businesses comply with underwriting and credit standards. It also ensures appropriate checks and balances, as well as compliance with the organization's credit policies and procedures. Moreover, trouble indicators such as unapproved limit excesses or double-rating downgrades should be reported and addressed. An effective credit review process not only helps to detect potential credit problems, it also ensures the identification of exceptions or violations to credit policies and procedures.

The periodicity of the reviews, and specific actions to be undertaken for policy violations, should be defined up front by the risk management function and approved by senior management and the board. These actions include rerating the counterparty or transaction, revising the terms and conditions of the transaction, selling the asset to another market player, or executing a risk transfer strategy. It is good practice to document and report policy exceptions and establish a defined timeframe for resolution.

---

[11]A commercial loan held on the balance sheet of a financial institution is subject to double taxation given that both the financial institution and its equity holder must pay income tax. In contrast, an investor of the same loan held in a mutual fund or hedge fund is taxed only once.

BASEL REQUIREMENTS

Regulatory requirements are a key driver of industry practices, and none more so than the capital adequacy system developed by the Basel Committee on Banking Supervision. The members of the Basel Committee, established by the central bank of the Governors of the Group of Ten countries in 1975, are banking supervisory authorities. Today, the expanded group consists of senior representatives of bank supervisory authorities and central banks from Belgium, Canada, France, Germany, Italy, Japan, Luxembourg, the Netherlands, Sweden, Switzerland, the United Kingdom, and the United States.

The Basel Committee's guidelines on capital allocation against credit risk have done much to shape the credit markets and the development of credit risk management. In 1988, the Committee introduced a capital adequacy system for banking institutions that stipulates an 8 percent capital charge against the risk-weighted exposure of all balance sheet assets. The risk weightings were assigned by asset class, ranging from 0 percent for U.S. Treasuries to 100 percent for corporate loans and bonds. The Capital Accord became a global benchmark for regulatory credit risk capital standards, and as such a major driver for the behavior of banking institutions.

However, by the mid-1990s the Capital Accord was being disputed by a large number of practitioners who argued that it had a number of pitfalls. For example, the risk weightings were seen to be too crude and arbitrary, so that the Accord recognized no difference between lending to a triple-A-rated corporation and a C-rated small business. Also, the Accord paid little heed to the term structure of credit risk. Consequently, a 1-year loan was treated in the same way as a 20-year loan, although there is clearly more chance of default over 20 years than over 12 months. Nor did the original Accord allow for the use of collateral or portfolio diversification effects.

To acknowledge the fact that the financial markets have changed significantly in the past decade, and that risk management tools have improved significantly, the Committee developed a new capital framework during the late 1990s. The new framework consists of three pillars: minimum capital requirements, supervisory review process, and effective use of market discipline. To quote from the introductory report: "It is designed to improve the way regulatory capital requirements reflect underlying risks. It is also designed to better address the financial innovation that has occurred in recent years . . . The review is also aimed at recognizing the improvements in risk measurement and control that have occurred."[12]

---

[12]Basel Committee on Banking Supervision, "A New Capital Adequacy Framework," June 1999.

Scheduled for implementation in 2006, some aspects of the new framework have yet to be finalized or introduced. However, the new framework has already motivated many financial institutions globally to adopt more advanced risk management tools for credit risk and other risks. Sophisticated banks would be able to use internal models and ratings rather than public ones, subject to supervisory review and approval. Credit risk may be only one part of the new capital guidelines, since the Committee will include capital charges for other risks, namely market risk and operational risk.

"The Committee believes that the Accord must be responsive to financial innovation and developments in risk management practices. The Committee's longer-term aim is to develop a flexible framework that reflects more accurately the risks to which banks are exposed."[13] Most risk practitioners would agree that, despite remaining technical issues, the new approach is certainly a step in the right direction.

BEST PRACTICES IN CREDIT RISK MANAGEMENT

Best practices in credit risk management, as with other risk management disciplines, represent a moving target. What are considered best practices today will become industry standards in a few years. For credit risk intensive businesses, a key challenge facing management is to ensure that company practices are, at a minimum, consistent with industry practices, and ideally represent best practices. The following sections describe three categories of credit risk measurement and management practices:

- *Basic practice* represents the minimum controls required for sound credit risk management.
- *Standard practice* represents the next level of credit risk applications in terms of sophistication.
- *Best practice* represents the most advanced credit risk applications adopted by leading institutions.

It is important to note that a company does not necessarily need to establish best practices for all of its risk management areas. The appropriate level of sophistication in risk management processes really depends on the risk profile of the individual company. For example, a manufacturing company does not require the same level of investments in credit risk management as a commercial bank. Therefore, many companies have adopted what

---

[13]Basel Committee on Banking Supervision, "A New Capital Adequacy Framework," June 1999.

they considered to be "best in class" practices that incorporate the size, complexity, and risk profile of their businesses.

Basic Practice

A fundamental step in credit risk management is developing common definitions of risk and exposure measurement across business units. These definitions include items such as (1) counterparty names used to identify the legal entities involved and the associated credit exposures; (2) risk ratings, based on consistent underwriting standards; and (3) simple exposure measurement and aggregation methodologies such as loan and notional amounts. At the basic practice level, few risk ratings are established, and they are mainly used to accept or decline credits, and the majority of credit exposures are often lumped into two or so ratings. The use of credit limits is focused on individual transactions, such as maximum amounts by obligor and risk rating, with few if any portfolio risk limits. The use of credit risk models is limited to simple spreadsheet models, ratio analysis, and credit bureau reports.

The credit risk management function is mainly a credit policy, approval, and monitoring function. It establishes credit policies and underwriting guidelines on how credits should be rated and what ratings are acceptable. For transactions above a certain size, the approval by a credit analyst or committee is required. On an ongoing basis, the credit function also identifies problem loans, maintains a watch list, and plays a central role in the workout process. The performance of the credit risk function is mainly determined by the level of charge-offs and delinquent loans.

Standard Practice

Building on the basic practices described above, standard-practice companies establish more risk ratings to better differentiate underlying credit risks, and explicitly link risk rating to pricing, reserve, and capital requirements. For example, a loan with a certain rating would be priced based on a pricing model or pricing matrix, and it is tied to a risk-adjusted level of reserves and capital. Formula-based exposure measurement and aggregation methodologies are used to translate on– and off–balance sheet exposures into loan equivalent amounts. Credit exposure limits are established by counterparty, risk rating, industry, and country. The use of credit risk models is limited to the credit risk management function, and may include both internally developed and vendor models. These models take into account detailed financial information, stock and credit spread volatility, and economic indicators.

The credit risk management function is more integrated with the loan origination function. Relationship managers or teams are assigned to institutional clients while product managers are assigned to retail products. These managers develop relationship and product plans that take into account both the profitability and the risks of individual transactions, and the overall portfolio. As such, credit analysts and loan originators work together to structure and price specific transactions and products in order to address both business and credit considerations. The performance of the credit risk management function is determined not only by the level of charge-offs and delinquencies, but is also influenced by how they contributed to the growth and risk-adjusted profitability of the business units.

Best Practice

Going beyond what has been discussed above, best-practice companies develop more advanced tools and applications in each aspect of their credit risk management. These tools and applications include:

- *Integrated credit exposure measurement.* Indeterminate credit exposures (e.g., swaps, forwards, credit lines) are calculated by Monte Carlo simulation models so they can be aggregated with loan exposures. This provides management with a more accurate measurement of credit concentrations by counterparty name, industry, risk rating, country, and other defined credit segments. Aggregate credit exposures also incorporate the impact of netting and collateral arrangements. In addition to credit exposure aggregation, the credit database can be used to identify unusual credit behavior or patterns.

- *Scenario analysis and planning.* Best-practice companies develop the ability to measure how adverse credit events and market changes would affect the institution's risk positions. It is important for management to assess the potential impact of multiple events. For example, how would a global stock market crash, combined with a Mexican peso devaluation, affect the institution's direct credit exposures to Mexican companies and to other companies with significant economic ties to Mexico? Such scenario analysis is then followed by the formulation of risk mitigation plans and leading indicators so that the company can identify the emergence of various scenarios and take appropriate actions.

- *Advanced credit risk management tools.* These tools include (1) credit scoring models that assist credit analysts in rating counterparties and tracking the probability of default over time; (2) credit surveillance systems that provide early warning signals by monitoring stock and bond prices, credit spreads, company news stories, and other market and competitive data; (3) credit migration models that help management to assess potential future credit losses and reserve and capital requirements, by projecting how current credit ratings would migrate over time under expected and stressed scenarios, (4) pricing models that help relationship managers determine risk-adjusted product pricing and relationship profitability; and (5) portfolio management tools that help management determine the optimal asset allocation based on business risk and return relationships.

■ *Active portfolio management.* Based on the information and tools above, best-practice companies develop strategies to optimize the risk/return of the overall credit portfolio. This includes changing the institution's existing credit portfolio through loan sales, securitization, credit enhancement, credit derivatives, and other techniques, as well as defining trigger points and exit strategies for the institution's current or projected credit concentrations. A centralized portfolio investment unit drives the active portfolio management approach. This unit sits between the bank's loan originators and the secondary market. It assumes ownership of credit assets, and exercises profit and loss responsibility for the portfolio as a whole. The portfolio unit is intended to act like an asset manager, that is, to make decisions about what to buy and sell, and at what price, based on a portfolio assessment of risk and return. A significant virtue of the active portfolio management approach is its transparency. Individual functions are held accountable for the sources of value within their control, such as pricing and productivity for origination; credit returns and economic capital utilization for portfolio investment; and scale and cost efficiency for servicing. This added transparency goes a long way toward eliminating the cross-subsidies that often make credit a loss leader, and toward establishing pricing and underwriting discipline based on market developments.

Best-practice institutions are characterized by a credit culture where credit risks are managed at both the transaction and portfolio levels, and where there is an optimal balance between business and risk management objectives. This culture is supported by the appropriate credit training and incentive programs that reinforce the organization's credit policies. Building a best-practice credit risk management capability is expensive: it requires highly skilled staff and extensive systems investments. However, there are significant benefits. First, credit approval and pricing decisions are improved at the transaction level. Second, concentrations in credit risk at the portfolio level are controlled to prevent large ULs. Third, more accurate projections of credit losses and reserve requirements result in smoother earnings. Fourth, advanced credit metrics and reporting help facilitate management decisions and actions before credit problems deteriorate further. And finally, active portfolio management and risk transfer strategies will help to optimize the overall risk and return of the credit portfolio.

Ultimately, the true test for a best-practice company is not simply the advanced models and methodologies that it employs, but the difficult management decisions that it needs to make in the face of earnings pressure. A recent example is the large credit write-offs of telecommunication loans by the large banks in 2002. Many of these banks had developed sophisticated credit risk models but nonetheless built up significant credit exposures to the telecommunication industry because they offered huge investment banking fees and attractive growth prospects in the previous years.

Lenders beware: "Concentration kills."

CASE STUDY: EXPORT DEVELOPMENT CORPORATION (EDC)

EDC is a Canadian crown organization with an important mission. Since 1944, EDC has been helping Canadian businesses grow and prosper through international trade and foreign investment. EDC is accountable to the Canadian Parliament through the Minister for International Trade and operates as a Commercial Crown Corporation.

Patrick Lavelle (chairman at the time this case was written) explained: "Overall, our results are a tangible reflection of our public policy mandate: to support and develop, directly or indirectly, Canada's export trade, as well as Canadian capacity to engage in that trade and to respond to international business opportunities. We do so by taking on trade risks in a financially sound manner, through credit insurance, bid and performance bonds and guarantees, and by making it easier for foreigners to 'buy Canadian,' through a multitude of financing options." Mr. Lavelle added, "As Chairman of EDC, one of my key objectives is to ensure that we can meet our public policy objective by striving towards best practices in risk management."

Lines of Business

With financial assets of about CAD$25 billion, EDC provides a wide range of financial products and services in support of its customers. The Corporation delivers its products and services through sector-based business teams. EDC's financial products and services can be classified into five general categories:

- *Credit insurance services:* Protect EDC's policy holders (generally, Canadian exporters) against nonpayment by buyers or banks, whether it is due to commercial risks such as insolvency, default, repudiation of goods or termination of contracts, or to country risks outside the control of the buyers/banks, such as difficulty in converting or transferring currency, cancellations of export or import permits, or war-related risks.

■ *Financing services:* Provide EDC's customers and enable them to provide their customers, with flexible, medium- and long-term financing using a variety of structures (lines of credit and protocols with foreign banks and agencies, note purchase arrangements, direct buyer loans, long-term preshipment financing, leveraged lease financing, and project risk financing packages).

■ *Contract insurance and bonding services:* Come into play in many international credit commitments, particularly for capital equipment and projects, where purchasers of EDC's customers may require them to post bonds guaranteeing their bid, performance, or any advances received from the purchasers.

■ *Political risk insurance services:* To support EDC's customers with investments in foreign countries and to support lenders who finance transactions pursued by EDC's customers abroad. Political risk insurance protects the policyholder against transfer and convertibility risk, expropriation risk, and war, revolution, and insurrection risk.

■ *Equity services:* Provide equity and other forms of related investments in EDC's customers or their projects, or companies operating abroad or through participation in market- or sector-focused investment funds.

Credit Risk at EDC

Credit risk at EDC is broadly defined as the possibility of financial loss resulting from credit commitments within EDC's business activities. Credit risk generally manifests itself as the risk of a payment default resulting in a financial loss for EDC's direct credit commitments, or a risk event that could lead to a claim for EDC's indirect credit commitments. Depending on the type of credit commitment, credit risk may include (1) financial solvency risk; (2) performance risk; (3) industry risk; (4) unwillingness to pay on the part of the obligor or related parties who may have an influence on the possible loss associated with the credit commitment; and (5) country risk of the country in which the obligor or related party is domiciled.

Because the acceptance of credit risk is such an important component of EDC's policy mandate and long-term success, it is critical for senior management that best practices are in place. As such, in the summer of 1999, EDC initiated a major initiative to establish a credit policy framework that would represent industry best practices. Peter Allen, Chief Financial Officer (CFO), and W. James Brockbank, Vice-President for Risk Management (who was promoted to Chief Risk Officer in 2001), provided the executive sponsorship for the initiative, while Christopher Clubb, a senior member of the Risk Management Office, acted as the overall project manager. The key objectives of EDC's credit initiative include:

1. Articulate and document the organization's credit philosophy and processes.
2. Make significant improvements in its credit policies and practices.
3. Shift the role of the Board of Directors from transaction approval to credit policy and portfolio management.
4. Develop a Credit Risk Policy Manual that will establish the overall credit risk management framework at EDC.

This project represented a significant step for EDC in moving toward best-practice credit risk management. At the conclusion of the project, all parties involved felt that the project was highly successful in achieving its objectives. Several key success factors contributed to the positive outcome of the project. These key success factors include:

- *Board Involvement.* Members of the Board, particularly Patrick Lavelle, Chairman, and Pierre MacDonald, Chair of the Board's Risk Management Committee, took on a highly visible, engaged, and supportive role throughout the project. At times, their personal commitment and participation resulted in more aggressive development of EDC's risk management capabilities.
- *Executive Management Commitment.* A. Ian Gillespie, Chief Executive Officer, and Peter Allen, CFO, were both fully committed to the project. To ensure compliance with the credit policies, a policy compliance and reporting procedure was put in place at the end of the project. As part of this procedure, Gillespie and Allen would sign a "compliance certificate" each month that ensures the Board that they are monitoring EDC's credit activities against the policies, and that any exception is reported as required.
- *Executive Management Steering Committee.* The project evolved over the course of approximately six months. Over this time, the executive Risk Management Committee served as the steering committee in completion of the project. In addition to Gillespie, Allen, and Brockbank, the Committee is composed of Eric Siegel, Executive Vice-President of Medium and Long-Term Financial Services, Rolfe Cooke, Senior Vice-President of Short-Term Financial Services, and Gilles Ross, Senior Vice-President of Legal Services and Secretariat.
- *Stakeholders Management.* The Risk Management Office, led by Brockbank and Clubb, paid significant attention to communication with key stakeholders. For both the board of directors and line management, they introduced each section of the Credit Risk Policy Manual in a phased approach to obtain buy-in. Additionally, they held "open house" meetings with small groups of directors to further educate them about credit risk management objectives and practices.

■ *Open Debate and Resolution.* There were no "sacred cows" during the project. All issues were open for debate and discussed until resolution is reached. In one defining moment for the project, Allen put forth a number of critical issues regarding EDC's credit approval process. These issues were fully debated until final agreement was reached on the appropriate policies for credit approval. This agreement alone resolved open issues that had caused confusion for many years.

■ *Credit Culture Change.* This project resulted in real change in EDC's credit culture even before the Credit Risk Policy Manual was finalized. Credit risk considerations were integrated into senior management decisions at both the transaction and portfolio levels. Additionally, line management was increasingly seeking the guidance of the Risk Management Office.

EDC'S CREDIT RISK POLICY MANUAL

The following sections summarize the major components of EDC's Credit Risk Policy Manual.

Organizational Structure

Patrick Lavelle: "Given that EDC is targeting higher-risk markets on behalf of Canadian businesses, as well as operating in an increasingly uncertain global economic environment, a Risk Management Committee of the Board has been established to ensure that the principal risks of the Corporation's business have been identified and that appropriate systems are in place to manage our risk strategy."

The organizational structure for risk management at EDC is shown in Figure 12.5.

The Risk Management Committee of the Board was established in May 1998. Pierre MacDonald, an independent board member, chairs the Committee. Its immediate focus is to ensure the appropriate credit policies are in place. It is also responsible for reviewing and approving business transactions, as well as monitoring the overall risk in EDC's risk portfolio. The Risk Management Committee of the Board consists of:

■ The Chairman of the Board of Directors
■ The President
■ Four directors appointed by the Board, including Pierre MacDonald

The Risk Management Committee of the firm and the Risk Management Office, headed by Brockbank, were established to provide a second

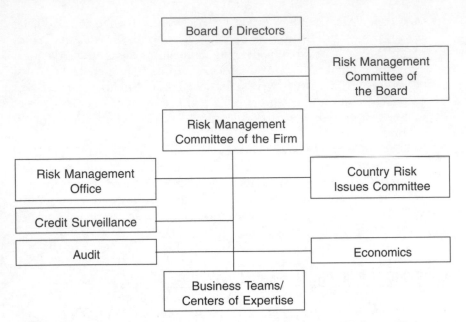

FIGURE 12.5 Organizational structure for risk management at EDC.

and impartial perspective as to the acceptability of the assets and exposures being recommended by the Business Teams. Their mandate is to optimize the corporation's capacity and appetite for timely origination of credit exposures consistent with corporate business plans and objectives.

Philosophy Statement

As mentioned previously, a credit-intensive firm should have a documented credit risk philosophy that underpins the credit risk management framework. This statement presents the credit risk culture that exists within the organization and underlies the credit risk policies, methodologies, and procedures. EDC's statement was developed by senior management and is provided in the following section.

EDC'S STATEMENT OF CREDIT RISK PHILOSOPHY

Due to its unique business mandate, EDC's credit risk philosophy can be best described as follows:

1. To fulfill our business mandate, we balance the dual responsibility of maximizing EDC's capacity to help create enduring prosperity

for Canada while at the same time safeguarding the Corporation's financial sustainability.

2. We are prepared to originate/underwrite credit commitments that have a risk profile that may be higher than what would be present at other Canadian credit providers, and hold portfolios of credit commitments at higher concentrations than at other Canadian credit providers.

3. At origination, we are committed to the appropriate level of due diligence to ensure that the risks of the credit commitment have been properly analyzed, fully disclosed to the authorizing and endorsing bodies, and appropriately characterized (e.g., rated). We apply leading edge commercial principles to ensure the credit commitment has been appropriately structured, priced, and documented with the goal of maximizing, when applicable, the marketability of the credit commitment in secondary market activity. We price credit commitments with respect to market practices.

4. When originating credit commitments, we recognize the differences between originating commitments within our financial services programs. Generally, the granting of credit within the credit insurance services and some of the contract insurance and bonding services concentrates on the risk/return of pools of credit commitments, while the granting of credit within other EDC Lines of Business concentrates on the risk/return of the individual credit commitment.

5. We strive to manage credit risk and ensure financial sustainability in order to continue to grow and fulfill our mandate.

6. We maintain reserve and capital levels adequate to absorb expected and unexpected losses.

7. We establish corporate portfolio pricing and profitability objectives that balance EDC's commercial financial requirements and EDC's public policy mandate to provide value-added benefits for Canada.

8. We establish credit limits (obligor, country, and industry) to manage portfolio concentrations.

9. We utilize risk transfer abilities to manage credit exposures within portfolio concentration limits and portfolio targets.

10. We strive to incorporate relevant credit risk management "best practices" within EDC where appropriate.

The Credit Risk Policy Manual

EDC recognized the need to have documented and approved policies and procedures to ensure that all credit risks are identified, measured, monitored, controlled, and regularly reported to the Board of Directors. The Credit Risk Policy Manual was developed in 1999 and describes EDC's perspective on the prudent origination and management of credit commitments of the corporation's portfolio. The Manual is designed to help ensure that EDC will always be in a position to provide value-added commercial financial solutions to companies of all sizes by using its own internal financial resources.

The Manual also serves to fulfill the Risk Management Committee of the Board's responsibility to ensure that appropriate policies are in place to maintain an acceptable level of credit risk to the Corporation. Credit risk policies remain the oversight responsibility of the Risk Management Committee of the Board, for which Management is responsible for ensuring and reporting adherence.

The Manual is divided into three chapters. The first chapter puts the Manual and its Policies into EDC's context by examining its mission, business objectives, credit risk philosophy, and credit risk principles. The second chapter presents EDC's Credit Risk Policies, each of which are structured as follows: executive summary, purpose, policies and methodologies, exceptions, and reporting to Management and to the Board of Directors.

The Policies are as follows:

- Risk Rating Policy
- Credit Granting Policy
- Credit Exposure Measurement Policy
- Country Risk Limits Policy
- Industry and Obligator Risk Limit Policy
- Credit Loss Reserve and Capital Adequacy Policy
- Credit Monitoring and Review Policy
- Credit Portfolio Management Policy
- Risk Transfer Policy
- Management and Board Reporting Policy

The third chapter defines the organizational structure for credit risk management, roles and accountabilities of various departments and committees, and responsibility of maintaining the Policies.

The Board of Directors approved the Manual and its Policies upon the recommendation of the Risk Management Committee of the Board of Directors and EDC Management. Management will provide reports to the Board of Directors on a regular basis evidencing adherence to the Policies. The Manual will be subject to review and revision on an annual basis to reflect changes in EDC's business environment and evolution in best practices in credit risk management. Management, the Risk Management Committee of the Board, and the Board of Directors acknowledge that full implementation may require several years. Accordingly, Management will review the Manual and its Policies on an annual basis, and recommend any changes to the Risk Management Committee of the Board. All changes to the Manual require the approval of the Board of Directors.

In developing the Credit Risk Policy Manual, EDC took a significant step forward in implementing best practices in credit risk management at the organization. This development involved the active participation of various parts of the organization. The Risk Management Office provided the technical resources in drafting the credit policies, as well as gaining business unit support and educating board members through a series of "workshops." Senior management, led by CFO Peter Allen in this effort, engaged in healthy debate as to the appropriate credit philosophy and policies for EDC. The Board of Directors, and the Risk Committee of the Board, allocated significant time in reviewing and approving the credit policies. The EDC case study is a good example of the components of establishing a credit risk policy, as well as one of the key requirements for success—the active involvement of senior management and the board. In December of 1999, the Credit Risk Policy Manual was approved by the Risk Committee of the Board, as well as the full Board of Directors.

CHAPTER 13

Market Risk Management

What is market risk? A general definition might go something like the following: Market risk is the exposure to potential loss that would result from changes in market prices or rates. All companies are exposed to some forms of market risk. The level and form of market risk exposure differs by industries, and by companies within an industry. The relevant prices or rates (sometimes called the market risk factors) might include equity or commodity prices, interest rates, and foreign exchange rates. So one form of market risk faced by a financial institution would be its exposure to changes in interest rates if the durations of its assets and liabilities are mismatched. Other market risks at financial institutions might arise from proprietary trading and market-making activities.

An international corporation, on the other hand, might be exposed to foreign exchange movements if its offshore revenues and expenses are denominated in different currencies. Even if these were denominated in the *same* currencies, foreign exchange risk would exist when it came to repatriating offshore earnings into the corporation's home currency. An energy firm is exposed to energy price movements if a change in an input price (e.g., the price of crude oil) is not matched by a change in an output price (the price of petroleum or jet fuel). Additionally, the value of an energy firm's reserves is directly linked to market prices.

While different industries face specific forms of market risks, there are some market risks that are faced by all companies. For example, the performance of a company's investment portfolio directly impacts its financial performance. All companies will only stay solvent by ensuring that all cash obligations can be met by a combination of investment liquidity, funding sources, and contingent liabilities. Another example of a common market risk is the obligation to fund pensions and other defined benefit plans. For example, in its third-quarter earnings release in 2002, General Motors announced a $1 billion pension fund loss due to the bear market. General

Motors was not alone, as many large corporations announced large pension losses.

In this chapter we will discuss the various types of market risk, approaches to measuring and managing it, and best practices today.

TYPES OF MARKET RISK

There are three types of market risk: trading risk, asset/liability mismatch, and liquidity risk. Trading risk encompasses the risks that a company faces in its investment and trading portfolios due to changes in interest rates, exchange rates, equity prices, and commodity prices. The exposures involved in trading risk are generally short term, and can typically be closed out or hedged over a period of several days. Trading risk is the major market risk faced by investment banks and dealers. Energy firms with market-making activities and nonfinancial corporations with a trading book would also face trading risk.

Asset/liability mismatch arises from a difference in the interest rate sensitivities of assets and liabilities held on the balance sheet. This interest rate risk is distinct from trading risk in that it is generally less liquid and can therefore only be adjusted or closed out on an infrequent basis, although they can be hedged and rehedged more often. Asset/liability mismatch is the major market risk faced by commercial and retail banks. Insurance companies and investment banks are also faced with this type of balance sheet risk. For energy firms, the risk of mismatches between input and output prices also can be analyzed in an asset/liability management framework.

Liquidity risk is the risk that a company will be unable to obtain the funds to meet its financial obligations as they come due, either by increasing liabilities or by converting assets without incurring significant losses. All corporations face this risk. Liquidity risk may occur even in a trading portfolio, when either a large position is unloaded on the market or when trading in "thin" markets (e.g., as commonly found in emerging markets).

Figure 13.1 illustrates how the three major types of market risk can be further subdivided into individual risk types, some of which overlap: interest rate risk, foreign exchange risk, commodity risk, equity risk, and basis risk. In addition, there will frequently be other (perhaps more complex) risks that arise from a change in a market risk factor. The major types of market risks are:

- *Interest rate risk:* The risk of financial loss due to interest rate volatility. Losses could result from changes in level or shape of the yield curve.
- *Foreign exchange risk:* The risk of an adverse variation in return or cost resulting from changes in foreign exchange rates.

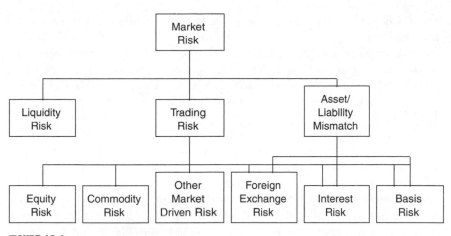

FIGURE 13.1 Types of market risk.

- *Commodity risk:* The risk of commodity price fluctuations.
- *Equity risk:* The risk of equity value fluctuations.
- *Basis risk:* The risk of changes in the relative rates of two indices [e.g., prime rate vs. the London inter-bank offering rate (LIBOR)].
- *Other market driven risk:* In addition to the most common market risk types listed above, there are other market risks, such as option risks (e.g., prepayment of mortgage loans and securities) and exposures to other market prices (e.g., real estate prices).

A key measure of market risk is value-at-risk (VaR). VaR measures the worst loss that might be *expected* over a given time interval, under normal market conditions and with a given confidence level. VaR is useful because it provides users with a standardized measure of market risk, expressed in terms of the money that might actually be lost. For instance, a bank might report that the daily VaR of its trading portfolio is $30 million at the 99 percent confidence level. In other words, there is only one chance in 100 that a daily loss greater than $30 million will occur, under normal market conditions. It also means in two or three days a year, losses would likely exceed $30 million. We will examine VaR and other useful and widely used techniques of market risk measurement.

MARKET RISK MEASUREMENT

Gap Analysis

Gap analysis is the most common and perhaps the best-understood technique for measuring interest rate risk, despite the limitations discussed below. It also can be applied in policy setting and risk limit definition. Most large banking corporations present gap analyses in annual reports to discuss their interest rate risk exposures.

In gap analysis, the organization's assets and liabilities are grouped into time "buckets" according to when they will be repriced. The difference between repricing assets and repricing liabilities is known as the gap. A negative gap would result if repricing liabilities were greater than repricing assets, indicating a risk exposure to increasing rates. Gap analysis, however, ignores mismatches that exist *within* the various time buckets. For example, repricing assets may equal repricing liabilities within the next year, but over the next month there may still be repricing mismatches. Additionally, gap analysis is usually not an effective measurement tool for more complex interest rate risk factors, including the treatment of accounts that don't have definite maturities (e.g., checking and deposit accounts), administered rate accounts (prime rate loans), basis risk (prime vs. LIBOR), and option risk exposures (mortgage loans and securities).

Duration

Duration is a fundamental technique in interest rate risk measurement, and determines a financial instrument's price sensitivity to changes in interest rates. Mathematically, duration is equal to the weighted-average time when all future cash flows are received, using the present values of such cash flows as weights. Duration captures the effects of differing coupon rates and market yields for debt instruments; an important property is that it is directly proportional to the percentage changes in asset prices that result from a change in market yields. For example, an asset with a duration of five years would drop by roughly 5 percent for every 1 percent increase in rates. Thus, duration can be used to calculate an investment's interest rate elasticity.

However, it only takes into account parallel shifts in interest rates; that is, those where all interest rates move by the same amount (so the three-month rate changes by the same amount as the five-year rate). In real life, shifts in the interest rate curve are often anything but parallel. To capture more realistic changes in the level and slope of the yield curve, other duration measures (e.g., key rate duration) are used to measure an instrument's or portfolio's price sensitivity to changes in various segments of the yield curve.

Value-at-Risk

The concept of VaR has rapidly become the industry standard for measuring and reporting market risk in trading portfolios. It translates the riskiness of an entire portfolio into a common standard: the potential loss stated in a single currency such as U.S. dollars. It is this simple common standard that makes VaR so appealing and powerful; it provides a consistent and comparable measure of risk across all instruments, products, trading desks, and business lines. In 1995, the International Swap and Derivatives Association stated that "The measure [of market risk] thought to be appropriate by most of the leading practitioners is some form of Value-at-Risk" (see Figure 13.2).

VaR is a measure of the likely loss of market value for a given portfolio over a predetermined confidence level and holding period. That is, there is some fixed probability (the confidence level) that any losses suffered by the portfolio over the holding period will be *less* than the limit established by VaR. There is also a fixed probability that the losses might be worse. The VaR limit does not, therefore, say anything about how bad losses could actually be, and definitely does not specify the worst possible loss—a common misconception. It simply suggests what loss might be suffered on a fairly bad day.

Another way of thinking about VaR is that it draws the line between everyday losses and exceptional losses. Clearly, this makes it useful for considering the market risks run by an organization. However, there is as yet no single industry standard for what constitutes a severe loss, and thus no industry standard for what actually constitutes VaR. The Group of Thirty, a think-tank that issued widely used standards for risk management, recommends the use of two standard deviations of daily market movement for calculating VaR, which corresponds to a 97.5 percent confidence level for

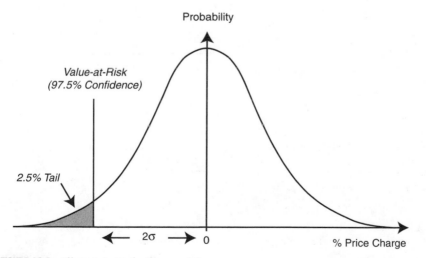

FIGURE 13.2 Illustration of value-at-risk.

normal distribution. Another widely used standard, RiskMetrics[1] defines VaR as the 5 percent event (a 95 percent confidence level), whereas the Bank for International Settlements (BIS) stipulates a 99 percent confidence interval. Individual institutions may choose other confidence levels; a level somewhere between 95 and 99 percent is most common. It is more important that an institution choose a consistent level across the entire enterprise than any one particular number.

The BIS has developed specific guidelines for the parameters that determine VaR calculation for risk in the trading room (Table 13.1). These choices were determined by the needs of a regulatory agency rather than from the point of view of active risk management in a sophisticated trading operation. As such, the 10-day holding period is unreasonably long for all but the most illiquid securities. The BIS-specified calculation method is simple and transparent, but less effective at predicting future volatility than the common approach where market behavior in the recent past is given more weight than the distant past. However, there is nothing to preclude any institution calculating both a regulatory VaR and an economically rational VaR for internal consumption, and most leading players do in fact calculate both. Most commercially available VaR systems allow for such dual calculations as well.

The VaR methodology also can be applied to the measurement of balance sheet interest rate risk. A smaller set of risk factors than the trading risk VaR analysis are used, restricted to those associated with the yield curves that affect the pricing of the assets and liabilities on the balance sheet. Since the balance sheet represents a longer-term portfolio than those associated with daily trading, a modestly different approach is required. The main difference is that the changes in the risk factors are measured less frequently than the daily measure taken for trading risk measurement.

TABLE 13.1 BIS Recommended Parameters for VaR Calculation

BIS Guidelines	
Confidence level	99%, one-tailed
Holding period	10 days
Observation period	1 year
Model type	No particular so long as it captures all material risks

Source: Basel Committee, January 1996.

---

[1]RiskMetrics is a set of tools originally developed by JP Morgan that enables participants in the financial markets to estimate their exposure to market risk under the VaR framework.

Calculating VaR

VaR is calculated as the product of three basic factors:

1. The size of the open position at risk, called the exposure amount
2. The price volatility of the instrument, called the price volatility factor
3. The time required to close out a position following an adverse price movement, called the liquidity factor

The exposure amount is the net exposure of an open position. It is typically calculated for a business unit or for a portfolio that consists of related instruments. The process of marking positions to market is essential to the accurate measurement of exposure amount and, therefore, market risk. Proper aggregation is also crucial to the calculation of exposure amount (e.g., all exposures to changes in the U.S. dollar/Japanese yen).

The risk inherent in holding any market position is dependent on the volatility of the underlying market. The most important volatility measure is the price volatility factor, which is the "best estimate" of the future daily volatility of market prices. While historical volatility can be observed, future volatility can only be estimated using past data, judgment about the future condition of the markets, or the implied volatility from traded options.

If a company is dealing with a portfolio instead of just a single asset (which is usually the case), it should include the correlations between market movements, usually estimated by using the historical correlations between each pair of market prices. The company itself can do this, but it is also possible to obtain third-party correlation matrices that cover the most commonly traded market prices. Again, the correlation matrix is ideally a forward-looking measure, so it may be necessary to adjust historical results to reflect current market conditions.

The liquidity factor represents the time (in days) required to liquidate a position in an orderly fashion and in *adverse* market conditions. Abnormally large positions or markets that can "dry up" will require more than a day to liquidate. This factor is often overlooked in VaR analysis. In order to incorporate the liquidity factor, the holding period should be adjusted given the market liquidity of the various instruments.

Three Flavors of VaR

There are three main approaches to calculating VaR: parametric (also called the variance-covariance) approach, Monte Carlo simulation, and historical simulation. Each has its strengths and weaknesses; taken together, they give a more comprehensive perspective of risk. We will describe each of these approaches briefly.

The Parametric Approach This is the simplest approach to VaR. It makes two basic assumptions about price movements and the consequent changes in portfolio value:

1. Changes in risk factors are *normally distributed* and linearly correlated.
2. The change in value of the portfolio resulting from a change in risk factor is *linear*.[2]

The first assumption simplifies the VaR computation dramatically, although it is not always true in practice. If the assumption is made, all we need to measure and model is the variance and correlation between assets or instruments. We should then be able to predict the likelihood of severe market fluctuations and their impact on loss. The second assumption is true for some simple financial instruments, but is violated by many other instruments, particularly those with option characteristics. The VaR estimates produced by this approach will therefore be most accurate when the portfolio is mostly composed of products with minimal optionality (or nonlinearity) and price changes are approximately normally distributed.

Despite its limitations, parametric VaR is often a reasonable approximation of a firm's risk profile. For example, the portfolio that brought down Barings Bank was dominated by positions in Japanese government bond futures and Nikkei futures. Not only was this portfolio highly concentrated (there were only two instruments), but it also contained derivative products (albeit of the simplest variety). Nonetheless, parametric VaR would have revealed that rogue trader Nick Leeson had placed almost $1 billion at risk! His final loss amounted to approximately $1.3 billion. Given the unusually large drop in the Nikkei following the Kobe earthquake, the highly concentrated nature of the portfolio, and its high proportion of derivatives, this loss was still remarkably close to the parametric VaR estimate. That number would have been very useful to senior management at Barings.

Monte Carlo Simulation This method generates a distribution of changes in portfolio value by revaluing the portfolio under a large number of scenarios. Each scenario represents one way that the portfolio's value might evolve over time, with the collection of risk factors changing in a different, randomly chosen way each time. The overall effect of these random changes on the portfolio value can then be found using the volatility and correlation information described above. A combination of the portfolio values found under each scenario gives an estimate of its likely behavior.

---

[2]Linear means that if the value of the portfolio changes by x when a rate changes by 1 percent, then the change due to a 2 percent move is $2x$.

Recall that the parametric approach to VaR rests on the two assumptions of normality and linearity. The Monte Carlo approach relaxes the assumption of linearity. To understand the distribution of changes in value for nonlinear instruments such as derivatives, consider Figure 13.3.

Panel A describes the payoff function of an option as the value of the underlying changes; here it is nonlinear. The next panel is the normal distribution of the underlying risk factor. While Panel C combines the two, it describes the distribution of value changes of the derivative product. In simulation, we generate the data for B randomly and recompute the value of the derivative product using A to obtain C. Note that C does not look normal even though B looks quite normal. This is because the nonlinearity we see in A results in a non-normal distribution of changes in the derivative's value. Only a simulation-based approach will capture this.

The Monte Carlo approach is, therefore, most useful when nonlinear instruments represent a significant fraction of the total portfolio and where the underlying risk factors are normally distributed. For example, mortgage securities react in a nonlinear manner to rate changes due to the prepayment option, yet changes in interest rates are normally distributed. In practice, Monte Carlo simulation is widely used to provide valuation and risk management for holders of mortgage securities.

Historical Simulation   This approach to VaR uses historical data about actual price movements to generate scenarios, and then reprices the portfolio according to these historical scenarios to generate the distribution of changes in portfolio value.

Historical simulation is therefore similar to the Monte Carlo simulation approach, except that the changes in the risk factors are determined by historical experience, not chosen randomly. The historical simulation approach allows the relaxation of both the linearity and normality assumptions of parametric VaR. In addition to the nonlinear characteristics of Panel A in Figure 13.3, Panel B becomes non-normal in this case. A good example

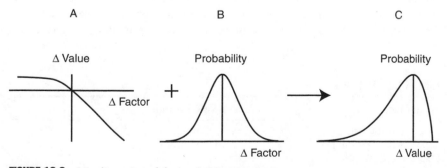

FIGURE 13.3   Nonlinearity of derivative instruments.

of a non-normal underlying risk factor is electricity prices, where there can be extreme upward spikes in prices.

Historical simulation is clearly the most generally applicable of the three approaches to calculating VaR, and there seems to be a move toward its use among the most sophisticated global trading houses. Its single main drawback is that we can only use information about market movements that actually occurred in the past. These may not include all the movements that are actually possible, or even likely. This shortfall has led some sophisticated companies to develop a set of stressed scenarios to use in addition to historical scenarios.

Consider an example of a European call option on a futures position in a non-G7 currency (e.g., the Mexican peso) to compare the three approaches to VaR. The VaR estimates are summarized in Table 13.2. The result implies that the amount of nonlinear risk in the position is US$7,689 (Monte Carlo minus parametric), and the magnitude of non-normal risk is US$3,414 (historical minus Monte Carlo). Note that relying on the computationally straightforward linear parametric VaR underestimates market risk by over US$11,000.

Estimating the Market Risk of Extreme Events

As we have already seen, VaR is good at describing the type of adverse events that occur perhaps three to four times a year (for an event that has a 1 in 100 chance of occurring under daily VaR). However, it is relatively poor at capturing the events that might happen once every five years but can wreak havoc on a portfolio.

There is therefore a need for a different kind of analysis that can tackle the potential impact of extreme events. This kind of analysis, which we will describe below, is called stress testing or scenario analysis, and is now required by regulators in most jurisdictions. Chase Manhattan, for example, uses both VaR and stress testing as its principal risk measurement tools: "VaR measures market risk in an everyday market environment, while stress testing measures market risk in an abnormal market environment . . . This dual approach is designed to ensure a risk profile that is diverse, disciplined and flexible enough to capture revenue-generating opportunities during times

TABLE 13.2　VaR Estimate Example

Technique	VaR Estimate
Linear parametric	US$24,935
Monte Carlo simulation	US$32,624
Historical simulation	US$36,038

of normal market moves, but that is also prepared for periods of market turmoil."[3]

The terms *stress testing* and *scenario analysis* are frequently used interchangeably in the context of risk management. However, we will make a subtle distinction in their definitions. We will consider stress testing to be a bottom-up analysis, based on the effect of large changes ("shocks") made to key risk factors. We will consider scenario analysis, on the other hand, to be more of a top-down approach, in which we begin by defining an alternative state of the world (such as a crisis in Southeast Asian financial markets) and then draw out the implications for portfolio value. There is sometimes no clear distinction between stress testing and scenario analysis, in practice, but equally, there is sometimes a very clear distinction. In any case, clear definitions will help to sharpen understanding of the issues involved.

Stress Testing

Stress testing quantifies the loss under extreme "outlier" events, without assigning any *likelihood* to such events or the consequent loss. Its goal is to provide insight on the portfolio behavior that would result from large moves in key market risk factors: What if the Fed announced a 50–basis point (bp) increase in interest rates? Or what if the price of oil doubled? How would a 30 percent devaluation of the Thai baht affect portfolio profit and loss (P&L)? All of these events, although unlikely under normal conditions, are certainly possible, and can quickly become more likely as conditions change.

The process of stress testing therefore involves identifying these potential movements, including which market variables to stress, how much to stress them by, and what time frame to run the stress analysis over. In general, stress testing involves the following steps:

1. Determine which variable(s) should be stressed and to what level(s).
2. Develop assumptions for price correlations within the portfolio.
3. Measure the impact of the stress test on the portfolio.
4. Develop alternative strategies that can be implemented.
5. Evaluate the cost-benefit of each alternative strategy.

In 1995, the Derivatives Policy Group (DPG) published "A Framework for Voluntary Oversight" to address derivative activities by U.S. brokerage firms. Among other things, the DPG proposed standards for the stress testing of key risk factors and their impact on P&L:

---

[3]Chase Manhattan Corporation Annual Report, 1998.

- Parallel yield curve shifts of 100 bp up or down
- Steepening and flattening of the yield curves (2s and 10s) by 25 bp
- Each of the four permutations of parallel yield curve shift of 100 bp concurrent with a tilting of yield curve (2s and 10s) by 25 bp
- Increase and decrease in all three-month yield volatilities by 20 percent of prevailing levels
- Increase and decrease in equity index values by 10 percent
- Increase and decrease in equity index volatilities by 20 percent of prevailing levels
- Increase and decrease in exchange value (relative to the U.S. dollar) of foreign currencies by 6 percent for major currencies and 20 percent for other currencies
- Increase and decrease in foreign exchange rate volatility by 20 percent of prevailing levels
- Increase and decrease in swap spreads by 20 bp

The above analysis represents the typical stress tests that are carried out by various financial institutions. However, it is critical that companies develop a stress testing methodology that is customized to their own portfolio and business environment, and not rely on standard tests.

Scenario Analysis

Scenario analysis typically goes beyond the immediate effects of predefined market moves and tries to draw out the broader impact that events may have on the revenue stream and business. It is meant to help management understand the impact of unlikely but catastrophic events, such as major changes in the external macroeconomic environment that will have an effect well beyond any immediate impact on the value of a trading portfolio. The crises triggered by the 1998 Russian debt restructuring, 1997 Thai baht devaluation, and 1994 Mexican peso devaluation are historical examples of extreme situations where the tried-and-tested assumptions made in the past simply ceased to apply.

The design of scenario analysis is a complex and difficult process that typically draws on the expertise of many people with diverse backgrounds in various departments. It is a very subjective way of assessing the long-term strategic vulnerabilities of a firm. The following are some guidelines for effective scenario analysis.

Defining Scenarios The first step is to define a plausible scenario. There are two ways of doing this. The first is to consider historical situations (such as the 1987 stock market crash, 1994 Mexican peso crisis, 1995 Kobe earthquake, and 1997 Asian crisis) and what would happen if something similar happened today. The second is to imagine entirely new circumstances that might be caused by catastrophic events (such as a natural disaster or war), long-term changes in the macroeconomic climate (such as a U.S. recession or failure of the European Monetary Union). One way to generate such scenarios is to ask business managers or traders what the worst thing they could imagine for their business might be.

Inferring Risk Factor Movements from the Scenario   Once a scenario (or set of scenarios) has been chosen, the second step is to identify all the relevant risk factors that will be affected by the scenarios, and the magnitude of the effect that the scenario will have. For example, a crisis in the Middle East might be modeled in terms of a set of shocks to foreign exchange rates, to the yield curve, and to oil prices.

Responding to the Results   The next step involves defining the early warning indicators that would precede the scenario and the management actions that should be taken in response. The scenario analysis reports should be circulated to line managers, risk managers, and senior management. Specific action plans and hedging strategies should be developed to address any high concentrations or exposures that are identified.

Reviewing the Scenarios Periodically   Once a scenario analysis has been developed, the methodology should be reviewed periodically (e.g., quarterly) to see if it needs to be modified due to changing portfolio or market conditions.

Verifying the Measurements: Back-Testing

Back-testing is the practice of comparing results of valuation or risk models to historical experience to evaluate the accuracy of the risk analysis. In other words, if the analysis had been carried out at some point in the past, would it have provided useful information in the light of what actually did happen next? This process is a critical part of the market risk control. There are three key objectives of the tests:

- To test whether the software and database have been properly installed and implemented
- To test whether the modeled probability distribution (VaR) is consistent with experience
- To test whether the modeled P&L matches actual P&L

If actual results are materially different from modeled results, then risk management must determine the underlying reasons, such as the methodology used by the model, the integrity of data and assumptions, or simply unexpected market behavior. Regulators also require back-testing. For example, banks operating under the Basle Committee's 1996 rules on trading risk may be allowed to use their internal VaR models to calculate their capital requirements. If they do, they are required to review the accuracy of the model-generated estimates by back-testing its results at least quarterly. More specifically, the actual trading results over the prior 250 trading days are compared with the bank's daily VaR, and the number of times that an actual loss exceeded daily VaR is noted. As shown in Table 13.3 the number of exceptions then determines the capital multiplier over 250 days.

This approach—to count the actual number of exceptions—is a simplified test, and financial institutions should consider developing their own criteria for back-testing. The audit function may be ideally suited to provide independent testing. The back-testing process must establish the appropriate time periods, variables (e.g., VaR, P&L), and acceptance levels. If back-testing reveals a failure of the risk analysis, there should be an immediate model and methodology review.

MARKET RISK MANAGEMENT

Although risk management cannot *eliminate* losses, it is nonetheless crucial, because it can ensure a company's awareness of and comfort with the level of risk that it is undertaking. This chapter is devoted only to market risk, but it is important to keep in mind that market risk management should be considered together with credit risk and operational risk in an enterprise-wide risk management framework.

TABLE 13.3   Back-Testing Results Determine Capital Requirement

Exceptions in 250 days	BIS Zones	Capital Multiplier
0		3.0
1		3.0
2	Green Zone	3.0
3		3.0
4		3.0
5		3.4
6		3.5
7	Yellow	3.65
8	Zone	3.75
9		3.85
10 or more	Red Zone	4.0

Source: Basel Committee.

Market risk management, like credit risk management (which we discussed in the previous chapter), requires participation on the part of five main groups of the company: the board and senior management, front office, back office, middle office/risk management group, and audit. While the different groups play different roles in the risk management process, each group's effort is essential for the proper control environment. The elements of market risk management include policies, limits, reporting, economic capital management, and portfolio strategies. We will discuss each briefly.

Policies

Like credit risk, an organization should have documented policies on market risk to ensure that all market risks are identified, measured, monitored, controlled, and regularly reported to senior management or the board of directors. These documents reflect the firm's perspective on the prudent management of market risks, and should be approved by the board of directors. Such policies should take into account the nature and complexity of the firm's activities, business objectives, competitiveness, as well as the regulatory environment and its staff and technological capabilities.

The human side is important to consider. Neither VaR nor any other more or less sophisticated risk measurement technique will safeguard against incompetent or rogue traders. Many of the most significant "trading" losses of recent times would be more accurately considered as fraud or other forms of operational risk. A risk measurement system cannot replace strong audit and process control functions. Market risk policies should therefore be monitored to ensure compliance on a regular basis. The policies also should be reviewed periodically to take into account internal and external changes (e.g., new financial products, new markets, or changes in regulatory environment).

There is no single set of market risk policies that is applicable to all companies. Rather, policies should be tailored to the investment, funding, and trading activities of the company. There are two important benefits of establishing any risk management policies. First, the process of developing a risk policy facilitates management discussion of, and consensus for, important issues. Second, the end product is a document that clearly lays out how risk management will be performed within the company. In general, market risk policies should cover the following areas:

- *Roles and responsibilities.* This section should define who is responsible for each aspect of market risk management within the company, as well as the organizational and reporting lines. For example, the board reviews and approves risk policies and limits, the treasury and trading units develop the strategies, and the risk management unit monitors and reports on overall portfolio risks. Review and approval processes should be developed for new businesses and products, as well as for new trading strategies and models. In addition to the responsibilities of individual functions and units, the structure and charters of various market risk committees should be established.

- *Delegation of authority and limits.* This section should specify who is permitted to execute market risk positions for the company. This includes specific authorities with respect to individuals, types of products and strategies, transaction limits, as well as approval processes. Most companies have centralized the authority to execute capital markets and derivative transactions within a few organizational units. Explicit risk limits should be defined for each type of market risk exposure faced by the company. Another key control procedure is to segregate the functions that initiate the trades, and the functions that execute and record the trades.

- *Risk measurement and reporting.* To ensure that there is a consistent measurement of portfolio risks against policy limits, the metrics, methodologies, and assumptions for various market risk measures should be defined. Reporting and escalation procedures also should be established in terms of periodic reporting of key measures to specific executives and committees, as well as immediate escalation of critical issues (e.g., limit violations, unauthorized trading activities, etc.). This section is critical to the board and senior management because they rely on other people and functions to inform them of critical risk exposures and trends.

- *Valuation and back-testing.* Accurate and timely financial statements and risk reports are prerequisites for effective market risk management. As such, this section should define how positions are "mark-to-market" when actual market prices are obtainable, and how they are "mark-to-model" when they are not. For example, some companies require at least three bids to establish a new valuation. A company also should define what prices are used (i.e., bid, offer, or mid) for various positions. For model-generated prices, back-testing procedures and criteria should be developed to ensure they truly reflect the underlying value of the instruments.

- *Hedging policy.* A hedging policy defines the type of risks that are to be hedged, the target risk levels, and the products and strategies that can be used. A definition and measurement of "hedge effectiveness" should be established so that management can be assured that the hedging programs are accomplishing their objectives. If hedging strategies are not performing as expected, then that should trigger a review and resolution process. Many companies encounter hedging losses because they didn't have a hedging policy in place that required them to understand the products, as well as the objectives and risks of the underlying hedging strategies.

■ *Liquidity policy.* The management of the company's liquidity is one of the most important aspects of a market risk policy. This section should define what measurements are used to monitor the liquidity position of the company. Measuring liquidity is not straightforward. Alternatives range from balance sheet measurements (e.g., liquid assets minus short-term liabilities), cash flow measurements (sources and uses of cash), and scenario-based measurements (in the event of a downgrade in the company's debt rating). In addition to liquidity measurement, this section should establish target liquidity positions, as well as the contingency plans that could be executed during financial distress.

■ *Exception management.* A market risk policy also should establish how exceptions are handled and reported. For example, what happens when a market risk limit is exceeded due to large market movements (vs. new trading activities)? One management response would be to reduce the risk position immediately, while another would be to reduce the risk position over a predetermined period of time. Some exceptions are intentional, such as those to accommodate a legitimate customer request. Regardless, this section should provide specific guidelines on the monitoring and reporting of exceptions, as well as the processes for approval and resolution.

BEST PRACTICES IN MARKET RISK MANAGEMENT

Of the three risk management disciplines—credit, market, and operational—market risk management is perhaps the most mature with respect to industry standards and best practices. As we did with credit risk in the previous chapter, we will discuss the range of market risk management applications in three categories: basic practice, standard practice, and best practice.

Basic Practice

At the most basic level, a company evaluates the earnings impact of various market risk factors, such as interest rate and foreign exchange changes. Gap analysis is performed between repricing assets versus liabilities, or projected revenues versus expenses denominated in a foreign currency. This type of gap analysis is then used to estimate how a change in a market variable will likely impact the company's earnings. To manage the company's market risk exposures within policy limits, asset/liability management and hedging strategies are developed and executed. This level of market risk analysis is generally what is required for regulatory and public reporting purposes. The use of market risk models is limited to spreadsheet models or basic vendor models.

The market risk management function is mainly a policy, analysis, and reporting function. It establishes the market risk policies and limits, analyzes the company's risk exposures against these limits, and provides risk measurement and hedging reports to senior management. The line and treasury units usually perform the execution of balance sheet and hedging strategies. As a monitoring and reporting function, the performance of the market risk function is dependent on its policy development, reporting effectiveness, and analytical skills with respect to earnings volatility estimation.

Standard Practice

Standard-practice companies have developed more robust modeling capabilities, including VaR, earnings and equity-value sensitivity analysis, and simulation capabilities. These companies also have implemented internal transfer pricing mechanisms so that all interest rate risks and foreign exchange (FX) risks are consolidated and centrally managed. This way, internal hedges are considered before external hedges are executed, thereby saving on hedging costs. Financial engineering capabilities are developed to evaluate the risk/return trade-offs of different market risk strategies. Beyond risk limits, market risk policies establish targets and ranges (e.g., target duration of equity of five years, with a range of three to seven years) so that the investment and market risk functions can take advantage of market opportunities.

The market risk function at standard-practice companies manages the balance sheet much more actively. It implements balance sheet strategies—including investment, funding, and hedging transactions—that would optimize financial return given market risk constraints. Earnings derived from the assumption of interest rate risk and FX risk exposures, as well as all hedging costs, are recorded in a central "market risk book." As such, the market risk function has a P&L, but its corporate mandate is not to maximize profits. The performance of the market risk function is therefore determined primarily by compliance with policy risk limits and secondarily by the earnings derived from the market risk book.

Best Practice

At best-practice companies, market risk management is both a corporate control function and a full-fledged profit center. As a corporate control function, market risk management ensures that changes in market prices and rates do not result in excessive losses. As a profit center, the market risk functions that reside in trading, investment, and treasury units seek to maximize their profits within the risk limits established by the corporate control function. These companies have developed very sophisticated real-time trading and risk management tools that allow them to take advantage of mispriced securities in the global capital markets. They also seek a competitive advantage by developing better research, more advanced analytical models, and more timely market intelligence based on access to deal flow information.

For these best-practice companies, sophisticated market risk management represents a core competency. Any slight advantage—such as the early discovery of an arbitrage opportunity or the development of a more accurate mortgage prepayment model—can mean millions of dollars in extra profits. Examples of these advanced risk management tools include:

- *Hot spot analysis* refers to the process of desegregating the total portfolio risk (measured by portfolio VaR or portfolio volatility) into contributory components. The breakdown of the risk can be done along one or more of the following dimensions: by risk factors, asset class, geography, trading desk, instrument class, and positions.
- *Best hedge analysis* refers to the calculation of the amount of purchase or sale of each asset that is required to reach the risk-minimizing position in the portfolio. This tool can support optimal hedging of the portfolio given changes in the balance sheet and hedging costs.
- *Best replicating portfolio* is a simplified representation of the overall trading portfolio of a company in the form of a small combination of assets that replicate the primary risks of the portfolio. By summarizing the risks in just a few assets, the report demonstrates the market views expressed in the portfolio.
- *Implied view* (also called implied bet) analysis takes the current portfolio as input, and reverse engineers a set of implied views on asset returns. This way, management can clearly see what market trends would most benefit (or hurt) the current portfolio.

Unlike credit risk and operational risk, where there is significant downside and limited upside, the risk/return profile of market risk is more symmetrical. As such, the role of the market risk function—as a corporate control function or profit center or both—is a fundamental question that is critical for the board and senior management. For companies that take on significant market risks, the culture of the market risk function is also critical. In contrast to the many stories of large market losses due to unauthorized trading or aggressive traders who "double down" on their losing bets, my favorite and factual story is about a trading desk manager. One day, a senior trader at a major investment bank produced a daily profit that was twice his daily trading limit. When the trader could not produce a good answer as to why he exceeded his limit, the manager fired the trader on the spot. A lesser manager would have simply looked the other way. I would take this trading desk manager with less sophisticated tools over a manager with less integrity and the most advanced tools.

CASE STUDY: MARKET RISK MANAGEMENT AT CHASE

Chase Manhattan (subsequent to the writing of this case, Chase acquired JP Morgan to form JP Morgan Chase), one of America's largest banks, has a venerable history. It can trace its antecedents all the way back to a water supply company founded in 1799, but the current institution is, by and large, the product of two mergers, each the largest in U.S. banking history at the time. The first was the 1991 merger of Manufacturers Hanover and Chemical Bank; the second, the 1996 merger of Chase Manhattan (founded in 1877) and Chemical Bank (founded in 1823). This Chase Manhattan is a holding company operating three main lines of business:

- The Global Bank, which offers commercial and investment banking services
- Global Services, which offers processing and settlement
- National Consumer Services, which serves retail customers through a wide variety of financial products and services

During the 1999 fiscal year, Chase boasted more than $400 billion in assets, operating revenue of $23 billion (up 17 percent from $20 billion in 1998), operating earnings of $5.4 billion (up from $4.0 billion in 1998), and return on average common shareholders' equity of 24 percent.

Chase attributes this performance to a number of factors. Prominent among these is a highly successful risk management system that emphasizes the creation of shareholder value and links it to employee compensation. It claims to view risk as a central aspect of its business and risk management as an area of competitive advantage, a claim supported by the fact that it devoted 19 of the 94 pages of its 1999 annual report to risk management. As the Chairman's letter states:

Let me begin by stating the obvious: We are in the "risk" business, and managing risk smartly and proactively with sophisticated risk management systems can create significant strategic advantages.

This may be stating the obvious, but it certainly helps to set the tone for the organization. Risk management at Chase focuses on the following principles and activities:

- Formal definition of risk management governance
- Risk oversight independent of business units
- Continual evaluation of risk appetite, communicated through risk limits
- Diversification
- Disciplined risk assessment and measurement, including VaR analysis and portfolio stress testing
- Allocation of economic capital to business units and measuring performance on the basis of shareholder value-added

Three committees carry out the above activities: one dedicated to credit risk, one to market risk, and one to capital. Their responsibilities are discussed in Figure 13.4, and each has decision-making authority within these areas. The Executive Committee, however, takes responsibility for major

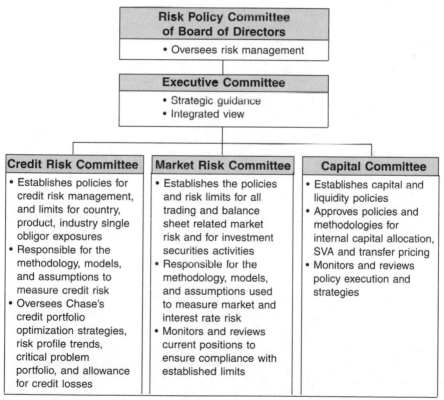

Source: Chase Manhattan Corporation.

FIGURE 13.4 Chase Manhattan's risk management structure.

policy decisions, determines the company's risk appetite, and formulates the company's risks; it in turn reports to the Risk Policy Committee of the Board of Directors.

Chase's Market Risk Management Group employed some 70 professionals around the world prior to its merger with JP Morgan. The group's mandate is to develop appropriate risk measures, set and monitor limits, and keep the company's risk profile within the boundaries of the risk appetite mandated by the Board. Part of the reason for that team's success is that it was born out of the global markets business, not from a traditional watchdog like audit, credit, or compliance. The market risk management approach also strives to balance business and risk management needs, and was developed by Don Layton and Leslie Daniels-Webster, both from the business side.

Development of the market risk group accelerated sharply with the 1996 Chase/Chemical merger. Daniels-Webster, now Executive Vice-President and head of Market Risk Management, said that the merger came at a fortuitous time: technology had just reached the point where it was possible to take the huge book of business created by the merger and evaluate it from the bottom up, position by position. Neither company's legacy systems were up to the job, however, and it was the bank's willingness to spend heavily on new technology that proved critical.

The market risk group continues to enjoy the backing of Layton, now Vice-Chairman of Global Markets, and Marc Shapiro, Vice-Chairman of Finance and Risk. "Having these two senior people behind us gives us a lot of credibility, changing our role from one that's there for the sake of the regulators to one that is there for adding value to the business units," says John Duddy, a Managing Director of Market Risk Management. The group manages the market risks generated on a number of different fronts:

- Market risk in its trading portfolios due to changes in market prices and rates (i.e., interest rate risk, foreign exchange risk, equity risk, and commodity risk)
- Asset/liability mismatch in its investment and commercial banking activities
- Basis risk in trading, investment, and asset/liability activities

The bank recognizes that market risk measurement and management should extend across all three of these activities. It learned that lesson fairly cheaply back in 1994, according to Daniels-Webster. During that year, the Fed raised interest rates repeatedly and somewhat unexpectedly, one result being considerable disruption in the market for mortgage-backed securities (MBSs).

"What we found was that we were fine on the trading business side, but one of our small S&Ls that was state chartered had invested its primary capital in MBSs," says Daniels-Webster. "The financial impact was very small, but what turned out to be much bigger was that we learned that you can't look at a firm like Chase just in terms of trading activities." That helped redefine market risk management in terms of the total economic return of an activity, not just its mark-to-market accounting valuation—a definition that ties into Chase's goal of pursuing and managing shareholder value.

Risk Measurement and Management

Chase does not believe there is a single statistic that captures all aspects of risk and therefore employs a number of complementary metrics. These include VaR, stress testing, and nonstatistical measurements such as net open positions, basis point values, option sensitivities, position concentrations, and position turnover. These nonstatistical measurements provide extra information about the size and direction of risk exposures that can be particularly useful when the statistical measurements break down (e.g., in anomalous market conditions).

Chase views stress testing and VaR as equally important in managing revenue volatility. Recognizing that VaR numbers change relatively little once their calculation is well established, and say relatively little about the potential extremes of loss, Chase is more actively interested in stress tests. "Stress testing is the backbone of our risk management, not VaR," says Duddy. "The beauty of VaR is that once you agree upon the statistical process, there's nothing to argue about. With stress testing, it's something that's really evolving. It's a very key part of our risk management tools to the extent that we allocate capital based on it."

Stress tests are built around both actual events (e.g., the 1994 bond market sell-off, the 1994 Mexican peso crisis, and the 1998 liquidity crisis) and hypothetical economic scenarios. As of December 31, 1999, Chase was using six historical and five hypothetical scenarios to perform stress tests about once per month. The tests assume that no actions are taken during the event that change the company's risk profile, an assumption that simulates the decreased liquidity often seen during market crises. Each stress scenario is extremely detailed, specifying more than 11,000 individual shocks to market rates and prices and involving data on more than 60 countries. Stress tests are performed on all material trading, investment, and asset/liability portfolios. Chase believes that one key to successful stress testing is the continuous review and updating of scenarios to ensure that they remain relevant and are as detailed as possible.

Chase's VaR methodology is based on historical simulation, reflecting a belief that historical changes in market indices are the best predictor of possible future changes. VaR calculations are performed daily on end-of-day positions, using the most recent one-year historical changes in market prices. The historical simulation is performed on individual positions as well as on aggregated positions by business, geography, currency, and type of risk. Because it realizes that historical VaR is dependent on the quality of the data available, Chase performs "back-tests" for its VaR estimates against actual financial results and uses confidence intervals to examine the reasonableness of its VaR calculations.

The bank manages the market risks that it has measured through the use of various types of limits, approved by the Board of Directors as falling in line with the risk appetite desired by the bank. The limit structure is specified at both the aggregate and business unit levels, going down as far as desk-level activities; it addresses authorized instruments, maximum tenors, statistical and nonstatistical limits, and loss advisories, and is based on relevant market analysis, market liquidity, prior track record, business strategy, and management experience and depth.

Risk limits are updated at least twice a year in order to reflect changes in trading strategies and market conditions. Chase uses stop-loss advisories to inform line management of losses that are being sustained. A review of the portfolio is automatically triggered if a Board-approved limit is breached. Chase believes that these procedures for tracking limits significantly reduce the likelihood that the daily VaR limit will be exceeded under normal market conditions.

Obstacles and Successes

One of the barriers to implementing the market risk program is the tension that arises naturally between risk managers and traders. This tension is usually a healthy one, ensuring that the bank balances business and risk objectives, but care must be taken to ensure that it does not turn into conflict or disregard for the rules. The problem tends to be at the desk level or below; senior business managers tend to understand and trust the risk managers more than those whose dominant concern is hitting their performance targets.

One way to deflate this problem is to make sure that risk management helps good, if complex, trades to get done, and does not just stop potentially troublesome ones. "We're like cops. If someone tries to rob you and we're there, you love us," says Duddy. "But if you're speeding and we catch you, you hate us." If the risk managers can persuade the traders that they want them to make money—but safely—they gain credibility.

A good example is unusually large transactions. "One-off trades undertaken for reasons of market opportunity or client demand usually involve hedging, structuring, and pricing issues such that we can either wring the risk out of it or price it smartly," says Daniels-Webster. Balancing the academic smarts of the risk managers with the market experience of the business managers can reap great rewards in this respect.

The most obvious evidence of Chase's success in implementing market risk management is the strength with which the company weathered the market turmoil of 1998. For that year, Chase reported earnings of $4.02 billion, up some 4.4 percent from the prior year. Chase had recorded larger rises in other recent years, but the circumstances of 1998 made it remarkable that it posted any increase at all; many of its peers and competitors suffered significant losses.

Chase's success in weathering the collapse of the Russian economy in 1998 can be attributed to two of the guiding principles of its risk management program: the value of learning from the past, and the importance of stress testing. Until 1997, Chase had aimed to lose no more than $500 million in the event of market turbulence. That year, however, it lost around $100 million in Latin American trading. That alerted it to the possibility that losses might exceed $500 million fairly quickly under extreme market conditions, and that its risk exposure was therefore greater than it had believed. The company reset its target loss limit to $250 million. The second lesson that Chase gleaned from this incident was that financial blowups could be global in nature, contrary to the previous assumption that economic problems in one part of the world would be unlikely to affect the performance of financial positions in another part of the world.

This realization was, in turn, a factor in Chase's decision to begin stress testing its entire trading and loan portfolio in late 1997, using scenarios that included global incidents. Stress testing using hypothetical scenarios enabled Chase to counterbalance the historical dependence implicit in its use of historical simulation in its VaR methodology. "We started doing these stress tests and got a number of about $500 million, which was a shock," remembers Daniels-Webster. "We didn't know what to do with such a large number except be skeptical of it."

The tests were soon borne out, however, as the economies of Southeast Asia started to nose-dive in fall 1997. Chase's losses looked very similar, if smaller, than those predicted by the stress tests. The postmortem proved a turning point in the risk management group's interaction with the business units. "This was the cultural watershed where people who didn't want to lose their jobs, who wanted discipline in their business, turned around and said they really needed these stress tests to understand the vulnerabilities in their businesses and hedge them."

Chase had no more inkling than any other bank that the 1997 Asian crises would rumble on into 1998, lead to a global drought of liquidity, and briefly threaten the stability of the global financial markets. However, it had prepared for a general scenario that coincided remarkably well with what actually happened—a sudden, pronounced flight-to-quality as investors swarmed out of stocks and into bonds and liquidity all but vanished in many markets. Because Chase had already used stress testing to examine the impact this event would have on its portfolio and had taken steps to mitigate its risks accordingly, its losses were less than they otherwise would have been.

Although the company did take a $200 million charge related to the liquidity crisis, the changes the company had made to hedge against such a crisis put the bank in a strong position to take advantage of the financial opportunities that followed the panic. Its diversity and business mix (e.g., the lack of a large equity business), coupled with sound risk management, put it in a strong position to carry on with its business. This allowed it to capitalize on market opportunities that others were too paralyzed to take advantage of, such as the plentiful opportunities for lucrative foreign exchange trading in October 1998. While competing banks stopped extending credit to clients during the market crisis, Chase continued to lend, a move that the company believes increased its prestige, won new clients, and increased business from existing customers.

A Look to the Future

The Russian crisis did leave its mark even on Chase, however. "A business that runs the same notional risk today as it did in 1997 will generate much more stress risk now, since we now include that scenario in our stress testing," says Duddy. A simple business goal—growing back to the volume of business done before Russia—is therefore not easy to achieve. One of the market risk group's new challenges is finding ways for that to happen.

Another new frontier for the market risk group is in addressing the increasingly liquid loan market. "It is extremely important to look at credit risk from the perspective of loss upon default. The market is evolving very rapidly into a much more transaction-based and market-based approach," says Daniels-Webster. For Chase, a market leader in loan syndication, it is extremely important to stay abreast of this evolution. The concept of risk as variation in economic value is key here; not only in recognizing the differences between loans, but also in the differences between loans and other credit instruments such as bonds. The next challenge will be to meaningfully integrate the market and credit risk management of the loan book.

CHAPTER 14

Operational Risk Management

In many respects, operational risk is nothing new. Businesses have had to deal with human fallibility, defective processes, and unreliable technologies since time immemorial. However, the advent of enterprise-wide risk management, the introduction of new regulatory capital requirements, and the increasing emphasis on sophisticated quantitative models for other types of risk (such as market and credit risks) has jump-started interest in the active management of operational risk.

Operational risk has been the subject of increasing management attention over the past few years. A 1997–1998 survey conducted in the United Kingdom and Australia by PricewaterhouseCoopers and the British Bankers' Association found that 73 percent of banks thought that operational risk was as or more significant than either market or credit risk. Twenty-five percent had experienced individual losses in excess of $1 million in the preceding three years.[1] With the recent corporate scandals (e.g., Enron, Worldcom), the interest level in operational risk management should continue to grow, in conjunction with related discussions regarding corporate governance and compliance.

Is this interest justified? Operational risk has traditionally been managed informally, as part of the everyday work of a manager who might never have even thought of that part of his or her job as an exercise in risk management. Beyond day-to-day management, operational risk issues are generally addressed through traditional audit and compliance functions. However, the episodic approach used by audit and compliance functions often results in operational risks being identified at a later stage. There are three major reasons why a more focused and proactive approach is desirable. First, investigations of the major financial disasters over the past decade (e.g.,

[1] Carmen Rossiter, "Operational Risk: The New Frontier in Risk Management," accessed at *pwcglobal.com*.

Barings, Kidder, Daiwa) have identified operational risk issues as the main culprit in the majority of these cases. As such, senior management recognizes that operational risks must be addressed as part of any enterprise risk management program. Second, operational risks are often interrelated with credit and market risks, and an operational risk failure during stressed market conditions can potentially be very costly. For example, in the Barings case it was the confluence of events—ineffective management oversight of its Singapore trading operations and a steep drop in the Nikkei after an earthquake—that bankrupted the 233-year-old bank with a billion-dollar loss. And third, if operational risk is not managed as a distinct discipline of risk, it tends to be managed differently in different areas of the company. This lack of consistent treatment can lead to the neglect of key risk issues and to a bias in various performance measures that may ultimately lead to management decisions based on inaccurate information.

Operational risk is an inherent part of any business. In many businesses a significant portion of revenue is consistently lost due to run-of-the-mill processing errors and human mistakes. In addition to these everyday losses, businesses also face operational risk incidents of greater magnitude. Some of these events are unintentional, the result of accidents and failures; others are intentional, such as fraudulent or other criminal activity. For instance, in 1994–1995, Citibank sustained losses totaling $1 billion as a result of three separate events—a wire transfer error, a failure of loan approval controls, and a computer hacking incident. The widely publicized collapse of Barings Bank in 1995 because of one rogue trader and the 1996 demise of Kidder, Peabody as a result of alleged fraud are other potent examples of what can happen when controls over operational risk are lacking. Bankers Trust and Enron, two remarkably similar corporate disasters that spanned two volatile industries, failed due to operational risks. Ironically, both companies were once considered leaders in financial risk management (i.e., market and credit risks).

Although these operational risk incidents have a low probability of occurrence, their consequences were tremendous. What's more, the effects may spread further than just a single institution. In our increasingly global, networked economy, the failure of a single company could have a devastating effect on an entire industry, and even on the economy as a whole. The threat of global systemic risks is why the Federal Reserve Bank of New York worked so hard in September of 1998 organizing a consortium of leading investment and commercial banks to orchestrate the $3.5 billion bailout of the Long Term Capital Management hedge fund.

Quite apart from the impact on the bottom line, operational risk can make it seem as though a company is ill equipped to prevent or deal with fraud, errors, or lack of controls. That in turn can result in enormous damage to a company's reputation. It is exceedingly difficult to quantify reputational loss, but such a loss is likely to impact customer relationships as well as current and future partnerships. Furthermore, damage to a company's reputation is also likely to negatively impact its dealings with the capital markets. Debt may become more expensive to obtain, and the stock market may lower its valuation of a company's stock if it is not able to effectively manage its operational risk.

If operational risk management is not treated as a discrete area of risk, it tends to be implemented differently in various areas of the same company. That means risk assessments and quantification may be performed differently by each business unit, resulting in inconsistent treatment of similar risks. For example, some business units might report operational losses on a gross basis, while others might report net losses, and still others might subtract losses from revenues and not report them separately at all. That in turn may bias measurements of those units' performances, ultimately resulting in suboptimal management decisions. The same is true in situations where responsibility for operational risk is not clear. For example, one business unit might be held responsible for risk events that should have been addressed by another unit. As a result, the return on equity of the first business unit might be artificially pushed below hurdle rate, leading senior managers to decide not to expand that business. In this instance, inaccurate performance measures would have obscured the business's true value, resulting in the loss of a growth opportunity.

Effective operational risk management has the potential to deliver three clear benefits:

1. Rigorous operational risk management should both minimize day-to-day losses and reduce the potential for occurrences of more costly incidents.
2. Effective operational risk management improves a company's ability to achieve its business objectives. As such, management can focus its efforts on revenue-generating activities, as oppose to managing one crisis after another.
3. Finally, accounting for operational risk strengthens the overall enterprise risk management system. A company with a good understanding of its operational risks will have a more complete picture of the risks and potential rewards run by its various businesses. That paves the way for sophisticated enterprise risk models that incorporate the correlations between the various components of risk: credit, market, and operational.

Although operational risk management may only be in its early stages, one can safely make three comments about its development. First, it has already been widely accepted that all companies face operational risks and should develop systematic programs to measure and manage it. Second, given the complexity of operational risks, a comprehensive approach should be used. As we will see later in this chapter, such an approach will ideally incorporate both process-oriented methods such as total quality management, and statistical methods such as economic capital and extreme value theory. Lastly, the focus of operational risk programs should be on management, not measurement, including the integration of operational risk with market and credit risks. A company cannot claim that it has an enterprise risk management program without fully addressing the issue of operational risk. In the rest of this chapter we will discuss the definition and scope for operational risk, tools that can help measure and manage it, and the range of industry practices.

OPERATIONAL RISK: DEFINITION AND SCOPE

A common business adage is that you cannot manage what you cannot measure. In the case of operational risk, there is another step: you cannot measure what you cannot define. Unlike market and credit risks, the definition of operational risk represents a challenge for most companies. In the early stages, operational risk was defined in negative terms, as the collection of risks that are *not* credit or market risks. Over time, industry sources converged to a more common definition:

> *Operational risk is the risk of direct or indirect loss resulting from inadequate or failed internal processes, people, and systems or from external events.*[2]

While this definition represents a common ground, there is still considerable debate on how it should be applied. For example, many organizations differ on whether business risk (e.g., margins, competition) and reputational risk (e.g., tarnished brand, loss of market confidence) should be included in the definition of operational risk. Both of these risks are explicitly excluded in Basel II, yet both risks are important risk management issues and key drivers of potential loss.

Individual companies should establish an overall definition of operational risk, as well as its subcomponents. In this chapter, we will apply the above definition to include process risk, people risk, system risk, and event risk. We will also add business risk, and will define each of these terms in turn.

---

[2]British Bankers' Association, International Swaps and Derivatives Association, PricewaterhouseCoopers, and RMA, "Operational Risk: The Next Frontier," 1999.

Process Risk

Operational risk occurs through ineffective or inefficient processes. Ineffective processes can be defined as those that fail to achieve their objectives, whereas inefficient processes are those that achieve their objectives but consume excessive costs. At times there is a natural conflict between the two. For example, reengineering and cost-saving efforts focused on improving efficiency may inadvertently end up reducing the effectiveness of control processes because certain checks and balances (which tend to be redundancies) are eliminated. A balance must therefore be achieved between effective and efficient processes.

A common process risk for any business relates to the processing of transactions. This includes the potential for errors in any stage of a business transaction, including sales, pricing, documentation, confirmation, and fulfillment. In any stage of transaction processing, a company is faced with risks that can cause a financial, customer, and reputational loss. For example, a pricing error can result in lower profitability, whereas a fulfillment problem can cause a customer to stop doing business with the company. Furthermore, companies need to make sure that operations remain within the limits of legal and regulatory provisions. With the adoption of a new regulation (e.g., Sarbanes-Oxley Act, USA Patriot Act), the consequences of violations increase for corporate executives from both a professional and financial perspective. Compliance is also an important issue with respect to a company's internal policies and procedures. For example, in managing a fund, an investment company must be in compliance with both its internal investment policies as well as any agreed client provisions.

Another significant element of operational risk can result from documentation processes. Improper or insufficient documentation may result in miscommunications between the parties to a contract, creating additional, unnecessary risks if there is a dispute. Consider the example of master agreements for financial products transactions. Nowadays master agreements play a major role in trading: they provide a uniform way of minimizing credit and legal risks across different financial products between two or more counterparties. They also provide the benefit of netting, which reduces the total credit exposures between frequent counterparties.

Many global derivatives dealers, however, struggle with master agreements. In 1998, the U.S. Federal Reserve reported that 20 to 30 percent of banks had incomplete International Swaps and Derivatives Association (ISDA) master confirmations documentation regarding settlement procedures and counterparty risk management.[3] Larger dealers can be managing hundreds of active master agreement negotiations at any given time, and some have

---

[3]*Capital Markets Report*, March 24, 1999.

thousands of master agreements in place, many of which also undergo amendments over time to accommodate new products, industry developments, or mergers. They often experience delay, disorganization, and miscommunication in the course of executing these essential contracts, putting significant revenues in jeopardy.

One potential answer, favored by some regulators, is to automate the process. Charles Fishkin, a risk consultant, has brought this idea one step forward, saying that all master agreement activities should be managed in *one* system—from initial discussion to execution to amendments for both new and existing customers.[4] With each of these phases executed and recorded in a controlled electronic environment, all of the participants (traders, marketers, credit officers, lawyers, documentation professionals, or operations staff) can check their status at any time significantly more easily than before. Comprehensive reports also can be easily produced and sorted by categories (business unit, product type, geography, etc.). Information flow has become more consistent and transparent. Issues like incomplete documentation realized at the time of need or transactions booked under the wrong master agreements can be minimized. As a result, decisions can be made faster and operating risk (and credit risk in this case) can be reduced.

People Risk

People risks typically result from staff constraints, incompetence, dishonesty, or a corporate culture that does not cultivate risk awareness. Staff constraints occur when companies cannot fill critical open positions because of labor shortages or because compensation and other incentives are not attractive to new candidates. Incompetence becomes an issue when employees lack the necessary level of skills and knowledge to do their jobs correctly. Lack of professional training and development would further compound human errors. Dishonesty within a company can lead to fraudulent activities such as employee thefts (interestingly, a University of Florida study showed that retail inventory managers attribute 31 percent of inventory losses to shoplifters and 46 percent to employee theft[5]). And corporate cultures that do not actively incorporate risk awareness, or encourage profits without regard to the methods used to make them, also can result in adverse employee behavior.

Every employee in an organization must be considered a risk, which is why background checks are essential in mitigating this risk. An alleged scan-

---

[4]Charles A. Fishkin, "Controlling the Documentation Vortex," *MiddleOffice* Spring 2000, pp. 13–17.
[5]2001 National Retail Security Survey Final Report, University of Florida.

dal at Disney World, whose business stands or falls on its reputation for safe, innocent fun, graphically demonstrated the danger of overlooking employee-related risks. In July 1998, a 17-year-old cook at Disney World was accused of raping a 16-year-old tourist in the bathroom of a hotel. Were this not appalling enough, it was compounded further by the revelation that the cook had been hired despite having an extensive juvenile arrest record, including charges of aggravated assault, burglary, theft, and grand auto theft. At the time of his employment at Disney, he was on probation for a break-in in which he had been accused of putting a gun to a victim's head.

How could such an individual have come to be hired in the first place? Because Disney did not carry out background checks on all of its employees at that time. Such checks were only seen as necessary for jobs such as security guards and child-care workers, as well as jobs that would require handling cash transactions. Nor was Disney's response a model of clarity: it initially said that it would not change its policy on background checks, but later recanted, saying it would perform such checks on new employees only. Furthermore, the company said it had no written guidelines, but would assess hiring on a case-by-case basis. By contrast, Universal Studios Escape, one of Disney's major competitors, already ran criminal background checks on all new employees.

System Risk

As technology has become increasingly necessary, in more and more areas of business, operational risk events due to systems failures have become an increasing concern. Companies today often use systems that are both integrated across the firm and specifically tailored to their particular business needs. If the development of a company's technological infrastructure does not keep pace with the development of its business, however, there is the potential for new risks. System risks include systems availability, data integrity, systems capacity, unauthorized access and use, and business recovery from various contingencies.

Another example of system risk is the risk of loss from faulty financial models. The institution may use inappropriate methodologies, assumptions, or parameters in evaluating a business or investment opportunity, and thus underestimate the risks it is taking on. Exposures to model risk can range from strategic decisions based on economic value-added–based models that understate the costs of risk, to investment decisions based on inadequate assumptions of how a complex derivative should be priced. The financial press is filled with stories of corporate losses due to inaccurate financial models.

In addition, the risks associated with programming errors and lack of planning can be significant. A small error in one algorithm can easily propagate through several models and across networks, causing great damage before the error is detected. The immense expense associated with remedies for the Y2K bug is a good example of how costly small oversights can quickly become. Finally, systems failures constitute a large risk for businesses, as a breakdown of the system may force revenue-generating activities to stop.

Security is rapidly emerging as another key technology risk, particularly given the rise of e-commerce. In early 2000, a web "hacker" successfully obtained a collection of more than 300,000 customer credit card files from the Internet music retailer CD Universe. This was possible because CD Universe had stored unencrypted credit card data on the web server itself, a fundamental design flaw that allowed the cracker to download the personal information using weaknesses in the card-processing software.

Although events such as this can and do occur with alarming frequency, it is a stark reminder that all organizations that conduct business in today's highly networked environment should specify data security as a primary goal in designing business processes and systems. Although sufficiently motivated and resourceful hackers will probably be able to compromise almost any computer software, there are several basic guidelines that can be taken to avoid becoming easy prey.

Event Risk

Event risk is the risk of loss due to single events that are unlikely, but may have serious consequences if they do occur—for example, internal or external fraud, system failures, market dislocations, and natural or man-made disasters. It is also a risk that can be controlled through effective planning and management. Incidents of event risk are often random and therefore difficult to predict. Although such events are unlikely, a business must "expect the unexpected." It is also important to note that major events often result in implications for all types of risk—market, credit, liquidity, and operational. Moreover, unlikely events occur in much greater frequency than one might expect. Leslie Rahl noted that there has been at least one major market move exceeding 10 standard deviations every year for the past 10 years.[6] These market moves included the Brazil Crisis (1999), the Russian Crisis (1998), and the Asian Crisis (1997).

The most unthinkable recent event is the September 11, 2001, terrorist attacks in which thousands of lives were lost and insurable losses exceeded $40 billion based on estimates from the Insurance Information Institute. Other notable loss events include Bank of Credit and Commerce ($17 billion), Long Term Capital Management ($4 billion), Texaco ($3 billion), and Sumitomo Corporation ($2.9 billion). In fact, between the 1980s and today, there have

---

[6]*Risk Budgeting* (London: Risk Books, 2000).

been 22 incidents (about one a year) of operational risk losses of $1 billion or more.[7] The corporate frauds associated with the likes of Enron, Worldcom, Adelphia, and others will only add to a growing list of "unthinkable" operational risk events.

Business Risk

Business risk is the risk of loss due to unexpected changes in the competitive environment, or to trends that damage the franchise or operating economics of a business. It includes "front-office" issues such as strategy, client management, product development, and pricing and sales, and is essentially the risk that revenues will not cover costs within a given period of time. Given the importance of a company's reputation and brand, reputational risk should be incorporated into business risk, or treated as a separate category. Business risk is heavily influenced by external factors, being primarily determined by environmental, competitive, and "evolutionary" factors and can be mitigated through effective management.

The most classic business risk example discussed in nearly every business school is the failure of railroad companies to redefine their businesses from railroad to "transportation," resulting in the collapse of most of these companies. On the other hand, one of the recent success stories in managing business risk is the transformation of IBM from a hardware company to a service and solution company. One of the key lessons learned from the Internet bubble is that every business must be based on a sound business strategy that will produce long-term growth and profitability. Achieving this objective is, of course, basic business management. The contribution of business risk management is to address key questions such as:

- What are the key vulnerabilities in our business strategy and plan?
- Do we have sufficient business and product diversification?
- Do we have the appropriate operating leverage (fixed vs. variable costs)?
- What if our business assumptions are wrong?
- When should we fix or exit a business? Do we have an exit strategy?

THE OPERATIONAL RISK MANAGEMENT PROCESS

Given the scope and importance of operational risk, management should establish a systematic process with respect to risk identification, measure-

---

[7]Douglas Hoffman, *Managing Operational Risk* (New York: Wiley, 2002).

ment, and management. The operational risk management process involves the following steps:

1. Risk policy and organization
2. Risk identification and assessment
3. Capital allocation and performance measurement
4. Risk mitigation and control
5. Risk transfer and finance

Let's discuss each of these steps in turn.

Risk Policy and Organization

As a first step, a company should establish an operational risk management policy that defines what it wants to accomplish, including how it is organized to achieve its stated objectives. An operational risk management policy should include the following:

- *Management principles for operational risk.* What is the company's philosophy and principles on operational risk? For example, as with credit risk and market risk, one common principle may be transparency. With respect to operational risk, it is critical that bad news travels up the organization so that emerging problems are addressed before they become full blown crises.
- *Definition and taxonomy for operational risk.* As discussed above, how is operational risk defined in the company, what is included and excluded, and what are the subcategories? A common language must be built around the discussion of operational risk within the company.
- *Objectives and goals.* Management should establish the overarching objectives (e.g., improved effectiveness and efficiency of core business processes) and specific goals that the company wants to achieve (e.g., a 20 percent reduction in operational losses, a 30 percent improvement in timeliness in resolving outstanding audit issues).
- *Operational risk processes and tools.* This part of the policy lays out the corporate-wide processes and tools that business units are expected to adopt, such as risk assessment, measurement, reporting, and management processes. This way, a consistent approach to operational risk is used based on common applications and standards for these processes and tools.
- *Organizational structure.* The policy should document the organizational structure for operational risk management. What are the key committees, memberships, and charters? What are the reporting

lines between the board, senior management, line management, and the risk management and oversight groups?

■ *Roles and responsibilities.* Given the complexities of operational risk, it is critical to clearly define the specific roles and responsibilities for every key aspect of operational risk management. At the highest level, the board is responsible to establish policies, and to ensure that the appropriate resources and controls are in place. At the lowest level, every employee is responsible for being knowledgeable about the operational risks that they are involved in, and for escalating problems and issues. Additionally, the roles and responsibilities of various risk management and oversight functions should be established (as further discussed below).

At most companies, there are a number of risk management, control, and oversight groups that have some connection to operational risk management. It is critical that specific roles and responsibilities be defined for these functions:

■ *Operational risk management* to ensure an overall framework is established to measure and manage operational risks

■ *Strategic planning* to ensure that business risks are addressed in business plans and reviews, as well as in new acquisition strategies and product plans

■ *Finance/accounting* to ensure timeliness, accuracy, and quality of books and records as well as business projections and profitability models

■ *Audit* to ensure business unit compliance with corporate policies and procedures

■ *Legal/compliance* to ensure that business activities are in compliance with applicable laws and regulations

■ *Information technology* (IT) to ensure that critical systems and databases are backed up, business recovery plans are established and tested, and information security safeguards are in place

■ *Corporate security* to ensure that corporate assets are maintained and protected

There are other important operational risk management functions, such as insurance, legal and compliance, quality management (or six sigma), human resources, and so forth. One of the key issues is whether a function is primarily established as a "consultant" or "checker" or both. For example, at many companies the operational risk management group acts mainly as a "consultant" for senior management and the business units, the audit group acts as a "checker," and the legal group acts as both. Other companies struggle

with trying to set up their audit groups as both consultant and checker, because
the former role can easily hinder the independence of the latter role.

Risk Identification and Assessment

Given the wide scope of operational risk, a company should employ a range
of qualitative and quantitative tools to assess, measure, and manage operational risks. Below is a summary of the main operational risk management
tools that companies use today:

- *Loss-incident database.* A company should capture operational risk
  losses and incidents for two main reasons. First, losses are easily
  measurable and can be used to show trends and ratios (e.g., loss/
  revenue ratio), whereas incidents can capture other events that should
  be noted. Second, every loss and incident within a company represents a learning opportunity, without which past mistakes are more
  likely to be repeated. As such, the loss-incident database should be
  used to support root-cause analysis and risk mitigation strategies, as
  well as to facilitate the sharing of lessons learned within the company. Additionally, there are a handful of industry initiatives to
  develop more robust loss-event databases, but it is too early to tell
  which one will become the industry standard. It is unlikely, however,
  that the management of operational risk will ever become a wholly
  data-driven process; given the nature of operational risk, it will always be more of a management issue rather than a measurement
  issue.
- *Control self-assessment.* A control self-assessment (also known as
  risk assessment) is mainly an internal analysis of key risks, controls,
  and management implications. It is important for each of the business units to assess their current situation with respect to these operational risk elements. By doing this, each business unit will develop a clearer picture of where to start and how to proceed in the
  operational risk management process. Each business unit would also
  have a greater sense of "ownership" through the self-assessment
  process. Tools that support self-assessments include questionnaires,
  issue-specific interviews, team meetings, and facilitated workshops.
  The output is an inventory of key risk exposures, key control initiatives, and sometimes even a Letterman-style "Top 10 Risks."
- *Risk mapping.* Building on the work from control self-assessments,
  the company's key risk exposures can be ranked with respect to their
  "probability" and "severity" so that management can have a com-
  parative view in the form of a two-dimensional risk map. For operations that are more complex (e.g., cash management, special pur-

pose vehicles), risk-based process maps can be produced to show how various risk exposures can arise. These maps will aid in the identification of the risks encountered in each business unit, indicating problem spots, such as single points of failures or where errors often occur. These maps will also enable each business unit to develop and prioritize their risk management initiatives to address the most important risks.

- *Risk indicators and performance triggers.* Risk indicators are quantitative measures that represent operational risk performance for a specific process. Examples include customer complaints for a sales or service unit, trading errors for a trading function, unreconciled items for an accounting function, or system downtime for an IT function. These risk indicators are usually developed by the individual business units and closely tied to their business objectives. Early warning indicators should also be developed to provide management with leading signals (e.g., employee absenteeism and turnover as an early warning indicator of future operational errors). To track the performance of processes against an expected range, trigger levels can be established in terms of goals (where you want to be) and minimum acceptable performance (MAP). If a key risk indicator falls below MAP, then that would trigger an escalation report to senior management, as well as initiate a corrective action plan. On the other hand, if a risk indicator is above goal consistently, then management should consider raising both the goal and MAP to facilitate continuous improvement.

Other sources of valuable information for risk identification and assessment include internal audit reports, external assessments (external auditors, regulators), employee exit interviews, customer surveys, and complaints.

Capital Allocation and Performance Measurement

Beyond risk identification and assessment, it is important to link risk to performance measurement through the capital allocation process. Unlike market risk and credit risk, where risk measurement methodologies have been developed and tested for many years, there are no widely accepted models for operational risk. In selecting a methodology (or combination of methodologies), each company should first establish its objectives and resources and choose accordingly. Different methodologies imply different interpretations of operational risk, and require various inputs to be useful. Given that there is likely to be no single solution, a combination of methodologies will allow the disadvantages of one model to be balanced by the strengths of another, allowing a more robust overall measurement to be developed. Some of the most common methodologies, including their strengths and weaknesses, are discussed below.

Top-Down Models   The top-down approach to operational risk modeling calculates the "implied operational risk" of a business by using data that are usually readily available, such as the overall financial performance of the company or that of the industry in which it operates. Top-down models use relatively simple calculations and analyses to arrive at a general picture of the operational risks encountered by a company.

These top-down models benefit from the sophisticated methodologies already developed for credit and market risk. Examples of top-down models on operational risk include the implied capital model, the income volatility model, the economic pricing model, and the analog model:

- *Implied capital model.* This methodology assumes that the domain of operational risk is "that which lies outside of credit and market risk." Thus, the capital allocated to operational risk must be the result of subtracting the capital attributable to credit and market risk from the total allocation of capital. Although this model provides an easily calculated "number" for operational risk, its simplicity presents several disadvantages. First, total risk capital must be estimated given the company's actual capital and the relationship between its actual debt rating and target debt rating. Second, it ignores the interrelationships between operational risk capital and market risk and credit risk capital. Finally, this model does not capture cause-and-effect scenarios for operational risk; it is accounted for only implicitly.

- *Income volatility model.* This model is similar to the capital allocation model, but it goes one step further, by looking at the primary determinant of capital allocation: income volatility. The volatility attributable to operational risk is calculated in the same way as in the capital allocation model—by subtracting the credit and market risk components from the total income volatility. One of the advantages of this model is that of data availability: historical credit and market risk data are usually easily obtained, and total income volatility can be observed. However, this model also has several shortcomings, the most dramatic of which is that it ignores the rapid evolution of firms and industries. Structural changes, such as new technologies or new regulations, are not captured in this model. The income volatility model also fails to capture softer measures such as opportunity costs or reputation damage. In addition, this model fails to capture the low-probability, high-consequence risks, as is true in all of the top-down approaches.

- *Economic pricing model.* The capital asset pricing model (CAPM) is probably the most widely used of economic models, and can be used to determine a distribution of the pricing of operational risk relative to the other determinants for capital. The CAPM assumes that all market information is captured in the share price; thus, the effect of publicized operational losses can be determined by evaluating the market capitalization of a company. The advantage of this approach is that it incorporates both discrete risks and softer issues such as reputational damage and effects of forgone opportunities. With this approach, a company's stock price volatility due to operational risk is derived by taking the company's total stock price volatility and subtracting from it the stock price volatility due to credit risk and market risk. However, the CAPM approach presents an incomplete and simplistic view of operational risk. It provides only an aggregate view of capital adequacy, not information about specific operational risks. Furthermore, the level of operational risk exposure is not affected by particular controls and business risk characteristics, so there is no motivation to improve operations, and while tail-end risks *are* incorporated in the model, they are not thoroughly accounted for. This is a significant omission. Such incidents can do more than just diminish the value of a business: they can lead to the end of the business completely. Finally, this model does not help in anticipating, and therefore avoiding, incidents of operational risk.

■ *Analog model.* The analog model is based on the assumption that one can look at external institutions with similar business structures and operations to derive operational risk measures for one's own organization. This model can be extended to look for the causes and effects of operational losses at such institutions. This method offers one way to proceed when a company does not have a robust database of operational risk losses. However, it takes some credulity to assume that the high-level numbers of another institution can accurately measure one's own operational risk, and many are suspicious of this approach. In the words of one analyst, "[The] intangibles within an institution—its risk-taking appetite, the character of its senior executives, the bonus structure of its traders—put so many wild cards into the operational risk equation that similarities in business volume, transaction volume, documented risk policies and other qualities that can be scored are swamped."

Bottom-up (Loss Distribution) Model   The bottom-up methodology applies loss and causal factors to derive predicted loss expectancies. This approach requires a company to clearly define the different categories of operational risk it faces, gather detailed data on each of these risk categories, and then quantify the risk of loss. A company often needs to augment its internal data with an external loss-event database. The final output of a bottom-up approach is a loss distribution model that can estimate operational risk capital for a given confidence level (e.g., target debt rating). According to a November 1999 study conducted by the British Bankers Association, the ISDA, and Robert Morris Associates, there is an increasing preference for risk-based bottom-up methodologies over the top-down approaches. The data needed for this methodology also can be used to derive a business's risk profile. For example, turnover or error rates can be tracked over time and combined with changes in business activities to construct a more robust picture of the business's operational risk profile. By tracking the risk factors over time, the company can assess its operational risk exposure on an ongoing basis and can upgrade controls in appropriate areas as needed. Furthermore, continuous tracking provides a company's management with better information about its operations and increases awareness of the causes of operational risk.

However, bottom-up models present several difficulties. Mapping loss data from the company with loss data from other companies is complex, given the differences in business mix, size, scope, and operating environment. Translating each cause of risk into a numerical value is often challenging, because losses are frequently reported as aggregates of multiple risk sources that are difficult to isolate. For example, an operational loss on a trading floor might result from personnel risk, lack of controls, expanding overseas business, lack of back- and front-office segregation, volatile markets, senior management confusion, and incompetence. In addition, robust internal historical data may not be available, and this model is inherently flawed with respect to low-probability, high-consequence events because it depends on a large database of values for its predictions. Bottom-up models are usually based on statistical analysis and scenario analysis.

Statistical Analysis   Traditional parametric statistical and econometric models strive to produce a good fit in regions where most of the data fall, potentially at the expense of good fit in the tails where few observations fall. A model of operational risk, however, must account well for the outer tail of the loss distribution in order to capture low-frequency, high-severity losses. Extreme value theory (EVT), which focuses on the extreme event data rather than on all the data, may be more appropriate in this context. EVT offers hope that reliable estimates of extreme probabilities may be achievable. A generalized extreme value estimation, for example, uses the largest loss observed in each of the preceding 12 months to obtain the distribution parameters best fitted by these 12 values. The results can be updated daily, weekly, or monthly on a rolling 12-month basis.[8]

Statistical analysis requires an ample supply of operational loss data that

---

[8]See Paul Embrechts et al., *Modelling Extreme Events for Insurance and Finance* (Heidelberg, Germany: Springer, 1997) for details.

is relevant to the business unit. The lack of appropriate internal data is therefore the greatest obstacle to the widespread application of this methodology; the use of external data as a proxy poses several problems, as mentioned earlier. However, the analytical power of this tool will hopefully become more widely applicable in the near future as increased awareness of operational risk leads to improvements in data collection.

Scenario Analyses Scenario analysis is perhaps more subjective than the other methodologies mentioned here, but it offers several benefits that are not addressed by the more quantitative models. A scenario analysis is used to capture diverse opinions, concerns, and experience/expertise of key managers and represents them in a business model. Scenario analysis is a useful tool in capturing the qualitative and quantitative dimensions of operational risk. Risk maps allow the representation of a wide variety of loss situations, and capture the details of the loss scenarios envisioned by the managers surveyed. Risk maps of each business unit identify where operational risk exposures exist, the severity of the associated risks, whether any controls are in place, and the type of control: damage, preventive, or detective. Cause and effect relationships can be captured with this methodology. The shortcoming of such a model, however, is in its subjectivity, which creates a potential for recording data inconsistently or for biasing conclusions if one is not careful.

Despite the shortcomings discussed for the above models, the application of several divergent models can in fact help management develop a more confident convergent view of how much operational risk capital is needed. Once an operational risk capital estimate is established, it can be integrated into the overall risk-return analytics of the company (as discussed in Chapter 9).

Risk Mitigation and Control

Assessing and measuring operational risk is important, but pointless unless directed toward the improved management of operational risk by improving and controlling key risk factors. Simply stated, the goal of operational risk management is to help management to achieve their business objectives. Once a measurement framework is in place, the next step is to implement a process that identifies actions that will reduce operational losses. These actions include adding human resources, increasing training and development, improving or automating processes, changing organizational structure and incentives, adding internal controls (e.g., more frequent or more extensive monitoring), and upgrading systems capabilities. The key to effective operational risk mitigation is to establish a cross-functional rapid response team that will address and resolve any emerging operational risk issues (at one business unit at Fidelity Investments these teams were called "turbo teams" and they would respond when operational risk indicators fell below MAP and report back to management on their assessments and actions within a few days or weeks). Finally, a mechanism for evaluating and prioritizing potential improvements must be created. Cost/benefit analysis and readiness assessments are useful tools that should be included in the evaluation process.

Some of the operational risk measurement approaches discussed above should naturally lead to improved operational risk management at the business unit level. A business unit can monitor and improve its operational risk levels by setting operational goals, exposure limits, and MAPs on the basis of data collection and analysis. For example, an operational goal might be a "stretch target," which a business hopes to attain over some period of time through the use of new procedures. A MAP level might be the maximum error rate permissible in a business process; if exceeded, the process would have to be reevaluated. The allocation of economic capital for operational risk, if it captures both performance and behavior effects, should motivate business units to improve their operational risk management in order to reduce their capital charges. For example, a business may set up procedures through which employees may respond immediately to operational problems and implement the controls necessary to monitor and improve operational risk performance. A key requirement for risk mitigation is to understand the root causes of operational risks, such as lack of training or inadequate systems, and then focus corrective actions on these root causes.

Besides risk mitigation through operational processes and controls, there are other financial solutions that management may consider. Companies can establish reserves to cover their expected operational losses. These reserves are considered a form of self-insurance. Expected losses should be embedded in the pricing of a product. Market and credit risks are already incorporated into some transaction prices as a matter of practice. Including an adjustment for operational risk makes for a more comprehensive picture and allows for more accurate risk-adjusted pricing. For example, if a business unit performs 10,000 transactions annually, with an expected loss of $80,000 a year, then a risk adjustment of $8 per transaction could cover such losses. Additionally, the cost of capital for operational risk (and other risks) should be incorporated into the pricing of a transaction.

Risk Transfer and Finance

For critical operational risk exposure, a company must decide if the best strategy is to implement internal controls or executive risk transfer strategies. The two are not mutually exclusive and are often complementary. For example, most companies implement workplace safety procedures and purchase workers' compensation insurance. In fact, the former can reduce the cost of the latter. Another example is product liability since a company can strengthen product development controls as well as purchase product liability insurance. Some risk transfer strategies are meant to be backstops to internal controls (e.g., directors and officers liability insurance provides protection against "wrongful acts"). In the past, insurance managers would purchase such insurance policies based on the structure, cost, and provider rating and service level. In the context of enterprise risk management (ERM) and operational risk management, a company should:

- Identify their operational risk exposures and quantify their probabilities, severities, and economic capital requirements.
- Integrate their operational risk with their credit risk and market risk in order to assess their enterprise-wide risk/return profile.
- Establish operational risk limits (e.g., MAPs, economic capital concentration).
- Implement internal controls and develop risk transfer and financing strategies.
- Evaluate alternative providers and structures based on cost-benefit economics (i.e., comparing the cost of risk retention vs. risk transfer).

There is an important difference between risk transfer and risk finance. Risk transfer is when a third-party insurance provider assumes the loss between the deductible and cap, whereas in risk finance the insurance company provides funding but is reimbursed over time. The economic capital and risk-adjusted return on capital (RAROC) framework discussed in Chapter 9 is also a useful tool for evaluating the impact of different risk transfer strategies. For example, in executing any risk transfer strategy, the economic benefits include lower expected losses and reduced loss volatility, whereas the economic costs include insurance premium, as well as higher counterparty credit exposures. In a sense, the company is both ceding risk and ceding return, resulting in a "ceded RAROC." By comparing the ceded RAROCs of various risk transfer strategies, a company can compare different structures, prices, and counterparties on an apples-to-apples basis and select the most optimal transactions. Moreover, a risk transfer strategy with a ceded RAROC below the firm's cost of equity would add to shareholder value, and vice versa.

BEST PRACTICES IN OPERATIONAL RISK MANAGEMENT

It is ironic that operational risk is the first and arguably the oldest risk that companies face, yet it is the latest and least developed component of ERM.

Today, operational risk is widely recognized as the most dangerous risk that companies must control, and it is an area where significant opportunities exist. There is also a wide range of industry practices in operational risk management, as discussed below in terms of basic practice, standard practice, and best practice.

Basic Practice

At the basic practice level, a company has recognized operational risk as a distinct risk management discipline. A definition of operational risk, and its subcategories, is in place (at this point, business risk is absent from this definition). An operational risk manager, who reports to the chief risk officer, is appointed to develop the overall operational risk management program. An operational risk committee is organized with representatives from the line and oversight units. This committee is held monthly to discuss the share information and coordinate operational risk measurement and management activities.

With respect to risk assessment and measurement, the company has initiated the tracking of operational risk losses as well as begun reporting on risk indicators. Moreover, control self-assessments by business and operational units are performed on an annual basis. An operational risk policy is developed and approved by the board of directors. The operational risk management group acts as a consultant to senior management and business units, and also provides support on crisis management situations. The audit and compliance groups act as the checker with respect to the operational risk policy.

Standard Practice

Building on the basic practices described above, the standard-practice companies have developed a full set of operational risk indicators by business unit. They also have established goals and MAPs for these indicators, and created monthly reporting and ongoing monitoring processes. These reporting and monitoring processes allow the board and management to understand their key risk exposures and trends. In addition, standard-practice companies have initiated the development of early warning indicators for their key operational risk exposures. To better understand their operational risk, risk-based process maps are developed to identify key areas of exposures within their business operations. Standard-practice companies have developed several years of operational risk losses and incidents, and also have linked their internal database with an industry loss-event database.

With respect to risk mitigation and control, standard-practice companies have developed response plans and contingency plans to mitigate operational risks when they arise. A team of operational risk professionals supports the operational risk manager. Their roles and responsibilities are well defined relative to the other oversight and control functions. To minimize gaps and redundancies, as well as maximize their effectiveness, they are integrated as part of the same organization. However, while audit is an active participant in operational risk management, they maintain their independence from the operational risk unit. To ensure organizational learning, the operational risk unit provides training programs, on-line risk policies, and postmortems of past losses and incidents.

Best Practice

Describing best practices in operational risk management is akin to describing true love after your first date. We are years away from really knowing what best practices in operational risk management will look like. Although few companies would claim that they have established best practices in this area, it is useful here to describe the more advanced applications that some of the leading companies have adopted.

Best-practice companies include business risk and reputational risk in their operational risk definition. Their assessment and measurement of operational risk is based on a convergent view supported by both qualitative and quantitative tools. They also have developed a full set of early warning indicators. These indicators not only provide leading signals on internal operational processes, but also the external business environment that the company operates in. Examples of external indicators include measurements that track public opinion, political uncertainties, regulatory changes, and competitive strategies. Best-practice companies allocate economic capital to underlying operational risks, along with credit risk and market risk. Economic capital allocation enables risk-adjusted performance measurement and provides corporate incentives for business units to improve their operational risk management. Additionally, they have initiated the development of scenario- or simulation-based operational risk modeling to quantify potential loss as well as evaluate various risk mitigation strategies.

The insurance function is fully integrated with the operational risk function. Based on the economic capital framework, risk transfer strategies are executed if the cost of risk transfer is lower than the cost of risk retention, unless the company deems a risk as undesirable to hold. To better manage operational risk, best-practice companies integrate operational risk controls into their business management. This includes risk analysis in business plans and reviews, as well as in new products and acquisitions strategies. As such, the operational risk management function has evolved from strictly a control function to one that supports better business decisions on pricing, growth, and profitability strategies.

CASE STUDY: HELLER FINANCIAL

Heller Financial was a commercial finance company with a market capitalization of over $2 billion. At year-end 1998, Heller had over $14 billion in assets and net income reached a record $193 million. Heller's vision is to become the leading provider of specialized financing solutions to mid-sized and small businesses in the United States and select international markets.

On May 1, 1998, Heller Financial returned to the New York Stock Exchange and the ranks of public companies. Previously wholly owned by Fuji Bank, over 42 percent of the company's stock was released in the initial public offering (IPO), generating over $1 billion. The IPO had raised the bar of competition: Heller must now not only compete for customers against its peers in the commercial finance industry, but also compete for investors' money against the broad spectrum of public companies. Chief Financial Officer Lauralee Martin explains: "The stakes are higher. The benchmarks of performance are not just your own standards; the benchmarks are set against all others. Tougher competition naturally raises you to a higher level of performance." The market's mandate is clear: maximize shareholder value by achieving exceptional risk-adjusted returns on investors' capital.

Heller's financial goals after this IPO are to:

- Consistently increase return on equity to at least 15 percent.
- Raise its credit ratings to mid-to-high single A.
- Grow earnings in excess of 15 percent each year by growing revenues, improving margins, increasing operating efficiency, and maintaining credit excellence.
- Maintain a strong financial position based on solid credit discipline, prudent risk management, and a balanced and well-diversified funding strategy.

Superior risk management is key to achieving each of these objectives. To increase return on equity to 15 percent requires efficient capital allocation. To raise credit ratings requires effective overall risk management. To increase operating efficiency while maintaining credit excellence requires solid understanding and management of operational risks.

Changes Within the Organization

Proactive focus on risk management is critical given the amount of change occurring within Heller's organization. During 1998, Heller consolidated its domestic operations around five core businesses: Corporate Finance, Commercial Services, Leasing Services, Real Estate Finance, and Small Business Finance. In addition, the Project BEST initiative restructured each of Heller's businesses to streamline processes, eliminating redundancies and reducing the workforce by 15 percent. Heller also acquired approximately $625 million in domestic and international assets associated with the technology leasing business of Dana Commercial Credit Corporation. Through 1999, Heller has continued to reorganize. Leasing Services has been broken out into Global Vendor Finance, Capital Finance, and Commercial Equipment Finance business groups. The Commercial Services business has been sold. The Healthcare Finance group has been acquired. Expansion into new international markets and integration of the acquired Dana Commercial Credit Corporation into the Global Vendor Finance group continues, widening the range of vendor leasing products Heller offers to customers and prospects.

In July 1999, the Chief Credit Officer, Mike Litwin, circulated a memorandum calling for Heller to change its risk management approach in response to this environment of increased risk. Litwin summarized:

> *The reality is that whenever an institution is in the process of change or is developing new activities, it runs into much higher operational risks than does a stable or existing business. A comprehensive and proactive focused enterprise risk management function must be in place to address the risks attributable to mergers, implementation of new systems and reengineering of processes, launch of new products or entry into new markets, and the acquisition of new staff and client relationships. In addition, I believe the entire organization is under stress as a result of Project BEST initiatives as well as the pressures of being a public company.*

This memorandum served as the catalyst for adopting a new approach to risk. In September of 1999, Heller Financial embarked on an ERM initiative to redefine its risk management vision, with a particular focus on management of operational risks.

ERM and Operational Risk Management

Senior management sponsors of the ERM initiative believed that managers and business leaders across the organization also saw the need for better risk/return management, but this belief had to be confirmed. Heller therefore conducted a thorough assessment of its current risk management practices as a first step in the ERM project. This process included:

- An internal survey of 38 members of the Leadership and Credit Councils regarding their overall attitudes toward risk/return issues.
- Over 35 one-on-one interviews with senior managers to discuss the company's current state and future direction.

■ Internal studies and benchmarking analysis of the company's current risk management practices (risk management organizational structure, policies, analytics, and reporting).

The assessment confirmed two key beliefs. First, that there is strong management support for the ERM initiative. Second, that the key gap in Heller's risk management included operational risk management and the integration of various risk management activities into an overall ERM framework.

Heller's Evolving Risk Profile

The changing nature of Heller's business calls for commensurate changes in Heller's approach to risk management. The structural change in the commercial finance industry from a "buy and hold" model to an "originate and distribute" model has shifted the risk profile of Heller's assets from traditional credit risks to integrated market–credit risk hybrids. The shift in Heller's businesses from transaction-oriented to more flow processes, such as small business lending and small-ticket leasing, also changes Heller's risk profile, creating the need for increased attention to operational risks.

Heller has always had a strong credit culture; the time has now come for Heller to integrate market risk and operational risk into its credit culture to develop a culture embodying the principles of enterprise risk management. Although the current credit risk management process has produced superior asset selection, liquidity, concentration, and diversification, it cannot be used to manage losses due to human error or system failure. Chief Credit Officer Mike Litwin argues:

> It is my view that at the present time we do not have significant credit risk issues in our company . . . the risks we should be focusing on and the ones that have potential to significantly impact our financial performance and market credibility are not limited to Credit and Market Risks, but must include . . . Operational Risks. Ultimately many of these non-credit risks could manifest themselves as write-offs, however, we're deluding ourselves if we think these are credit issues that can be appropriately addressed in the credit process. We will be attempting to address the "effect" rather than the "cause" of the problem.

In order to become best in class in the commercial finance industry and achieve superior risk-adjusted returns on capital relative to the market, Heller needs to incorporate a more sophisticated understanding of risk/return trade-offs in its decision making and become the best manager of risk in its class. An ERM approach is needed to go beyond management of credit risk to full enterprise-wide risk/return optimization. ERM looks at the risks Heller faces holistically, rather than separately addressing market, credit, and operational risk. The risks that Heller faces do not always lend themselves to easy categorization. Market and credit risks are interrelated; operational risks often manifest as credit losses. ERM integrates management of market, credit, and operational risk to ensure that risks that overlap categories are fully understood, taking into account all interdependencies among market, credit, and operational risks, and to ensure that all risks are addressed.

Objectives of ERM

The objective for the ERM initiative is both to protect the company against downside risks and to improve business performance through an integrated view of risk and return. The ERM approach will help management identify and grow businesses with the highest risk-adjusted returns and thus maximize shareholder value. The goals of Heller's ERM initiative are to:

1. Create an enterprise-wide awareness of the importance of risk management for the company.
2. Create comprehensive, enterprise-wide reporting of risk—credit, market, and operational.
3. Reduce long-term write-offs.
4. Enhance credibility with external stakeholders and potentially reduce Heller's cost of funds.
5. Increase Heller's market capitalization.

Organizational Changes

A chief credit and risk officer (CRO) position was created (Mike Litwin became the CRO), with overall responsibility for management of all types of risk. The CRO will be responsible for strategically managing the credit, market, and operational risks of the organization and will centralize the reporting and management of all the risks Heller faces in one position. An operational risk officer (ORO) position also will be created, with centralized responsibility for measurement, monitoring, and management of operational risks. This new position will enable Heller to implement a consistent operational risk management approach across all aspects of its business, provide an overall view of operational risk, and share operational risk management best practices and lessons learned across business groups.

Components of the ERM Project

The initial phase of the ERM initiative was completed in late 1999. There were substantial achievements during this first phase, which included the following:

- An ERM assessment was conducted to obtain a better understanding of Heller's risk management practices, as discussed in previous sections.
- A benchmarking study across all risk types for several dimensions of risk management practices was completed, and Heller's current state was benchmarked against other financial institutions' practices.
- An ERM framework document has been developed. It addresses the three main components for ERM—risk awareness, risk management, and risk measurement—and puts risk terminology in a "common language."
- Heller's vision for ERM has been defined and articulated with senior management.
- A detailed implementation plan for achieving Heller's long-term ERM vision has been developed. It also contains specific interim milestones to benchmark the company's progress.
- A framework for operational risk management and a standard operational risk report template have been developed that can be applied consistently across all business units and support services. The framework was piloted at two business units: Small Business Finance and Global Vendor Finance.
- An enterprise risk report template has been developed.
- An economic capital "proof-of-concept" exercise was conducted.

Implementation Phase

The implementation phase for Heller's ERM program addressed the following key challenges:

- *Organizational realignment:* The ERM and operational risk management objectives will be integrated into incentive compensation, roles and responsibilities, policies and procedures, and training programs.
- *Enterprise risk reporting:* The data environment needs to be improved to capture and aggregate information for the enterprise risk report and operational risk report.
- *Implementation of operational risk management methodology:* The new ORO will be working with the rest of the business groups and support services over the next year to apply the new operational risk

management framework and begin producing the new standard operational risk report.

ERM is like a journey, which will require the organization's commitment to fully reach all of its goals. There are, however, some quick wins that require relatively fewer resources, which Heller should pursue in the near term. With the right up-front preparation and a clear road map for heading forward, Heller will realize substantial successes and benefits, as other organizations have experienced on their similar journeys.

Post Note

On July 30, 2001, GE Capital announced that it was acquiring Heller Financial for $5.3 billion in a cash transaction, or $53.75 per share (a 48 percent premium over the preannouncement price of $35.90). In its press announcement, GE Capital noted Heller's risk management capabilities as one of the company's key assets.

CHAPTER 15

Business Applications

The application of risk management concepts was born thousands of years ago; we noted in Chapter 8 how references to insurance could be found in texts from thousands of years ago. However, it is only since the 1970s that risk management has really evolved as a business discipline, thanks to a combination of factors—economic liberalization, the rise of shareholder power, and regulatory pressures—and the increase in computational power among them.

There are three major business applications of risk management. The first is loss reduction. The second is uncertainty management. The third is performance optimization. The combination of all three is enterprise risk management (ERM). This order is both the order in which the applications were developed historically and the order in which a particular institution will typically develop its risk management capabilities. Let's consider these in turn.

STAGE I: MINIMIZING THE DOWNSIDE

The first stage in risk management, which emerged during the 1970s and 1980s, focuses on protection against downside risks. Risk management practices mainly involved establishing credit controls, investment and liquidity policies, audit procedures, and insurance coverage. The objective of these defensive risk management practices was to minimize losses:

- Credit risk management was designed to reduce the probability of default and to maximize recovery in the event of default, through credit approval at the front end and debt recovery at the back.
- Market risk practices were designed to minimize potential portfolio losses and liquidity crises. Portfolio risk was minimized through con-

servative investment policies, favoring government bonds and high-quality corporate debt.

- Operational risk controls focused on reducing the probability and severity of operational events, with audit and compliance procedures to ensure that books, records, and operations were accurate and orderly. Insurance was the primary means of risk transfer.

As it turned out, however, a simple focus on the downside was not enough, illustrated most clearly by the failure of portfolio insurance. Invented in 1980 by Professors Hayne Leland and Mark Rubinstein of the University of Berkeley, portfolio insurance was intended to reduce equity investors' downside risk by automatically trading out of stock into cash when the market fell.

Some $60 billion in assets were insured in this way by October 1987—but when the stock market crashed that month, portfolio insurance managers struggled to carry out sell orders fast enough to keep pace with the requirements of the model. Insured investors did only marginally better than their uninsured brethren, most getting out at or below their designated floors. Nonetheless, portfolio insurance fell out of favor, even being blamed in some quarters for worsening the crash.

More broadly, loss reduction has always been, and continues to be, a central objective for risk management, but the early focus on downside risk management was too restrictive. It gave rise to the destructive "offense versus defense" mentality described in Chapter 6, where business units taking risks are frequently at loggerheads with risk functions minimizing risks.

One way of overcoming this tension was to demonstrate how risk management can be a positive force in supporting profitability and business growth. That led to the development of the second application of risk management: managing uncertainty.

STAGE II: MANAGING UNCERTAINTY

In the second stage of risk management—originating from a string of insights during the 1990s—risk management focuses on managing volatility around business and financial results.

Over the past few decades, many new sources of volatility have appeared and the effects of traditional sources of volatility have become magnified. The 1970s saw a move from fixed to floating exchange rates, along with wildly fluctuating oil prices; the 1980s, double-digit inflation, interest rate volatility, and lending crises. The trends continued into the 1990s with derivatives losses, volatile equity markets, and the rapid "contagion" of turbulence from market to market. Finally, the turn of the millennium brought about the Internet bubble and accounting scandals.

At the same time, investors have shown less and less tolerance for earnings volatility. As companies faced up to the challenges of increased volatility, risk management practices evolved to help management anticipate potential loss and reduce the range of potential outcomes—in other words, to manage that increased volatility:

- Credit scoring and migration models helped credit risk managers to develop more precise estimates of the probability of default when extending or reviewing credit transactions. This allowed more accurate annual provisioning for losses and thus reduced earnings volatility.
- Significant advances were made in the management of financial market risks. Sophisticated simulation models projected potential changes in earnings and market value, while industry standard measures were established, notably value-at-risk and economic capital techniques.
- Recognition of the importance of operational risk management increased sharply during this period. Disasters such as Kidder, Peabody, the Exxon Valdez oil spill, and the 1990 Perrier benzene contamination scare brought crisis prevention and management to the fore. Moreover, numerous industry studies—the Treadway Report (1991) in the United States, the Dey Report (1994) in Canada, and the Turnbull Report (1999) in the United Kingdom—pointed out the need for effective corporate governance.

As risk managers focused their efforts to manage volatility, risk transfer products (including financial derivatives and sophisticated insurance) experienced a vast increase in popularity. However, derivatives can pose significant risks if used improperly; in particular, complex derivatives such as compound swaps and structured notes are often highly levered transactions that are extremely sensitive to market movements. Well-publicized debacles, such as those involving Barings, Metallgesellschaft, and Bankers Trust, convinced many people that derivatives, rather than reducing volatility, were themselves a threat to financial stability. This is probably unfair; most of the debacles were, at root, due to management or process failures.

Nonetheless, it became apparent in the late 1990s that conventional derivatives and insurance were by no means a complete solution to companies' risk transfer needs. The result was the emergence of new instruments covering previously uninsurable risks. Alternative risk transfer (ART) emerged as a way either to transfer previously uninsurable risks or to transfer traditional risks in a more efficient manner.

Another key development was the integration of various risk management "silos." ART products enabled corporations to transfer packages of risk, rather than individual risks. This mirrored the development of integrated internal models and controls for risk—for example, the integration of market and credit risk when assessing counterparty default risk.

This more holistic view of risk allowed the risk/return profile of a business to be considered more explicitly than before. This, in turn, spurred the use of risk management as a lever for performance optimization.

STAGE III: PERFORMANCE OPTIMIZATION

In the third stage, risk management is characterized by a more integrated approach to all kinds of risk. The partial integration of similar risks in stage II gives way to complete integration of silo risk management functions within the organization and the corresponding rationalization of risk control and transfer strategies.

However, a more important aspect of integration is that of risk and return. As we discussed in Chapter 4, ERM requires the integration of risk management into the business processes of a company. Rather than the defensive or control-oriented approaches used in stages I and II, designed to manage downside risk and volatility, ERM optimizes business performance by supporting and influencing pricing, resource allocation, and other business decisions. It is during this stage that risk management becomes an offensive weapon for management:

- Companies have developed pricing models for credit products that fully incorporate the underlying default risk of the counterparty and are priced accordingly. Combined with active portfolio management based on concentration limits, diversification, and hedging strategies, this has led to disaggregation of the overall credit business into underwriting, origination, portfolio management, and distribution.
- In market risk management, companies are making asset allocation decisions across all assets, liabilities, and off-balance sheet items held by the overall business, not just in their investment portfolios. In so doing, companies balance the expected profitability offered by the marketplace against financial and regulatory constraints.
- Operational risk management remains the biggest challenge in terms of knowledge and applications, but the level of awareness about operational risk has been raised significantly. The massive volumes of process maps produced by reengineering projects are enhancing understanding of business and operational processes. Activity-based costing techniques add to this understanding by quantifying the cost drivers for various business and operational activities.

Finally, the application of risk management to performance optimization has been accelerated by the acceptance of risk/return management by companies and regulators. The best example is the use of risk-adjusted re-turn on capital as a performance metric used by business management not only to measure business profitability but also to support key strategic de-cisions such as acquisitions and business unit strategies.

THE FURTHER EVOLUTION OF RISK MANAGEMENT

As we have already seen, good risk management is an integral part of busi-ness decision making, not something external to it. The other side of the coin is that changes in the business environment affect the practice of effec-tive risk management. Some obvious mega-trends affecting all industries are:

- *Globalization:* the growing interdependence of economies and mar-kets, and the internationalization of business operations through net-works
- *Technology:* the new operational risks associated with technology-driven businesses
- *Changing market structures:* the impacts of deregulation, privatiza-tion, and new competition
- *Restructuring:* the effects of mergers and acquisitions, strategic al-liances, outsourcing, and reengineering

Each of these trends gives rise to new risk management challenges. How-ever, that doesn't mean that these trends should each be considered in iso-lation—that would be a return to silo-based thinking. Most are intimately related to each other.

For example, improvements in communications technology have helped to bring down the barriers between markets that were historically distinct and contributed significantly to the globalization process. That in turn has forced deregulation, allowed new competitors to enter hitherto protected markets, and forced incumbents to rethink their organizational structures and practices.

Ultimately, it is safe to say that we live in times of great change, and the risks that these changes bring up require an integrated, enterprise-wide re-sponse. In this chapter, we discussed risk management applications from the perspective of any business. In the remainder of this section, we will exam-ine risk management applications from the perspective of different indus-tries and the specific challenges they face.

CHAPTER 16

Financial Institutions

The financial services industry is in the throes of a transformation that is redefining both the competitive landscape in which financial institutions operate and the dynamics of risk and return that shape their businesses. If existing financial institutions are to survive and thrive in this new business environment, they must adapt their business models and improve their risk management capabilities.

Financial institutions[1] are different from other companies in the sense that their ability to measure and manage risk is central to their competitiveness. Risk management has always been a core competence for financial institutions and risk performance a key determinant of profitability. As Gary Wendt, the former Chief Executive Officer of GE Capital, put it, "If you don't get the risk management part of the equation right, then nothing else will matter." Put another way, the key to a financial institution's survival and prosperity is its ability to identify, quantify, price, and manage risk better than its competitors. As a manager of other people's money, the ability to gain and maintain the trust and confidence of clients is an absolute requirement for business success.

Moreover, the business of financial risk management involves some level of expected losses, which represent an important business cost component. Financial losses traditionally make up a significant portion of the cost of doing business in the financial services industry. Unsurprisingly, then, financial institutions are keen to point out how good they are at risk management. Their annual reports normally include a detailed discussion of the company's risk management capabilities, including risk committees and strategies for different types of risk.

---

[1]Although our focus in this chapter is on banks, thrifts, securities firms, and insurance companies, the issues discussed are directly relevant to the financial and insurance operations of any corporation.

241

As we'll see in this chapter, however, it is not enough for a financial institution to rest on its laurels. The financial services industry has been changing rapidly since the 1980s, with the result that the challenge of risk management is dynamic, not static. First we'll examine the key industry trends that are changing the fundamental structure of the financial services industry. We will then discuss the risk management requirements of financial institutions, with the aid of a case study of the Canadian Imperial Bank of Commerce (CIBC). We will also briefly discuss the key challenges for the future management of financial institutions.

INDUSTRY TRENDS

To appreciate fully the risks facing financial institutions and the best approaches for managing them, we must first understand the fundamental business trends in the industry. There are four major, interrelated trends: consolidation, deregulation, competition, and convergence. Let's run through these in turn.

Consolidation

The financial services industry has been undergoing a massive wave of consolidation, beginning in the mid-1980s with American banks and subsequently spreading both to other types of financial institution and around the world.

For example, the number of banks insured by the Federal Deposit Insurance Corporation (FDIC) in the United States shrank from 14,500 in 1984 to 7,887 in 2002, a 46 percent decline. The number of banks acquired annually increased from 330 in 1985 to a peak of about 600 in the mid-1990s. While this number has dropped steadily to below 400 in 2001, the concentration of banking assets has continued. For example, in both the commercial loan and credit card loan markets, the top five players control about 60 percent of industry assets.[2] Insurance companies and insurance brokers likewise consolidated; 19 of the top 31 brokers in 1988 no longer existed 10 years later.[3]

Why this insatiable urge to merge? The first reason is simply that firms were now allowed to do so, thanks to deregulation (to which we will return below): changes in banking legislation first opened the floodgate to bank mergers and acquisitions. The 1927 McFadden Act and the 1956 Bank Holding Company Act had previously restricted interstate banking, but the

---

[2]Standard & Poor's Industry Surveys—Banking. November 7, 2002.
[3]Morgan Stanley Dean Witter Insurance Industry Quarterly Review on Insurance Brokers, March 10, 1999.

1994 Riegle-Neal Interstate Banking and Branching Efficiency Act overturned this, ushering in nationwide banking by October 1995. As mergers began, they apparently became self-perpetuating, as "one-stop shopping" and "economies of scale" became the buzzwords of the day. If a small bank did not merge, the belief was that it would be left behind by larger institutions that offered more products at more attractive prices.

For insurance companies, consolidation was facilitated by demutualization of their ownership structures. Insurers in the United States, the United Kingdom, Canada, Australia, South Africa, and other countries converted from their traditional mutual ownership structures to become shareholder owned, often publicly offering their stocks at the same time. Demutualization funded a number of mergers, either by allowing the insurer to purchase other companies using stock instead of cash, or by raising cash for the transaction through a public offering.

Consolidation comes with its own risks. In particular, the challenge of combining the different cultures and business systems of two financial institutions is considerable and should not be underestimated. This may be part of the reason why the expected economic benefits of a merger rarely turn out to be as great as anticipated. In fact, one recent study found that bank acquirers in North America lagged the market by an average of 13 percent in the three years following their mergers. "Instead of quickly and deftly improving customer service, newly merged companies spend their early years dealing with internal controversies. All the glittering benefits touted in merger press conferences tend to get lost amid the rigors of integrating two disparate entities."[4]

DEREGULATION

Deregulation in the financial services industry has been a double-edged sword. On the one hand, it removes "unnatural" regulatory barriers and allows greater competition. Customers should reap the usual benefits in terms of lower price, better service, and greater choice. On the other, it exposes previously protected institutions to market forces and discipline. This can result in the demise of weaker players that may be ill-prepared to face the new risks of market volatility and intense competition.

An economist might argue that the weeding out of weaker players is a good thing over the long run, despite the short-term costs of bankruptcy such as job loss and service interruptions. However, these short-term costs can be minimized if deregulation is planned and phrased in a thoughtful way. Sudden, poorly executed deregulation can give rise to undesirable

---

[4]*Banking Strategies*, March 1, 1999.

behavior and to the potential for significant losses, often ultimately borne by the taxpayers.

A dramatic example is the case of the savings and loan (S&L) crisis of the late 1980s. During this dark episode in the history of U.S. finance, relaxed vigilance on the part of thrift regulators—combined with increased rate volatility and lax internal risk management—led to vast losses to the taxpayer.

A wave of deregulation between the late 1970s and early 1990s reduced the minimum capitalization required of S&Ls, abolished the ceiling on the interest rates they could offer customers, and allowed them to enter new businesses like stock brokerage. S&Ls quickly found they had to raise interest rates paid out if they were to retain customers in the competitive market for deposits. The problem was that there was no practical way to raise the rates they earned on lending—their main use of funding—to match the increased deposit rates.

The result was widespread losses through the industry in the 1980s, exacerbated by risky real estate deals made in doomed attempts to bridge the gap. The subsequent losses put renewed pressure on the institutions to not only raise deposit rates but also extend their sources of funds from retail to wholesale customers, leading to a vicious circle in which rates continued to spiral and investments got riskier and riskier.

The rest is history. Huge swathes of the S&L industry went bankrupt, but the Federal Savings and Loan Insurance Corporation, which insured all S&Ls to the tune of up to $100,000 per depositor, was completely overwhelmed. Faced with bailouts costing $38.6 billion in 1988 alone, it was forced to keep more than 500 insolvent institutions open because it simply lacked the capital to shut them down and pay off their investors. The aftermath took years to clean up, at huge expense to the taxpayer.

Some good did come of the S&L disaster, albeit at far too high a price. Banks and thrifts created asset/liability risk management units that implemented gap, duration, and simulation techniques to analyze the interest rate sensitivity of their balance sheets. They also designed mortgage products that were less sensitive to interest rate changes. For example, adjustable-rate mortgages were invented that matched more closely with short-term liabilities such as deposits and certificates of deposit.

Banking regulators around the world revised capital requirements to more closely align capital with risk. In 1988, the Bank for International Settlements (BIS) issued risk-based capital requirements that for the first time tied capital explicitly to the assets held by banking institutions. Another lesson the banking regulators learned was how to deal more effectively with the trade-off between closing an ailing institution and maintaining any remaining franchise value: isolating bad assets in a "bad bank" so they can be disposed of while the "good bank" can be operated independently or sold to a buyer. This was the approach adopted by Japanese regulators a decade later as they worked through the massive credit problems in their country's banking system.

Competition

The wave of deregulation in the 1980s didn't just give established financial institutions enough rope to hang themselves. It also gave new competitors enough rope to trip them up. For example, mutual fund companies were allowed to grant customers check-writing privileges. That allowed them to compete with checking accounts at banks while offering the more attractive returns of mutual funds.

Together with the advent of new information technology and the increased liquidity of the capital markets, deregulation meant that established financial services companies often found themselves vying with new (and sometimes more efficient) competitors for business—indeed, this was frequently the actual motivation for the deregulation. Change came swiftly, as exemplified by developments in the retail banking sector. By 1998, only 23 percent of households' liquid financial assets were held in conventional bank deposits, down from 49 percent in 1980. Credit cards, mortgages, and commercial loans were also increasingly handled by nonbank institutions. The percentage of credit card loans held by nonbank institutions increased from 25 percent to 40 percent in just the three years from 1992 to 1995.[5]

Clearly, banks (in particular) needed both to cut costs and to find new ways to attract and retain customers in order to avoid further erosion of profitability and market share. The rise of e-commerce arguably allowed them to do just that, but it was nonbanks who were quicker to grasp the possibilities. That meant new entrants, particularly those who had the advantage of specialization, were able to further encroach on businesses that had traditionally been the sole domain of banks.

One particularly dramatic development was the emergence of a new breed of on-line banks and brokerages. Because they lacked the costs of physical branches and customer service personnel, these institutions could offer extremely attractive rates, as well as other attractive features such as free electronic bill payment and low (often zero) minimum balances and fees. On-line brokerages have likewise attracted investor dollars with the lures of efficiency and cost savings: on-line trading is cheaper and faster than trading by telephone, or in person, and most on-line brokerages also offer conveniences like free real-time stock quotes, on-line portfolio tracking, and easy access to research.

---

[5]Case 9-897-177, Harvard Business School Publishing.

But on-line brokerages face perils of their own. One key issue for the first wave of on-line brokerages, given the investment climate of the time, was the development and management of a strategy for rapid growth. On-line brokerages needed to win potentially nervous users away from the incumbents, so they often adopted aggressive marketing strategies; having attracted those users, they needed to deal with the rapid development of technologies and processes to handle them.

The impact of on-line services took longer to reach the insurance industry, and at time of writing it remains unclear how the competition between old and new providers will play out. The more complex nature and economics of insurance products make the case for on-line insurers rather weaker than the case for on-line banks or brokerages.

But competition did nonetheless change the face of the insurance industry during the 1990s. Rates for insurance decreased steadily from 1986 onward, largely as a result of increased competition within the industry. The soft market was a boon for insurance buyers, able to take advantage of rock-bottom rates, but put an enormous strain on the providers. For example, in 1998 premiums rose by a mere 1.4 percent, whereas incurred losses rose 6.5 percent and expenses rose 4.3 percent.[6] Many insurers' continued viability owed much more to the outperformance of their asset portfolios, driven by the runaway bull market, than to their prowess in underwriting. However, the recent bear market and post–September 11 claims have reversed these trends, as investment performance has declined but insurance premiums have increased dramatically.

Meanwhile, the nascent alternative risk transfer (ART) market threatened to further erode the insurance industry's market share and profitability (see Chapter 8 for more information on ART). Although it would be in insurers' best interests to see higher pricing in the market, the fact that ART providers are trumpeting savings as high as 20 to 30 percent over insurance premiums during a soft market does not make a hardening of the market seem feasible. ART products also provide greater flexibility and efficiency for the customer; such products can be customized to meet particular customer needs and offer greater efficiency, since they often cover the buyer for a number of years and may reduce the number of insurers needed. Just as the mortgage-backed security market has reduced the cost of mortgage financing, the ART market should reduce the cost of risk transfer by increasing the availability of cheaper sources of risk capital.

Convergence

A third consequence of deregulation has been the elimination of barriers between different kinds of financial services. In the United States, for ex-

---

[6]PaineWebber Industry Report, April 13, 1999.

ample, the Depression-era Glass-Steagall Act put a regulatory fence between securities business and commercial banking, as well as insurance. This meant that for nearly 50 years the United States was home to entirely separate securities, banking, and insurance industries, in contrast to the European situation in which "universal" banks and *bancassurers* carried out various combinations of these activities.

During the 1980s, however, it became clear that regulation in the U.S. financial services industry began to relax, so commercial banks began underwriting securities on a limited basis. Banks were also allowed to sell mutual funds, bringing them even closer to achieving the status of financial clearinghouses. In turn, money market funds offered by mutual fund companies were allowed to offer check-writing privileges, which had previously been limited to banks. Insurance and banking also began to overlap as banks viewed insurance policies—along with annuities, retirement funds, and mutual funds—as opportunities to increase fee income.

By 1998, it was clear that the old legislative framework had crumbled, as evidenced by the debut of Citigroup, the financial titan formed by the merger of the Travelers Group (predominantly an insurer), Citibank (a commercial bank), and Salomon Smith Barney (a securities house that had just been acquired by Citibank). Citigroup's very raison d'être was to realize value by cross-selling banking, insurance, and securities services, and it apparently worked because Citigroup's stock has outperformed those of other less diverse banks. However, there is growing public and regulatory concern that convergence comes with a steep price when it comes to issues such as conflicts of interest (e.g., research vs. investment banking), tying of financial products and services, and consumer rights.

The convergence of investment banks, commercial banks, and insurance companies has direct implications for enterprise risk management (ERM), both for better and for worse. The benefit: such companies are more diversified, which smoothes their overall risk profile; they can also provide products that offer the advantage of such diversification to their customers. The cost: the risk management of these multiline financial businesses needs to be integrated if such benefits are to be realized, a challenging task.

RISK MANAGEMENT REQUIREMENTS

The confluence of the trends discussed above has increased the stakes for risk management for all players in the financial services industry. Deregulation has removed the barriers that once protected the industry from competition and from its own mistakes; consolidation and convergence has resulted in companies that are far larger and more complex than those that have gone before.

Risk management has become absolutely vital in ensuring both that established players do not lose the race and that new ones do not fall at the first hurdle. In the modern financial services environment, the consequences of a failure of risk management frequently go well beyond financial loss or strategic setback; in fact, they may ultimately include the demise of the afflicted institution as an independent company. The bar has been raised: what might have been considered "best practice" a few years ago is likely to be seen as a "basic requirement" today. To ensure ongoing success and survival, financial institutions must continuously upgrade their risk management capabilities.

Let's first consider a number of types of institutions. We'll see that each type of institution faces market, credit, and operational risks, but these take on different forms according to a particular institution's businesses. In the next section, we'll look at the challenges that cut across industry sectors and are common to a number of different types of institutions.

Risks by Industry Sector

Depository institutions, such as commercial banks or thrifts, take credit risk by extending loans to borrowers. This credit risk must be managed through prudent credit analysis and effective portfolio management in order to prevent excessive credit losses.

One major source of profitability (and earnings volatility) is the interest rate spread between asset yields and liability costs. Interest rate risk arises from the difference in interest rate sensitivities between financial assets and liabilities. A depository institution's management must therefore establish appropriate asset/liability management and hedging programs in order to ensure a positive and stable interest rate spread throughout various interest rate cycles. As we saw in the discussion of the U.S. S&L crisis, the "one-two" that knocked out the industry was a round of higher interest rates followed by commercial real estate losses.

Another key source of profitability is fee income from services such as cash management and securities processing. The operational risks associated with these services must be managed to ensure accurate cash and securities movements and record keeping.

Securities houses such as brokerage firms or investment banks take on a variety of market risks. As securities underwriters, they earn a fee for assuming the risk that a new equity or debt offering will fail to win market acceptance at a favorable price. Failure can result in financial losses as well as tarnished reputation.

As market makers in certain securities, securities houses face the risk of market losses in a declining market. These losses may come from their existing inventories as well as from new commitments that arise in the course of their market-making activities. These risks are still more significant if a firm is engaged in proprietary trades on its own account as well as trades made on behalf of customers; it may face huge financial losses if its market predictions are wrong.

In addition to market risk, securities firms often take on default risk through margin lending to individuals and securities lending to institutions. They also face the counterparty risks associated with securities settlement processes and financial obligations such as swaps and other derivatives.

Insurance companies take actuarial risk when they issue insurance policies that may result in larger-than-expected claims in the future. Their primary sources of income are the premiums paid on insurance policies and the investment income generated by investing the cash flows from these premiums. These income sources must between them cover expenses and claims. The ratio between the sum of premiums and investment income and the sum of expenses and claims is known as the *coverage ratio* and is a widely followed indicator of industry profitability.

Insurance companies therefore face two key risks. The first is a function of the relationship between premiums earned and claims paid; the second is the performance of the investment portfolio. In addition, insurance companies often cede a portion of their premiums to other insurance or reinsurance companies, which in turn take on a portion of their insurance liabilities. Because the ceding insurer may have to call on the reinsurer if an insurable event occurs, it is exposed to the risk that the reinsurer may fail to pay up—a credit risk.

Insurance companies are also exposed to operational risks, often related to the complex distribution system for their products. Historically, insurers often have relied heavily on sales agents to distribute their products. The loyalty and discipline of these agents is variable, since they may be employees or free agents, with compensation linked heavily to commissions from one or more insurers. It is relatively easy for the incentive structure to become inappropriate, with potentially damaging results, as it seems in both the United States and United Kingdom with respect to various lawsuits on unfair sales practices on insurance policies and pension plans.

Cross-Sector Risks

In addition to the sector-specific risks discussed above, financial institutions as a group are faced with a number of financial risks that are more fundamental to their business activities than they are to the business of nonfinancial institutions. While these risks present particular challenges for financial institutions, they represent important issues for any corporation with significant financial operations and capital markets activities.

Monitoring Default and Counterparty Risks   As discussed above, financial institutions are exposed to a variety of default and counterparty risks. These credit risks arise mainly from lending activities, trading and settlement processes, insurance/reinsurance contracts, and derivatives transactions. The two key questions to ask are:

- What is my aggregate exposure to a single counterparty or a group of similar counterparties?
- What is the likelihood of default and loss?

These questions can only be answered if there is an adequate credit exposure measurement process and an accurate credit rating system.

Managing Market Risks On and Off the Balance Sheet One unique characteristic of financial institutions is that most of their assets and liabilities are sensitive to movements in one or more markets: interest rate, equity, foreign exchange, commodity, or real estate. Market risk exposures can originate both from on–balance sheet activities and from off–balance sheet transactions such as derivative contracts and forward commitments.

In order to manage market risks effectively, a market risk manager must first measure the sensitivity of the portfolio to external price changes. This analysis can be based on a combination of value-at-risk (VaR), scenario testing, and simulation modeling. Given an accurate and timely assessment of market risks, management can then decide on risk management strategies, including product design and risk transfer.

Incorporating Leverage and Liquidity Financial institutions are generally much more highly leveraged than their nonfinancial counterparts. This is because of the need to maximize asset risks given thin profit margins and pressure from shareholders for healthy returns on equity. However, just as leverage increases the absolute returns on assets, it also magnifies the effect that a decline in asset values would have on the equity value of the institution.

Another important consideration is the liquidity profile of an institution's assets and liabilities. For example, an institution can easily liquidate a large position in U.S. Treasury securities but may find it difficult to reduce its holdings in debt issued in an emerging market. Financial institutions must therefore be fully aware of how their market and credit risk exposures will be affected by leverage and liquidity. It is not enough to measure the 10-day VaR of an asset alone. The risk manager must establish a reasonable liquidation period over which price volatility should be measured, as well as quantifying the potential impact on equity value given the leverage of the firm.

Attributing Economic Capital and Managing Portfolio Risks Economic capital represents the amount of capital required to support a consistent level of potential loss across all risk exposures. In essence, economic capital represents a common unit for the measurement and management of risk and is an important concept for financial institutions to understand and apply. It is valuable because its attribution to risk exposures enables management to measure risk-adjusted profitability across different business activities.

For example, economic capital allows the profits from trading to be compared directly with profits from dissimilar businesses such as retail lending or securities processing. Economic capital can be used to support portfolio management decisions such as the allocation of financial and human resources to business activities that generate higher risk-adjusted returns. By explicitly incorporating the benefits of diversification, economic capital provides the appropriate signals and incentives for diversification and limit setting. Finally, risk transfer decisions such as hedging and insurance can be rationalized by comparing the cost of risk retention (i.e., the cost of economic capital for the underlying risk) with the cost of risk transfer.

Systemic Risk

It is in the nature of financial institutions that they are highly dependent on each other, with linkages created through business activities such as securities trading, foreign exchange, derivatives trading, reinsurance, syndicated underwriting, and stock lending. These interdependencies are the root cause of concerns about *systemic risk*, the possibility that problems at a single large financial institution could create a chain reaction that can result in large losses or defaults at other institutions.

Systemic risk is the primary concern of many regulators, whose attention has shifted from the stability of individual organizations to the stability of the industry or system. An individual firm's management also has cause to be concerned: even if the system survives, the company may nonetheless suffer collateral damage along the way. The challenge for management is therefore to understand fully these interdependencies with other financial institutions and to put in place appropriate contingency plans and exit strategies in the event of a significant disruption in the financial system. It is also important for management to establish indicators of early warnings, such as higher market volatility or lower liquidity.

The events that lead to systemic risk tend to be rare and idiosyncratic, but there are two points to bear in mind. First, financial institutions face risks that are highly intertwined. For example, a sudden market drop can cause the default of a major financial player, leading to a loss of confidence and a liquidity crisis, which may in turn exacerbate the market drop. Second, the interdependencies in the financial system are not only associated with discrete transactional risks, but also with the linkages between institutions, markets, and countries. These global economic linkages only reinforce the criticality of the risk management requirements discussed above.

Consider Russia's technical default on its debt in the early fall of 1998, which led to repercussions that echoed throughout financial institutions and markets around the world. Panic spread quickly throughout emerging markets, even those that had little to do with Russia. That hit financial institutions hard: the top 50 firms worldwide reported losses totaling over $17 billion during the third quarter of 1998.

But that was not the end. The general "flight to quality" in the credit markets and the accompanying dwindling of liquidity led to the unprecedented spectacle of investors discriminating between near-identical U.S. Treasury bonds on the grounds of credit risk. A slew of associated losses ultimately brought Long-Term Capital Management (LTCM), the supposedly state-of-the-art hedge fund run by legendary trader John Meriwether, to its knees.

A number of copycat hedge funds and proprietary trading desks also suffered enormous losses; LTCM itself had to be bailed out by its creditor banks, to the tune of some $3.5 billion. Its absence from the markets thereafter left some interbank markets, such as the market for option volatility, changed for good, and even two years later the debacle's aftermath was being blamed for the troubles of some smaller financial institutions.

A LOOK TO THE FUTURE

Financial institutions have only recently started to manage risk in an integrated fashion. Traditionally, different types of institutions specialized in different types of risk: investment banks in market risk, commercial banks in credit risk, and insurers/reinsurers in insurance risk. However, the industry is slowly moving toward specialization by function rather than by risk type.

In this framework, origination and customer service will be handled by risk brokers, separate conduits will handle underwriting and balance sheet management of all types, integrated investment banks will execute capital markets risk transfer, and portfolio managers will handle both financial and insurance securities. Similarly, risks that have traditionally been handled in "silos" are finally starting to be treated holistically, by risk management teams reporting directly to the board.

Given the squeeze on profitability that all types of financial institutions have been experiencing, coupled with the increasingly complex risks of a global financial world, financial institutions must continue to be careful in their quantification and analysis of risks. However, they must balance this with an increased emphasis on the soft side of risk management by realigning incentives to promote ethical, risk-aware behavior, setting a tone of openness from the top and developing communication channels to discuss risk issues.

As we saw at the beginning of this chapter, prudent risk management is not just about mitigating potential downsides, but also about maximizing profit in a safe way. In today's market, just one mistake could easily push a company out of the black and into the red.

CASE STUDY: CIBC

CIBC is a full-service financial institution with $270 billion in total assets and 44,000 employees operating around the world. In 2000, the bank generated $12 billion in revenue, earned $2 billion in net income, and achieved a 20.5 percent return on equity.

The financial services industry in Canada, like that in the United States, had been characterized by consolidation. Many Canadian banks had allied themselves with other financial institutions, often through outright mergers and acquisitions, either to benefit from economies of scale or in order to deliver the wide range of financial products that their customers were demanding. CIBC's critical move in this respect was its 1988 acquisition of majority interest in Wood Gundy, a well-regarded Canadian investment bank. The Wood Gundy purchase signaled CIBC's intention to broaden its financing capabilities for corporate customers; the decision to offer integrated, global financial services and offer an increasingly complex product portfolio (including exotic and structured derivatives) motivated a substantial rethink of risk management at CIBC.

At the same time, Canadian regulators were beginning to think more in terms of enterprise-wide risk management. This culminated in the December 1995 Dey Report, published by the Toronto Stock Exchange (TSE), which recommended that the board of every firm listed on the TSE take direct responsibility for risk management efforts within their firm, and report on those efforts in the annual report. For banks, in particular, the Canadian banking supervisors were among those who drafted the 1996 Amendment to the Basel Capital Accord, which similarly emphasized firm-wide risk reporting and control.

So CIBC had a twofold reason to invest in ERM. It was becoming more active in the capital markets at about the same time that regulators were looking closely at risk management. Its reaction was to start building an ERM team; its first significant high-profile hire was Dr. Robert Mark, who joined the bank in July 1994 to be the Corporate Treasurer as well as look after firm-wide market risk, operational risk, and sections of credit risk, which included responsibility for managing credit risk in the trading book. Mark was promoted to Senior Executive Vice-President and became CIBC's Chief Risk Officer in February 2000 and joined the CIBC Management Committee.

Mark articulated his vision from the very beginning, outlining his plans to build a strong ERM team, made up of experienced risk managers with strong business experience to work in partnership with, but independent of, the business lines. "I will need your commitment to support my vision," he explained to key senior management and the Board during his selection. He pointed out that "The objective is to be among the top five financial institutions in the world in terms of managing risk," Bob emphasized. "I'm going to come in and make changes. There's no doubt about that." The Board was not put off, and when Mark joined CIBC, he did so with a mandate to deliver world-class risk management.

Changes and controversy duly followed. Of the team he inherited, none were to be found doing the same job a year later. New executives with significant risk management and trading experience were put in place to execute the new vision. There was also a compensation differential between risk staffers and their colleagues on the business side that had to be evened out in order to attract and retain the requisite talent. Mark pointed out that his business partners were highly encouraging and supportive of upgrading the quality of risk personnel. In short, the change was nothing less than dramatic.

Today, risk data are collected from across the globe and risk reports are disseminated through a series of risk management and business committees (see Figure 16.1). Risk management committees at CIBC establish risk management policies, limits, and procedures; approve risk management strategies; and monitor portfolio performance and trends. The Risk Management Division works closely with both the lines of business and risk management committees to manage CIBC's exposure to market, credit, and operational risks. "One of the keys to success is getting business and risk people to work effectively together," says Mark. "If you have people from both camps sitting together, agreeing, disagreeing, asking questions, then we all have a clearer understanding of the problems we face, and a clearer path to the answers. Our business partners provided us with invaluable insight as we evolved our risk management function into a world-class team."

The kind of Socratic dialogue that Mark favors isn't always frictionless. There have been occasions when risk management has been obliged to restrict the amount of business that certain units can carry out. "The ability to generate revenues is clearly a function of the volume of business you do," notes Mark. By limiting business, risk management could be cutting into profitability and individual bonuses—one reason why CIBC links compensation to risk-adjusted return performance.

CIBC has defined several objectives for its risk management program, which include reducing surprises, reducing losses consistent with risk/return objectives, reducing regulatory capital requirements, and developing sophisticated risk metrics designed to capture various components of risk. While risk information and analysis can be highly technical, they must be trans-

```
┌─────────────────────────────────────┐
│          Board of Directors          │
└─────────────────────────────────────┘
```

Risk Management and Conduct Review Committee

- Ensures policy guidelines and systems exist and are adhered to (credit, market, operational).
- Reviews and approves policies on loan concentrations.
- Reviews and approves procedures for dealing with related party transactions and conflict of interest issues.
- Reviews year 2000 program.

Chair: External Director

Audit Committee

- Oversees CIBC's financial reporting process on behalf of the Board of Directors.
- Reviews CIBC's financial statements.
- Liaises with internal and external auditors.
- Reviews internal control procedures and loan loss provisions.

Chair: External Director

```
┌─────────────────────────────────────┐
│        Management Committees         │
└─────────────────────────────────────┘
```

Credit and Investment Policy Committee

- Approves credit risk management and investment policies.
- Reviews the diversity and composition of the asset portfolio.
- Approves specific business plans.

Chair: Chairman & CEO, CIBC

Asset Liability Management Committee (ALCO)

- Establishes and enforces market risk policies.
- Assesses strategies for management of assets, liabilities and capital.

Chair: Chairman & CEO, CIBC

Credit Committee

- Approves credit requests over $100 million.
- Presents new credit requests and certain renewals over $100 million to Board of Directors.

Chair: Sr. Executive Vice-President, Risk Management

Investment Committee

- Approves merchant banking investments within delegated limits.

Co-Chairs: Sr. Executive Vice-President, Risk Management & CEO, CIBC Wood Gundy Securities

```
┌─────────────────────────────────────┐
│       Risk Management Division        │
└─────────────────────────────────────┘
```

- Designs, recommends and implements infrastructure to manage risk.
- Develops, recommends and monitors adherence to risk management policy.
- Establishes methods and tools to give effect to risk management.
- Manages CIBC's global exposure to credit, market and operational risk through offices located across Canada, United States, London, Tokyo, Singapore and the West Indies.

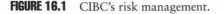

FIGURE 16.1   CIBC's risk management.

lated into a reporting structure that is meaningful and relevant for senior management. Mark suggests that the risk management program has succeeded in meeting those objectives.

Mark highlights the bank's reaction to the regulatory and market pressures of 1998. At the start of 1998, the BIS implemented a new set of revisions to its Capital Accord, the regulatory standard used by regulators and central banks the world over. The revisions gave sophisticated banks the freedom, subject to regulatory approval, to use their own risk models as a basis for calculating the minimum required regulatory capital against market risk in the trading book (rather than a crude standardized multiplier system). It was a change that banks had long campaigned for.

When the new rules became effective at the start of 1998, CIBC was the only bank in Canada and one of the few banks in the world to receive the approval for all aspects of the Accord in 1998. Mark explains, "As a bank, you'd almost have to be crazy not to take advantage of BIS 98. From the get-go, we saw that if we invested in risk management, we'd get capital relief, and the savings were huge."

Later the same year, CIBC's risk management team proved its worth in a very different way. The volatility that swept the globe during the third quarter was a test of fire for banks around the world, largely because almost every market was affected by the turmoil, but also because the early warning signs made little sense at the time. "During June and July we were seeing a lot of highly rare events that we didn't like," says Mark. "Liquidity was drying up in certain areas, correlations were diverging from their normal patterns, and credit spreads were widening." This uncertainty prompted Mark and his team of experienced risk managers, working in partnership with the business lines, to cut limits across the business by 33 percent in an attempt to mitigate exposure to volatility.

Soon after the limits were cut, the market broke. The losses sustained by CIBC were not easily digestible, but it could have been far worse. For Mark, it was a painful experience tinged with a certain amount of professional satisfaction. More than 98 percent of the losses suffered by CIBC during the 1998 market crisis were from positions that risk management had previously identified and placed on a "hit-parade" of the bank's top 10 risks. "We knew that if we were going to get hit that it would be attributable to one of those exposures," says Mark.

CIBC has come up against a few challenges similar to many organizations that have faced the task of implementing integrated risk management practices. One issue it has faced is that of linking compensation to risk-adjusted performance. This is a key component of ensuring the effectiveness of each business and is a well-recognized practice at CIBC.

Another challenge to the risk management processes comes from one of CIBC's key competitive advantages—its culture. CIBC has long benefited from a culture that is decentralized, diversified, and entrepreneurial. This helps it to keep on its toes and respond quickly to the ever-changing demands of increasingly savvy customers. However, this type of culture can be difficult from an administrative perspective, and is sometimes a challenge to integrate into a system of risk reporting.

CIBC is also in the process of preparing for BIS 2000 by implementing credit VaR in the banking book. In this vein, CIBC has developed models for integrating risk measures such as market VaR and credit VaR, in order to better capture the intersection between market and credit risk.

CIBC also wants to further develop an integrated and centralized method of collecting data for operational risk VaR. In addition to planning to centralize data collection within CIBC within the next year, CIBC is also part of a global initiative to develop an operational loss database in conjunction with the Big Six Canadian banks, the British Bankers' Association, and the Risk Management Association.

CHAPTER 17

Energy Firms

The energy industry is one of the largest in the world. Energy sources are crucial to the functioning of modern economies, and global demand increased steadily during the twentieth century. The trend shows no sign of stopping: world energy consumption is forecast to grow by around 60 percent between 1997 and 2020, with most of that growth coming from the emerging markets. Presumably global energy production will grow similarly, to meet demand—it did, in fact, increase by some 10 percent between 1990 and 1997.

Such growth makes it even more important that energy companies manage their risks effectively, as we will see in the next section. The risks are, broadly speaking, the same as those for other corporations: credit, market, and operational. However, a number of factors have made energy companies more aggressive in establishing formal approaches for measuring and managing these risks, particularly market risks.

First and foremost among these is the trend toward deregulation in the natural gas and power businesses. Until recently, the energy industry was heavily regulated in most countries, creating an environment of relatively stable prices and providing utilities with the ability to pass any price volatility on to consumers. For example, a typical regulatory framework would ensure that a utility selling natural gas to residential customers would realize an adequate return, regardless of how much it paid its own suppliers for the gas.

Deregulation has, however, made the industry more competitive and more subject to the vagaries of a free and open market in the relevant commodities. Consumers now have more choice when selecting an energy provider, which, in accordance with the logic of free markets, has exerted downward pressure on prices and made energy providers shoulder more of the burden when it comes to managing price volatility. Price volatility has itself increased dramatically; the early days of deregulation, in particular, are typically times of enormous volatility. Although this may level off as the market settles down, price volatility typically remains far higher than was ever the case in the tightly regulated market.

INDUSTRY TRENDS

The environment in which the energy industry operates suggests a dire need for enterprise risk management. In many ways, this environment is evolving very similarly to that of the financial services industry: deregulation has encouraged competition, leading to consolidation within industry sectors and convergence across sectors.

The 1990s saw a wave of deregulation in the energy industry, beginning in the United States, United Kingdom, and Scandinavia and moving into other countries as the decade went on. For example, the U.S. Federal Energy Regulatory Commission has issued orders that have deregulated transmission in both the natural gas and electric power industries, with the aim of promoting price competition in these industries at both the wholesale and retail levels.

Such deregulation increases the onus on management to maximize shareholder value; if they do not, the company will not be able to attract capital sufficient to maintain or grow its operations. In the past, regulation made returns stable and predictable, and there were only minimal incentives to reduce cost. Shareholders in energy companies expected to earn stable returns while running minimal risks. As competition has increased, however, earnings have become more volatile, because energy companies have been forced to take on more risk, particularly price risk, instead of passing it directly to the customer. Shareholders have therefore begun to demand greater returns to compensate them for this greater risk.

This has had two major effects on the structure of the energy industry. The first is rapid consolidation, with companies merging both horizontally and vertically; the second is convergence, in that energy companies are no longer focusing on niches within the energy market, but rather on providing complete energy services for their customers. This convergence parallels the trend for "one-stop shopping" in financial services.

Consequently, the numerous niche players who previously populated the energy industry are giving way to a smaller number of firms that either own the entire chain in a given sector, from generation (or extraction) to delivery, or specialize in one part of the delivery chain but cross a variety of sectors. An example of the first might be an oil company that owns exploration, refinery, and distribution businesses; an example of the second might be a company that delivers both gas and electricity to retail consumers. A number of energy firms have established significant trading operations, but they have retrenched since the collapse of Enron and other players in the energy trading markets. These trends pose new challenges for risk management. Energy companies must now manage a wider set of risks, some of which were not typical of their former businesses. Moreover, merging two companies in different industry subsegments often means risk management systems must be integrated. This integration must be done at an enterprise level, since the new entity is likely to have an entirely different risk profile from its separate parts. Also, there are likely to be many more ways to manage risk with respect to distribution and trading activities.

Fortunately, a larger company can make more resources available for risk management, and the evidence is that this is happening. Integration is most complete in the oil business, and most large integrated oil companies have invested substantial resources in developing their capabilities in this area. Electric and natural gas companies are likely to follow suit as these markets continue to deregulate.

As in other industries, senior management and boards of directors have become increasingly accountable for developing risk management policy and guidelines for risk tolerance levels. "The Boards of large-cap and super-cap diversified energy and utility holding companies are making risk management one of their top three priorities in 1999. This means active involvement in establishing and enforcing risk management policies . . . For the best managed of such firms, the attention is on enterprise rather than functional risk."[1] Senior management can no longer afford to delegate the risk responsibility to individual business units.

The second effect of deregulation is the creation of full-fledged energy marketing and trading groups. These groups tend to be more active in the market, and thus more exposed to its risks and vagaries, than their parent institutions. In many respects, they act like "energy banks." A traditional bank or financial institution makes markets between buyers and sellers of financial products and risks. Energy banks carry out similar functions, but with a focus on energy and related risks, such as the variability of the weather. In this regard, the value that these groups add is generated from the fact that they are making markets in energy-related exposures, managing a book of these risks, and hopefully making a spread that is generating an adequate return based on the level of risk being taken.

Increased trading in volatile markets quickly led to an increased focus on risk management, just as it had in the financial markets. However, unlike financial services firms, where taking and managing risk was an essential part of the business's value proposition for many years, most energy companies were not nearly as comfortable with the idea of managing market

---

[1]*Energy Central,* April 5, 1999.

risk. One answer was to adapt popular tools from the financial services industry: value-at-risk (VaR),[2] stress testing, and the use of limits to mitigate unwanted levels of risk.

Adapting VaR for energy companies is not a trivial task, however. The applicability of a VaR model to the energy industry is strongly affected by a number of factors unique to the energy industry; we'll examine these below. Furthermore, VaR models are not universally applicable to all of an energy company's market risk exposures: they are most useful to energy companies in the management of market making and trading activities.

VaR refers by definition to the potential loss in value of a position (or portfolio of positions) over a particular time frame (typically one day), based on a specific statistical confidence interval (typically 95 or 99 percent). This provides an effective measure of the potential short-term loss associated with an energy company's market-making activities.

However, energy companies, like other nonfinancial corporations, frequently hedge energy prices (as well as other types of market risk), to shield themselves from any impact on cash flow and earnings. VaR is of limited value when it comes to assessing these kinds of activities, and needs to be used in conjunction with other metrics such as earnings-at-risk and cash-flow-at-risk. For simplicity, in the rest of this chapter we will use VaR to refer to the set of risk analytics used by an energy company.

A VaR model developed for the financial services industry is not of much use to an energy company even when it comes to market-making activities. A VaR model for an energy company must recognize a number of market risk issues specific to the industry: risk sharing, optionality, basis risk, and price transparency. Let's consider these in more detail.

RISK MANAGEMENT REQUIREMENTS

Thanks in part to deregulation, the price of an energy commodity is significantly more risky than financial market risks like those associated with interest rates, foreign exchange rates, and equity prices. Figure 17.1 shows how varied price volatility can be in the financial and energy markets. Whereas U.S. real estate has an annualized volatility of 12 percent and the S&P 500 had an annualized volatility of approximately 14 percent, natural gas and electricity had volatilities of 121 percent and 228 percent, respectively.

These price fluctuations pose a risk to energy companies from both the buy side and the sell side. An oil-refining company, for example, faces market risks from fluctuations in the price of the crude oil it buys; it also faces market

---

[2]See Chapter 9 for detailed discussions of VaR models.

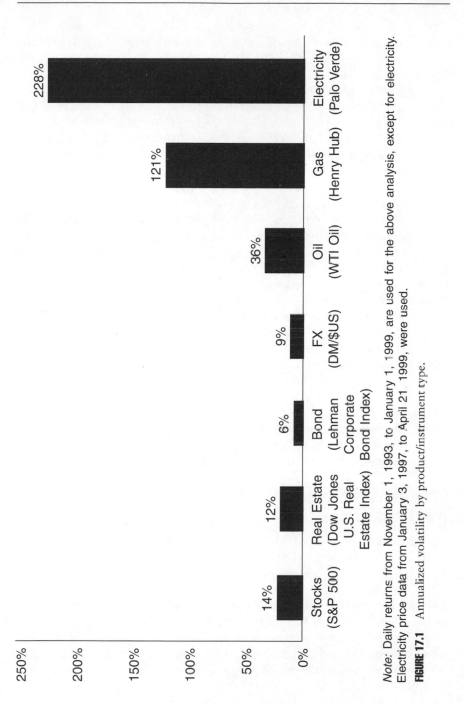

Note: Daily returns from November 1, 1993, to January 1, 1999, are used for the above analysis, except for electricity. Electricity price data from January 3, 1997, to April 21, 1999, were used.

FIGURE 17.1 Annualized volatility by product/instrument type.

risks from fluctuations in the price of the refined products that it sells. Its profit margin is basically the difference between these two prices (the "crack spread," in the jargon), and is thus doubly subject to market risk.

Some of this market risk can be hedged away. For example, the company might hedge its crude oil needs using futures contracts. However, this leaves it exposed to the *basis risk* that the oil specified by the futures contracts will not exactly match its needs—it might be delivered to the wrong location or at the wrong time, for example, or be of a different chemical composition. Not only does this mean that the oil may not meet the company's operational needs, but it means that the company's position is not actually neutral.

The risks do not end there. For example, the company might also face currency risk if the crude oil is obtained from foreign sources or its products are sold in foreign markets; and it also faces the risk that its suppliers or customers will default on their obligations. As is so often the case, this credit risk is intimately intertwined with market risk. As market prices increase, so does the value of a supply agreement, along with the credit risk associated with any default on that agreement.

Not surprisingly, defaults typically occur when market conditions are least favorable, and therefore when there is most stress on the system— the result can be a succession of failures. For example, summer 1998 saw an enormous spike in electricity prices in the midwestern United States, with prices reaching hundreds of times their normal levels. Among those who could not cope was a company called Federal Energy Sales, which defaulted on its obligations to supply power to a number of other companies. One of those, Power Company of America, was, in turn, forced to default on an estimated (and hotly disputed) $236 million of obligations to its own customers.

Price and Volume Risks

Business risks in energy companies take the form of pricing pressures and volume risks. Different sets of risk exposures exist at different points along the value chain, so a given company's portfolio of risks will reflect both its sector (e.g., oil, gas, or electricity) and its role in that sector (whether it is a generator, refiner, or distributor). For example, an upstream oil company involved in exploration and production will have risks materially different from those of a downstream oil company involved in refining and distribution. And both will be materially different from gas companies that convert oil inputs into wholesale and retail gas products.

As discussed above, energy prices are extremely volatile. Pricing pressures can occur when deregulation changes the competitive environment. Managers at natural gas companies and electric utilities have been faced with the prospect of declining prices as industry deregulation continues; they must now compete for customers and capital without the protection of the government. Moreover, energy companies have been forced to manage their volume risks as market competition makes long-term contracts less prevalent.

To ensure the future viability of their operations in the changing competitive environment, energy companies must increasingly broaden the scope of enterprise-wide risk management to encompass all types of risks in their business and trading activities. Many industry analysts have predicted that the next two decades will be a time of unusual pressure for change, both for environmental and economic reasons, in which companies will be driven to compete for survival and dominance in a new energy system.

Event Risks

Event risk losses for energy companies include litigation, equipment failures such as oil spills or well failures, or losses incurred by violations of company policies (e.g., rogue speculative trading).

Lawsuits have become an increasing concern for energy companies over the past 20 years, particularly due to the activism of environmental lobbies. For example, after the Exxon Valdez oil spill in 1989, Exxon agreed to pay approximately $1.15 billion to settle the civil and criminal cases against it, not to mention the cost of the lost oil and the ensuing cleanup.

One type of risk that is particularly relevant to energy companies is weather risk. Weather risk can impact a company by impacting credit, market, or operational risk exposures. A severe heat wave can cause electric power shortages in certain markets. It is possible that a counterparty might default on contracted electricity if the shortage is severe enough, as in the case of Power of America discussed earlier. That was an instance where a weather event directly caused a counterparty default.

There are several ways that energy companies can benefit from using an enterprise risk management approach. Each energy company can set limits as to the amount of risk it can tolerate, measure its exposure to each risk type, and then hold sufficient capital to cover its risks at the appropriate level. Most energy companies face several if not all of the risks outlined above. An enterprise approach can comprehensively address all of the risks and their interdependencies in an energy company.

Risk Sharing

Settlement in the energy markets will often involve an exchange of both cash and of the physical underlying commodity, something that is becoming increasingly uncommon in the financial markets. In some instances, these physical positions are very straightforward, meaning that they are exclusively associated with the exchange of the physical commodity on some prearranged terms—for example, a contract to physically deliver the commodity at some agreed future date and price. In many instances, however, some of the "portfolio" of exposures may be embedded in an agreement between the energy producer or intermediary and their customers or suppliers. Such clauses must be quantified and factored into the overall VaR calculation.

Given that the energy industry is still at least partly regulated (and likely to remain so for some considerable time in many places), there are likely to be regulatory limits on the risks that companies can take in search of returns. There are also likely to be limits on the extent to which their customers can in turn be exposed to those risks and returns. In some regulatory environments, a company may only be able to pass along a portion of any cost increase when acquiring energy supplies, and may be required to pass along a portion of any "savings" resulting from their hedging strategy. These must be quantified and incorporated into the VaR model.

Even if the industry does become fully deregulated, VaR models will still need to account for such limits—albeit imposed not by a regulator, but by industry practices. For example, a company that passes on more risk to its customers (through price adjustments) than the industry average will likely lose customers. The first step in developing a VaR model that accurately reflects these structural elements is the assessment of the regulatory (or market) environment that affects a particular company's activities. These should then be built into the model in the form of assumptions, which accurately identify "risk ownership": the ability to pass on the costs or profits of the commodity business to the ultimate consumers.

Optionality

Most energy suppliers implicitly offer some "optionality" in the amount of energy they provide to consumers (whether retail or commercial); they also may have complementary options to increase the supply of energy when market conditions are right. These two sets of optionality—demand and supply, respectively—have value that must be included in the VaR calculation.

Individual consumers usually have the option to use more or less power over a given time period than the historical average. A number of factors will affect the exercise of this option, one of the most important being the weather. An unusually warm summer may increase demand for electricity to power air-conditioning, for example, while an unusually warm winter may reduce the demand for gas for heating systems. The power consumption of large manufacturing companies, on the other hand, may be more reflective of the macroeconomic environment and demand for their goods.

This option has some value, which the supplier needs to consider in its pricing. Put another way, the potential distribution of demand must be factored into the overall VaR framework, thus providing insight into an oft-ignored element of risk. The approach taken typically includes two steps:

- Build a mathematical model for the demand as a function of various likely factors. The underlying relationship can be derived from historical data, but care must be taken to choose a time period, geographic area, and customer breakdown that is a reasonable match for the current situation. This may require the company to build a number of models for different areas and customer segments.
- The various forecasting models can then be used to create a distribution of potential usage. This distribution can be used in combination with the correlations of prices to determine potential shortfalls in generation capacity or pricing.

A company that possesses either power generation capacity or some form of generation or storage capacity for the basic energy commodity (e.g., natural gas) is holding a physical position with inherent optionality. As with any option, this position has inherent value, which can be assessed in terms of the factors generally considered in option pricing—strike price, volatility, time to maturity, and so on.

In the case of physical assets, the greatest difficulty arises in determining the strike price and time to maturity. Typically, the strike price is a function of the variable costs associated with producing power or of obtaining the energy commodity from a production or storage facility. For example, consider a company that owns both a power plant fueled by natural gas and a source of natural gas. The spread between the price of power and the price of natural gas would have to reach a certain level (the strike price) before the company would find it worthwhile exercising its option to produce power from the natural gas, rather than simply selling the gas off in the spot market. That level will be determined by the cost of obtaining the natural gas and the efficiency with which the plant turns it into power.

If the company owned several power plants or sources of natural gas, it might own a number of options corresponding to different combinations of plants and sources. Each of these options would have to be priced individually. Furthermore, each generation asset would need to be modeled individually to accurately reflect potential risks. Operating characteristics that must be considered include the type of fuel, historical reliability including both forced and scheduled outages, and total operating costs, as well as heat rates and marginal production and distribution costs discussed previously. These characteristics should be used to produce a distribution of the available capacity versus the total capacity for each period (e.g., hour, day, etc.) over a predefined forecast horizon. The results of this simulation will determine total capacity, as well as excess available for sale (e.g., total capacity net of service load or obligated sales).

Basis Risk

In the financial markets, a security traded in one geographic market can easily be arbitraged with a similar security in another geographic market, thus eliminating pricing discrepancies. By contrast, commodities like natural gas and power cannot be arbitraged across locations so easily—for most practical purposes, a store of natural gas on the West Coast of the United States is not the same thing as a store of natural gas on the East Coast. Prices for the same commodity in different areas can diverge under the influence of local factors. Under these conditions, an organization that needs the commodity in one area is exposed to *basis risk* if it has to find it elsewhere.

Basis risk can be a function of several independent factors, which must be incorporated into VaR models. It tends to be a major consideration in markets where physical transportation of energy is not feasible—for example, in electric power, where electricity produced in the western United States cannot readily be transmitted into the eastern power grid. Where physical transportation *is* possible, basis risk arises if an organization does not own the rights to use that transportation at a useful time or price.

Another important factor in basis risk is regional variations in weather, regulatory framework, or market environment. For example, many natural gas producers hedge their physical stocks of the gas (their natural long positions) by selling natural gas futures (acquiring short positions), hoping that a loss in either position will be offset by gains in the other.

This strategy went badly awry in the first quarter of 1996, however. At that time, the only futures contracts available were listed at the New York Mercantile Exchange and stipulated that the gas was to be delivered at the Henry Hub, which serves the Northeast. An exceptionally cold snap resulted in extremely volatile prices for natural gas, particularly in the Northeast. Prices rose at the Henry Hub even as prices remained relatively flat in the remainder of the U.S. regional gas markets. The result was that natural gas producers suffered large losses on their futures positions that were not offset by corresponding gains on their national physical positions.

Many of the producers thus affected did have risk management policies and procedures in place, some of them quite well regarded. However, their exposure to the weather-related basis risk between their long (physical) and short (futures) positions led them to suffer losses.

Price Transparency

One significant issue in many physical energy markets is the lack of reliable pricing information. In this case, a proxy needs to be found, in the form of a similar market where pricing information is more readily available and whose long-term correlation to the target market is well known. VaR can then be approximated, but it becomes critical that stress testing be carried out efficiently, since the correlations on which the model is based frequently break down during stressed market conditions.

Prices within commodity markets also tend to move differently from prices in capital markets such as foreign exchange or interest rates. For example, a VaR model for energy commodities such as power or natural gas should in principle account for the characteristics observed within the price movements of power and natural gas: price jumps, continuous price or diffusion, and mean reversion. These characteristics need to be modeled to determine the various paths of potential price movements and their range. In practice, these characteristics do not require a substantially different treatment from those in the financial markets.

A more significant difference involves the weighting of historical information. It is widely accepted that future volatility is best predicted on the basis of an exponentially weighted average of historical volatilities. An exponentially weighted average gives more credence to recent observations than past ones, and thus captures recent trends better than a simple average over the same period. It is therefore important that the weight and time period concerned reflect the characteristic trends of price movements, which tend to be shorter and more seasonal in the energy market than in the financial markets.

For example, analysis of recent price movements indicated that an optimal weighting factor for foreign exchange and interest rates would result in 99 percent of the volatility calculation being based on the past 151 days of historical observations, whereas it would be based on the past 42 days for natural gas markets and 23 days for power markets.

A LOOK TO THE FUTURE

In the longer term, the most important issue facing energy companies may be the move toward new technologies and alternative energy sources, motivated both by environmental factors and the possibility of resource shortages. Globally, petroleum is the most important of the various energy sources available today, accounting for 39.1 percent of total energy production in 2000. Coal and natural gas follow, with 23.3 and 22.9 percent, respectively, while other sources (e.g., geothermal and nuclear power) account for the remaining 15 percent or so.[3]

This is likely to change in coming years. While coal remains important,

---

[3]Energy Information Administration, *International Energy Annual 2001*.

the fastest growth is in the natural gas sector, driven by environmental considerations and technologic advances. It looks increasingly likely that gasoline will gradually give way to natural gas and electrical power for smaller machines (most obviously cars), while alternative energy sources such as biomass, wind, geothermal power, hydropower, solar power, and nuclear power will account for an increasingly large chunk of energy production.

The way companies handle this transition may result in a drastic shift in market share as some of the most successful companies are supplanted by up-and-comers who make the transition more smoothly. Given the importance of environmental issues in driving the transition process, reputational risk may prove a key issue.

Already, BP, one of the world's largest energy companies, has rebranded itself as "beyond petroleum." Energy companies that do not prove able to evolve fast enough may end up as extinct as the prehistoric life that makes up the fossil fuels they rely upon.

LESSONS LEARNED FROM ENRON

No chapter on energy risk management is complete without a few words about Enron. While the shocking story of Enron will be unfolding for many months to come, there are three lessons that are already evident: Keep your eye on the cash; manage *all*, not just some of your risks; and get auditors back to basics.

Keep Your Eye on the Cash

Prior to the restatements of its accounts, Enron reported $3.3 billion in net income over the five years ending 2000. Over the same period, it reported only $114 million of total cash generated—a mere 3 percent of reported income. A long time delay between reported earnings and actual cash flows should be a warning indicator for any company. This is especially true in financial markets and derivative businesses, where "paper profits" are prevalent and expected future cash flows are often counted as current revenue. If the gap cannot be closed, the company is liable to implode, as at Barings and Kidder, where reported profits were never reconciled with the cash positions of the firms. To quote one analyst, "Cash is king. Accounting is opinion." The lesson here is to focus on the cash.

Manage All of Your Risks

Ironically, Enron had a chief risk officer (CRO) who reportedly oversaw a 150-person staff, a $30 million annual budget, and a suite of market and credit risk controls that were widely believed to be state of the art. However, it was not a credit or market bet that bankrupted Enron—it was operational risk, in the form of basic failures of governance and accounting controls. There are uncanny parallels between Enron's rise and fall and those of Bankers Trust. Both companies were labeled "masters of risk management" in their respective industries; both ultimately met untimely ends due to "soft" operational risks associated with people and culture. (In the case of Bankers Trust, bad sales practices and mismanagement of client accounts broke the company's franchise as a sophisticated trading house.) Ironically, Enron's CRO, Rick Buy, was previously a Bankers Trust executive before joining Enron in 1994. The lesson here is that companies must manage all of their risks on an integrated basis, not just the obvious ones.

Get Auditors Back to Basics

Auditors should by no means get the full blame for the Enron disaster. However, the profession has lost sight of one of its key roles, which is to ensure that books and records are accurate. I can't remember the last time I met an auditor who told me that his or her main focus is to ensure the accuracy of books and records. Yet I meet hundreds of auditors each year who describe their roles as evaluating the effectiveness of controls and processes, helping business units perform "self-assessments," or providing operational risk consulting. Some of them also fail to recognize that the term *internal audit outsourcing* is an oxymoron. Who, when all is said and done, is minding the books? The lesson here is that the audit function should return to one of its basic and most valuable functions: to provide an independent assessment of the accuracy of a firm's books and records.

By the time the saga comes to its end, the financial losses and business repercussions of the Enron debacle could easily eclipse those of five other notorious corporate disasters: Barings, Kidder, Bankers Trust, Orange County, and Long-Term Capital Management. Those who wish to be wise, not foolish, in risk management, should take this opportunity to learn for free what Enron and its stakeholders learned at a very high cost indeed.

CHAPTER 18

Nonfinancial Corporations

As the twenty-first century begins, corporations from a range of industries and from around the world face unprecedented opportunities and risks. Globalization, technology advances, changing market structures, industry consolidation and intense competition, and outsourcing and reengineering: combined with the stock market's increasing proclivity for earnings stability, these trends have placed new importance on the role of risk management.

Whereas financial institutions have long-recognized risk management as a core competence in their business, nonfinancial corporations are beginning to realize that risk management tools can help them improve their financial performance beyond the traditional applications in hedging currency or interest rate exposures or buying corporate insurance. Leading corporations are turning to enterprise risk management as a means of enhancing shareholder value, ensuring financial stability, and facilitating the achievement of strategic and corporate objectives.

In this chapter, we will examine the major changes affecting corporations from a wide range of sectors, such as consumer products, durable goods, high technology, pharmaceuticals, chemicals, and agriculture.

RISK MANAGEMENT REQUIREMENTS

A negative risk event incurs significant costs for a corporation. In addition to financial loss, it can damage a company's brand and customer relationships, as well as its reputation in the industry. It can also represent a strategic setback in terms of lost momentum for new businesses and products, since management time and attention is diverted to fixing the crisis.

However, while a company may die a quick death if it does not manage its critical risks, it will certainly die a slow death if it does not take enough risks. It will lose its customers if competitors introduce better service, or its competitive advantage will decline if it does not take sufficient research and development (R&D) risks and other corporations launch more innovative products.

Thus, as with financial institutions, the objective for enterprise risk management at nonfinancial corporations should be to optimize the company's risk profile by controlling undesirable risks and taking desirable risks. In this chapter, we'll examine the major risks faced by most corporations.

Credit Risks

Most corporations face some form of credit risk. The most common is the risk of customers defaulting on their obligations. Whether the business is a small tailor or a major car manufacturer, there is always some risk that customers will not pay in full or on time, unless payment in full is always received before services are rendered. This may be no more than a nuisance if the business rarely experiences significant credit losses, but it can jeopardize the success of the corporation if it gets out of hand.

Another credit risk that corporations face is counterparty risk—the failure of a counterparty to perform under the terms of a financial transaction, including trade finance and derivative transactions. A nonfinancial form of counterparty risk is the failure of a strategic partner or vendor to provide critical operations and services because of credit problems. For example, a company that uses vendors to provide critical services such as technology or order fulfillment is faced with the risk of disruptions and serious business problems if the vendors fail to perform because they are bankrupt.

Because the implications of credit losses for corporations can be wide ranging, it is essential that executives have a clear sense of their overall credit risk, and what, if anything, should be done differently. Which accounts are questionable? How much do these questionable accounts amount to? Can corporate policy be changed to reduce credit risk without losing customers? Do we have an allowance for questionable accounts, and, if so, is it sufficient? Do we have a system in place to review accounts receivable regularly and assess their status? Are our business partners reliable? What is our backup plan if they do not perform? Do our legal contracts protect us somewhat from credit loss? Regularly reflecting on questions such as these can help any corporation keep their credit risk exposure to an acceptable level, while not jeopardizing the growth and success of the company.

Market Risks and Hedging

Market risk involves any risk of loss due to market price fluctuations. Changes in market variables such as interest rates, foreign exchange rates, equity prices, commodity prices, and real estate prices can impact a corporation's financial positions in three ways.

First, the company has *transaction exposures* that represent the direct impact of changes in market variables on its revenues and expenses. Second, it is faced with *economic exposure* with regard to how such changes affect its competitive position, as well as buyer and supplier behavior. Finally, the company may have *translation exposures* when it converts the financial statements of foreign operations to its home currency.

These three types of exposure are frequently interconnected, with a change in the level of one kind of exposure leading to a change in the level of some other kind. For example, a U.S.-based car company might make cars in the United States but sell them in Japan. The company would therefore face the following risks if the U.S. dollar strengthened relative to the Japanese yen:

- The revenues from sales in Japan will represent fewer U.S. dollars and thus the net profitability of Japanese sales will be reduced (transaction exposure).
- The U.S. car company might be forced to raise prices in Japan, thus losing customers and market share to other car companies (economic exposure).
- The financial statements of the company's Japan subsidiary will be translated into fewer U.S. dollars when the parent company consolidates its financial statements (translation exposure).

Stock Price Risk

One major market risk—and one that is not often considered as such—is that publicly listed companies can be very exposed to fluctuations in their *own* stock prices. When investors favor specific sectors, a company's stock price can soar, resulting in a higher market value for that company. This higher stock price acts as a stronger "currency," which the company can use in pursuing strategic initiatives such as business development and mergers and acquisitions.

By contrast, even a company with the strongest fundamentals can be at risk from significant devaluations in stock prices when investors are spooked. A reduction in stock price can limit a company's capital-raising opportunities as well as leaving it vulnerable to a hostile takeover. A clear and recent example of this type of stock price risk is the Internet crash of 2000, where the market meltdown for Internet stock prices and subsequent withdrawal of venture capital funding forced many dot-coms into bankruptcy and the rest to rethink their business plans.

Traditional brick-and-mortar companies are not exempt. In the current market environment, any negative surprises in corporate earnings can lead to dramatic declines in stock price. For example, in March 2000, Procter & Gamble announced that it expected first quarter earnings to come in 11 percent lower than earnings for the same period a year earlier, sending its stock price tumbling 30 percent in one day. By the end of that week, the stock had lost 40 percent of its value and Procter & Gamble had lost $4.3 billion in market capitalization.

Investment Risks

More conventional market risks affect companies that hold investment portfolios. Most firms hold a significant portion of their available cash in fixed income securities, a practice that exposes the firm to rising interest rates, particularly if the company has short-term liabilities and long-term assets. Furthermore, many firms take equity stakes in other companies, either in their investment portfolios or venture funds, and are therefore affected by the changes in stock prices. Finally, some firms with defined-benefit pension plans face market risk in the form of pension liability. If their pension funds are invested unwisely, a company may face a risk of being required to pay out more in pension liabilities than it holds in pension funds. This is becoming less and less of an issue as more and more firms turn to defined contribution plans, in large part to avoid this issue.

Hedging Risks

In addition to price fluctuations in the financial markets, companies are faced with uncertainties relative to their input and output prices. For example, as discussed in the previous chapter, energy firms are faced with price volatility in the oil, gas, and electricity markets. Agricultural firms are affected by commodity prices. Technology firms are not only affected by the volatile prices of computer chips, but also by the costs of bandwidth for transporting data. Hedging is often used to offset some of a company's exposure to market risk, by allowing the hedger to benefit from "adverse" fluctuations in foreign exchange rates, for example.

Some hedging strategies, however, can be quite risky and can actually *increase* a company's exposure to market risk. For example, in April 1994, Gibson Greetings announced that it had lost $20 million on trading in derivatives for hedging purposes. Thinking that it understood the derivatives proposed to it by its banker, Bankers Trust, Gibson entered into derivatives contracts that bet on the movements of interest rates and financial indexes, but quickly found that it had bet the wrong way. Bankers Trust was ultimately found responsible for misleading Gibson Greetings and charged a $10 million fine. Gibson, meanwhile, had lost 40 percent of its share value in less than four months, and it was three and a half years before its stock regained its value of early April 1994.

In response to the high profile of derivatives losses and public outcry for improved transparency, the Financial Accounting Standards Board (FASB) issued a standard, FAS 133, for accounting and reporting derivatives transactions. Many corporations claimed that this standard exposed them to significant earnings volatility by requiring them to reflect changes in the market value of derivative instruments in their income statements and balance sheets. Given these concerns, they requested that the FASB amend the standard. Although the FASB partially met that request and issued an amendment to FAS 133, the implementation of the new standard still poses a number of operational headaches for companies that they will have to contend with in the near future.[1]

Secondary Risks

In addition to these primary exposures to market prices, companies are also exposed to secondary price drivers. For example, temperatures can significantly affect a utility's revenues, while snowfall can affect the revenues for an airport. These secondary exposures are not strictly market risks, but share many similar characteristics, and market makers in the financial and insurance markets are fast developing new and innovative hedging products, as discussed in Chapter 9, to help companies cope with these price uncertainties. Beyond financial and commodity derivatives, these risk transfer products offer protection against price uncertainties with respect to bandwidth, temperature, and yes, even snowfall.

Operational and Insurable Risks

As outlined in an earlier chapter of this book, operational risk encompasses virtually any risk that is not a market or credit risk, and stems, broadly speaking, from potential loss due to a failure in people, processes, or technology. Operational risk is rapidly gaining acceptance as a critical risk because failures stemming from operational problems can be enormously damaging. As a result, operational risk management has been the subject of significant attention from risk managers, regulators, and the press as a critical challenge for all companies. Nonfinancial corporations face many forms of operational risk:

- Product liability resulting from defective products
- Failed mergers and acquisitions

---

[1]For further information on FAS 133, refer to the website: *www.fas133.com.*

- R&D underperformance risk
- Reliance on faulty financial models
- Changes in tax laws and regulations

Additionally, operational risks encompass organizational and technology risks. Organizational risks include shortages in management talent and skilled labor, negative public relations, or improper employee behavior due to poor hiring practices or adverse corporate culture and incentives. Technology risks include systems outages from older systems or untested applications, inadequate or faulty data, and information security breaches.

Catastrophic Failures

Examples of operational risk management failures, and their potentially catastrophic consequences, abound. One of the best known examples is the 1984 chemical leak from a Union Carbide plant in Bhopal, India. In December 1984, a Union Carbide pesticide plant in Bhopal, India, was the site of what was then called the "world's worst industrial accident" in history.[2] A tank in the plant leaked 5 tons of poisonous methyl isocyanate gas into the air, killing more than 3,000 people and injuring tens of thousands. The Indian government successfully sued Union Carbide for $470 million in 1989, and criminal proceedings are still outstanding.

Another very high-profile example of an operational failure occurred when, in 1989, the cargo tanks of Exxon's oil tanker, the Exxon Valdez, ruptured when the ship ran aground off the coast of Alaska, spilling more than 10.8 million gallons of crude oil into the ocean. Exxon spent $3 billion to clean up and to settle government lawsuits, and was in 1994 ordered to pay $5 billion in punitive damages to those harmed by the spill, an order that it contested publicly. The Valdez spill and Exxon's subsequent actions have damaged Exxon's reputation as a good corporate citizen. In fact, Exxon's corporate reputation reportedly led regulators to scrutinize Exxon's proposed 1999 merger with Mobil Oil more heavily than the similar merger between BP and Amoco, despite the fact that the latter posed more antitrust concerns. Exxon's opposition to the 1994 judgment in the Valdez spill caused it to be "known in the industry for never yielding an inch with legal opponents, including regulators."[3]

---

[2]"Big Chemical Firms to Halt Operations on New Year's Eve," *The Wall Street Journal,* October 3, 1999.
[3]"Exxon-Mobil Merger Faces Legal Threat: Wednesday Deadline Set for Accord on Asset Sale," *The Dallas Morning News,* September 24, 1999.

Business Risk

Adopting the wrong business strategy, or failing to execute the right strategy, also can be considered a form of operational risk. Because a company's strategy is of paramount importance to its success, strategic uncertainties such as business plan assumptions, competitor responses, and technology changes should be measured and managed along with any other risk management issue. In a rapidly changing business environment, even a company with a well-thought-out strategy must establish feedback mechanisms and contingency plans to ensure that the company's strategy is sound over time.

As history has shown with the railroads when automobiles were invented, or with large cars when gas prices escalated, companies with unbending strategies can face extinction. A more recent example would be Olivetti, which was one of the leading manufacturers of typewriters heading into the 1980s. Olivetti believed so firmly that the typewriter would always be commonly used that it did not follow the lead of other companies and start to manufacture personal computers. Thus, it nearly lost everything by not recognizing the need to change strategy to focus on new technologies.

In another recent example, Boeing and Airbus have each bet the futures of their companies on their vision of the future of air travel. At issue is the question of whether the air travel industry requires a new "super-jumbo jet" to fly passengers between major international hubs. Boeing believes that point-to-point service will be more important than travel through hubs in the future, necessitating smaller planes. Airbus, however, thinks that a super-jumbo jet with dramatically increased capacity will be greatly in demand, to satisfy the ever-increasing international appetite for air travel. Given the cost of developing new models of aircraft, these alternatives are, for most purposes, mutually exclusive—each company must pick the strategy it believes to be correct. Whichever turns out to be correct will stand to gain market share on the other's back and avoid potentially devastating losses from development costs. For the company that chooses incorrectly, the development costs and loss of businesses could be their undoing.[4]

Cultural Risks

The wrong culture also can be a form of operational risk. IBM is a classic example of a company whose culture turned from a strength to a weakness, ultimately posing a significant risk to its success. During the 1980s, IBM fiercely maintained its culture described by others as "bureaucracy run

---

[4]Jeff Cole, "Ante Up! Big Gambles in the New Economy—Flight of Fancy: Airbus Prepares to 'Bet the Company' as it Builds a Huge New Jet," *The Wall Street Journal,* November 3, 1999.

amok"[5]—epitomized by the nickname "Big Blue"—while all around it the high-technology sector developed a culture of golf-shirt-sporting executives leading organizations with flat hierarchies. IBM's "caution, obsessive training of employees, focus on following rather than anticipating customer needs, and a guarantee of lifetime employment to its workers" made it inflexible and were integral to its decision to focus on mainframes rather than personal computers in the late 1970s. That decision nearly cost the company its business. IBM went from earning a $6 billion profit in the early 1990s to a $5 billion loss just two years later; its stock price fell from $176 to the low forties.

Reputational Risks

One of the most valuable assets a company can have is its reputation. One measurement of a company's reputation is its brand or trademark value. In June 1999, Coca-Cola was considered the world's most valuable brand, with a trademark value estimated at $83.8 billion, nearly 60 percent of the company's market value.[6] However, that brand value and the company's reputation were seriously jeopardized when more than 100 people fell ill after drinking Coca-Cola products in June 1999. Coca-Cola products were subsequently banned by a number of European governments, including those of Belgium, France, Greece, Spain, and Italy, forcing the largest product recall in the company's 113-year history.[7] Coca-Cola reported that the impact of the European recall cost shareholders two to three cents of second-quarter earnings because of a "loss of sales in several markets, a fall in equity income and increased marketing expenses."[8] Coca-Cola Enterprises (one of Coke's bottlers) alone estimated that the recall would cost them US$60 million.[9] Furthermore, Coke's stock price lost nearly 13 percent of its value in one month, falling from $70 to $61 and eroding more than $22 billion in market capitalization.[10]

[5]Richard L. Daft, *Organization Theory and Design* (Mason, Ohio: South-Western College Publishing, 1998), p. 4.
[6]Richard Tomkins, "Assessing a Name's Worth," *Financial Times*, June 22, 1999.
[7]"Rat Poison Probe Under Way at French Coca-Cola Plant," *Financial Times*, June 24, 1999, and Neil Buckley, Michael Smith, and Robert Graham, "Coca-Cola Apology to Belgian Consumer," *Financial Times*, June 22, 1999.
[8]"Coca-Cola 21% Down on Earnings," *Financial Times*, July 16, 1999.
[9]"Coke Recall Cost Is Put at Dollars 60m," *Financial Times*, June 25, 1999.
[10]*www.bloomberg.com.*

BEST PRACTICES IN CORPORATE RISK MANAGEMENT

As discussed above, corporations are faced with a wide range of credit, market, and operational risks. To mitigate these risks, management can develop internal control processes and external risk transfer strategies. The risk management process for corporations includes risk identification and assessment; quantification and reporting; and management and control. Let's look at each of these in turn.

Risk Identification and Assessment

One risk identification methodology made popular by corporations is the use of risk mapping. Today, risk mapping is increasingly used by both financial and nonfinancial companies to identify and monitor enterprise-wide risks.

Figure 18.1 shows an example of a risk map, which ranks risk exposures by severity on the horizontal axis and by probability on the vertical axis (see Chapter 3 for a discussion of these concepts). The process of developing and implementing a risk map is as follows:

1. Establish a top-down framework—an overall taxonomy for classifying all types of risk.
2. Create a bottom-up list of specific risks by business and functional units, based on loss history and self-assessments.
3. Evaluate the probability and severity of each risk based on management judgment or risk models, and develop the risk map as shown in Figure 18.1.
4. Identify existing controls to incorporate their impact and determine whether new controls are needed at the business and functional levels.
5. Assign responsibilities for implementing new controls as well as for monitoring and reporting on specific risks.
6. Aggregate individual risk maps into an enterprise-level risk map, and determine whether new controls are needed at the enterprise level.
7. Go back to step 1 in order to update and refine the risk mapping process on an ongoing basis.

Few companies face many risks that are both highly severe and highly probable. One rare example is that of Internet companies that are projected to run out of cash within, say, 12 months. For these companies, the probability of depleting their cash positions is high, given their "burn rate," and the consequence of such an event—bankruptcy—is the most severe that can be faced by any company. Such exposures warrant significant management attention and the active deployment of risk mitigation plans. For the Internet

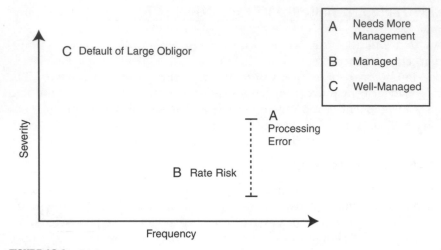

FIGURE 18.1 Risk map.

companies, cash management is a critical activity and the ability to raise additional funds often means life or death for the company.

On the other hand, all companies face risks that are of both low severity and low probability. For example, it is unlikely that a company would experience a malfunction in its voice mail system. Such an occurrence should in any case have little impact on its business and financial performance (unless, of course, it is a company that makes voice mail systems). Risks that are considered low probability and low severity should simply be monitored to ensure that they remain in an acceptable range. Such risks are often only important if they recur: the cumulative impact of many, repeating small risk events may be much more significant than that of a single risk event. For example, many investment banks have a high error rate in the settlement of financial transactions. The focus of attention for these banks has not been to achieve a zero error rate, but to make sure that any such errors are within an acceptable range and that they are resolved in a timely manner.

Risk exposures that are of high severity but low probability are excellent candidates for contingency plans or insurance policies. Examples include events such as fire, earthquake, or other natural or business catastrophes. Finally, risks that are of low severity but high probability may include minor theft, machinery breakdown, and expected levels of receivables charge-offs. These exposures are generally self-insured by a company. Some exposures, such as interest rate risk, currency risk, credit risk, employee turnover and product liability, may range in probability and severity depending on the company's specific exposures and the actual volatility. For these exposures, management should establish effective monitoring and reporting systems, including early warning indicators that would signal problems ahead.

Risk mapping has become a widely used risk identification and assessment tool because of its flexibility to incorporate both financial and non-financial risks. Given its flexibility, the risk-mapping process should exhibit the following qualities:

- *Comprehensive:* The risk map represents an overall framework for identifying and assessing all of the risks faced by the corporation.
- *Consistency:* A standard taxonomy establishes a common language to discuss risk exposures, and the standards for risk assessment provide a consistent methodology for evaluating their probability and severity.
- *Accountability:* Business and functional units are directly involved in the identification and assessment of risks, as well as in the risk monitoring and management processes.

If implemented appropriately, the risk map can be a highly effective tool for risk identification and assessment. However, the quality of a risk map is entirely dependent on the quality of the input and process that produced it. Without a sound methodology, risk mapping can become a bureaucratic exercise that yields little benefits other than a hodgepodge of risk exposures that are not well thought out.

A misuse of the risk-mapping process would be to gather a group of business and functional managers, brainstorm about risk exposures without a standard taxonomy, arbitrarily assign probability and severity without a methodology, and then create a risk map that would not be looked at until the following year. Such an approach might create risk awareness for certain issues, but is by no means a disciplined risk identification and assessment process. For a risk-mapping process to be effective, it should follow the steps discussed above and be supported by risk quantification and reporting, as discussed in the next section.

Quantification and Reporting

Nonfinancial corporations should benefit from the risk quantification and reporting processes discussed in the rest of the book. In this section we will discuss how corporations can apply value-at-risk (VaR) techniques to quantify and manage cash flow and earnings volatility, as well as make the appropriate risk adjustments in economic value-added (EVA) and net present value (NPV) models.

As described in Chapter 9, VaR is a summary statistic that quantifies the potential decline in asset or portfolio value given an adverse market price change over a specified period. For example, the VaR for a bond or bond portfolio can be calculated based on a 99 percent confidence level over a 10-day period. Such a number would indicate that, based on historical data, there is only a 1 percent probability that the company would suffer a value decline greater than the calculated VaR over any 10-day period.

VaR has become an industry standard for risk quantification and control for many companies, especially those involved in trading capital markets instruments such as financial institutions, energy firms, and nonfinancial corporations with significant capital markets activities. For these companies, VaR has been used to quantify risk exposures across financial risk positions as well as to establish trading limits. For financial institutions, which are increasingly managing their overall balance sheets on a mark-to-market basis, VaR represents an effective and concise tool for quantifying and reporting enterprise-wide risk exposures.

However, that is not the case for most nonfinancial corporations, because these companies use accrual accounting. Moreover, the financial and risk management objectives of corporations are focused more on cash flow and earnings management, and not on the market value of their assets and liabilities. As such, corporations have applied VaR techniques to measure and manage cash-flow-at-risk (CFaR) and earnings-at-risk (EaR). The objectives of CFaR and EaR are to quantify and control the key variables that contribute to the volatility in the cash flows and earnings of the company, respectively. Corporations can use one or more of three general approaches to estimating CFaR and EaR.

Pro Forma Analysis This analytical approach is based on a pro forma analysis for each item on the cash flow and income statements. The starting point is the company's financial forecast, which provides a "base case" number for each item. A risk analyst then determines the key variables that might affect the outcome of each item and the potential range of these variables. For example, the risk analyst might determine that the dollar/yen exchange rate is a key variable for revenues; the use of contract labor might have significant influence on expenses; and receivables turnover is a key driver of cash inflows. Next, the risk analyst would establish a range for each of these variables and estimate the sensitivity of the cash flow and income items to these variables. An adverse change in the dollar/yen exchange rate might be 15 percent, translating into a 30 percent decline in earnings. Based on such an analysis, the full impact of specified changes in key risk variables to the company's overall cash and earnings positions would be quantified under various scenarios.

Regression Analysis The regression method quantifies the exposure of the company's cash flows and earnings to various risk factors on the basis of time series analysis of the company's prior performance and historical data. The purpose of the analysis is to use historical data on the company's cash flows and earnings, as well as key variables—such as interest rates, exchange rates, or workers' compensation—to determine the beta coefficients for each variable. These beta coefficients measure the company's sensitivity to each variable. For example, a 0.5 beta for interest rates would indicate that a 10 percent increase in interest rates would lead to a 5 percent decline in earnings. Other statistical tests can be used to measure the accuracy of the model and the significance of each variable.

The regression model provides a linear estimate of the company's cash flows and earnings given a set of assumptions about the key variables. As such, management can quantify CFaR and EaR using a range of assumptions for the variables. The advantages of using the regression method are that it is a fact-based analysis using historical data, and can be updated regularly given new data. The disadvantages include the inherent assumption that the future will be like the past, and that nonlinear relationships between the variables and the company's cash flows and earnings will not be accurately captured.

Simulation Analysis   The simulation approach quantifies potential changes to the company's cash flows and earnings on the basis of computer-simulated changes in key variables. The key advantage of simulation analysis is that it can incorporate dynamic changes in the external environment, as well as internal management decisions. This allows the simulation method to quantify risk exposures that are time and path dependent.

For example, the company's interest expense sensitivity in the second year might be dependent on the first year's issuance of fixed versus floating debt, which in turn is dependent on the level of interest rates in the first year. A simulation model can be programmed to incorporate these relationships, given the potential changes and path of interest rates. An advanced from of simulation analysis is Monte Carlo simulation, in which the future distributions of interest rates and other variables are determined by random simulation of the values, volatilities, and correlations between these variables. The flexibility of the simulation approach allows management to evaluate the impact of competitive responses. For example, a pharmaceutical company facing the expiration of a key drug patent might want to evaluate the impact of various pricing strategies, including the likely responses from competitors with respect to their product and pricing strategies.

A corporation does not have to choose one of these three methods to the exclusion of the other two. It can select a specific method for specific business applications. For example, a corporation may use the simulation method for risk management, pro forma analysis for business and financial planning, and regression analysis for back-testing. The key is to effectively quantify and report on the company's risk exposures in order to reinforce risk identification and assessment, as well as support risk management and control.

Beyond risk measurement, the quantification of a corporation's risk exposures should provide management with analysis of its capital adequacy. A corporation holds equity capital for two main reasons: to fund cash and investment requirements, and to absorb unexpected losses. Greater quantification is useful in both these areas, and in particular the concept of economic capital—the capital held against risk (as explained in more detail in Chapter 9). If the economic capital is greater than the actual book capital of the company, the company is undercapitalized for the risks embedded in the business, and vice versa. Besides assessing the overall capital adequacy of the company, economic capital can be allocated to individual business units, products, or investments in order to evaluate risk-adjusted profitability on a consistent basis.

Many corporations use NPV and EVA tools to support investment decisions and business performance measurement. However, many of these applications allocate book capital or an average cost of capital to business activities, without fully adjusting for their risks. If the capital charge in these NPV and EVA applications does not fully reflect the underlying credit, market, and operational risks, then higher-risk investments and businesses would appear to be more profitable than the lower-risk ones. Over time, this would result in "adverse selection"—in other words the business portfolio would have higher risk exposures but not the higher returns that would compensate for such risks. To ensure the appropriate risk/return linkage, corporations should either adopt the economic capital methodology or make specific risk adjustments in their NPV and EVA tools.

Management and Control

The risk management process does not end with risk identification and assessment, or risk quantification and reporting. The final step is risk management and control. In this section, we'll highlight some of the key risk management and control strategies that corporations can implement. Generally speaking, corporations are paid to take strategic and business risks, manage financial risks, and mitigate operational risks. Based on the risk assessment and quantification of these risks, management can then decide on the appropriate strategies, including internal control and external risk transfer.

A company's management should start by establishing clear criteria for a business's acceptance of strategic and tactical risks and instituting ongoing processes for the monitoring of risks (see discussion of Policy 6.0 at GE Capital in Chapter 6). Beyond these, there are other strategic options that can provide the company with valuable flexibility. These include service level agreements with vendors that specify performance standards with penalty and exit clauses, as well as provisions that allow the delay or extension of projects. The company can further optimize its business risk by diversifying business and product lines, staging R&D projects, and shortening time to market for new project launches. Management also can reduce profit margin volatility by reducing the operating leverage of the company (i.e., reduce fixed vs. controllable expenses).

To reduce market and credit risk exposure concentrations, management can implement risk management policies and limits, as well as use internal and external hedging. Internal hedges for corporations include matching foreign revenues and expenses by sourcing supplies and locating plants abroad, or matching the interest rate adjustments of financial assets and liabilities. External hedging would involve financial derivatives, such as swaps, options, and futures contracts. The cost/benefit analysis between internal and external hedging should include hedging costs, administrative costs, and any residual basis risks associated with these alternatives.

Management should mitigate operational risks by developing quality control procedures for high-frequency but low- to medium-severity risk exposures, such as manufacturing defects. A corporation can also establish contingency plans and insurance strategies to mitigate event risks (low frequency but high severity) such as fire, earthquake, or a major systems outage. To mitigate risks associated with process or technology, single points of failures should be identified and redundant backup processes and systems should be developed. For critical operations such as customer service and core systems, excess capacity may be appropriate.

SUMMARY

Nonfinancial corporations face many of the same pressures to improve enterprise risk management as do their counterparts in the financial services and energy industries, namely, a dynamic business environment, an unforgiving stock market, industry mandates on corporate governance, and changes in regulatory and accounting requirements (e.g., FAS 133). Many corporations, particularly those with significant foreign operations and capital markets activities, have invested in the people, process, and technology for enterprise risk management. The case study below on Microsoft is a case in point.

CASE STUDY: MICROSOFT

Microsoft Corporation, the American software giant, began to implement its enterprise risk management program in 1994 and 1995. Scott Lange, the director of risk management at the time, began by developing a comprehensive list of the risks faced by the company and sorted them into a dozen broad categories: financial, reputational, technological, competitive, customer, people, operations, distribution, business partners, regulatory and legislative, political, and strategic.[11] "For the first time, management had a complete inventory of the organization's risk," said Lange. That helped them to recognize early on that their risk financing program, although "well-conceived and tremendously efficient," only covered about 30 percent of the risks the company faced.[12]

The recognition of the fact that much of Microsoft's risk exposure was not covered and the need to communicate that to senior management led Mr. Lange and his colleague, Jean-Francois Heitz, Microsoft's Treasurer, to develop an innovative communication tool: risk maps. The risk management map plots each risk's severity on the vertical axis and its frequency on the horizontal to show management easily what their risk picture looks like. The map then uses a color coding system to indicate whether the risk is insured, partially insured, or uninsured, helping Microsoft to best decide where to allocate its risk management resources. Obviously, uninsured risks that are high in frequency and severity demand more attention than ones that occur infrequently or are of small impact. According to Lange, the maps revealed at least two things. "One, Microsoft had a lot of risks that needed to be actively managed. Two, there was little consistency as to why some risks were insured and others weren't."[13]

In order to help direct Microsoft management's efforts to address those risks that were not being actively managed, Lange and Heitz used a risk grid. The grid outlines in a readily understood format the risk management process for any given risk. It is a simple matrix with what Microsoft considers the five main elements of the risk management process (identification, assessment, mitigation, financing, and services) as the first column. The next three columns are labeled "current," "goal," and "action required" and indicate, respectively, the current process for managing that risk, the ideal process, and what actions are required to move toward the goal. This tool is applicable to all risk types, and is easily used and understood by management throughout Microsoft, further enabling Microsoft to achieve its goal of enterprise risk management.

The process of going through this analysis helped Microsoft to realize that it had insurance policies with coverage or limits that were too small to be meaningful to their business, and were able to save premiums by discontinuing the policies or increasing the limits. Furthermore, risk analysis helped them to identify a risk of possible tort litigation for repetitive stress injuries that might arise from the release of a new keyboard. They determined the potential cost of repetitive stress injury suits and built that cost into the price

---

[11]Edward Teach, "Microsoft's Universe of Risk," *CFO, The Magazine for Senior Financial Executives*, March 1997.
[12]Scott Lange, "Going 'Full Bandwidth' at Microsoft," *Risk Management*, July 1996.
[13]Edward Teach, "Microsoft's Universe of Risk," *CFO, The Magazine for Senior Financial Executives*, March 1997.

of their keyboards, helping to mitigate the risk of future losses in that area.[14]

For the future, Microsoft wants to continue to manage its risks holistically, and may participate in the trend toward holistic risk transference. "Ultimately, we may package together our disparate risks and take it to market, if that makes the most sense for us," says Richard Sadler, Microsoft's current Senior Risk Manager.[15]

Another of Microsoft's innovative approaches to enterprise risk management is its use of information technology as a risk management tool. Microsoft's risk managers recognized early on that they would have to make risk management an easy process for employees in order to maximize their compliance with risk management procedures so as not to take their time away from customer service. Thus, Lange realized that they "had to advance a strategy of mixing technology and outsourcing to free up the human horsepower [they] needed to get the job done."[16] So they set up risk management information systems that track data on historical losses, both as a record and as the foundation for risk analysis in the future.

Next, they built an intranet that all Microsoft employees can access to "communicate everything from A to Z that is happening in risk management."[17] The intranet aims to integrate all Microsoft units' understanding of their risks and to give business units ready access to any information they might need concerning risks related to their businesses or business decisions.[18] Also, it helps to free up employee time by automating many repetitive tasks, such as loss claims. It enables employees to refine their needs so that risk management staff can provide focused and value-added information and services.

Microsoft's use of the intranet for risk management has strong buy-in from senior management, too. In the words of Mike Brown, Microsoft's Chief Financial Officer, "If you are a risk manager, the web is an incredible opportunity to take costs out of your model, to provide higher quality services and to be much more informed about company issues. If I could pick one item in our risk program that really turns me on, it's the continual improvements in using on-line technology."[19]

---

[14]Scott Lange, "Going 'Full Bandwidth' at Microsoft," *Risk Management*, July 1996.
[15]Russ Banham, "Kit and Caboodle," *CFO: The Magazine for Senior Financial Executives*, April 1999.
[16]Scott Lange, "Going 'Full Bandwidth' at Microsoft," *Risk Management*, July 1996.
[17]Scott Lange, "Going 'Full Bandwidth' at Microsoft," *Risk Management*, July 1996.
[18]Robert Ceniceros, "Sharing, Integrating Risk Management Information Made Even Easier with Companywide Intranet," *Business Insurance*, December 1997.
[19]Kimberley Birkbeck, *Integrating Risk Management: Strategically Galvanizing Resources in the Organization*, Proceedings of the 1998 International Conference on Risk Management (Ottawa: Conference Board of Canada, April 1998).

SECTION
four

A Look to
the Future

CHAPTER **19**

Predictions

We began this book by discussing the concepts and processes for risk management and made the case for an integrated enterprise-wide approach. We discussed the general principles of *enterprise risk management* (ERM) and then investigated the components of a well-founded ERM framework. Next, we reviewed the applications of ERM in the three key functional areas—credit, market, and operational—as well as specific industry sectors, including financial, energy, and nonfinancial corporations.

Throughout this book, from the title to the individual chapters, I have emphasized the importance of taking a balanced approach to ERM. One facet of this is balancing control over the downside (loss minimization) with support for the upside (shareholder value maximization). Another is the need to strike a balance between balancing internal controls over risk (policies, functions, and processes) with external risk transfer mechanisms (derivatives, insurance, and alternative risk transfer).

A final aspect of balance in risk management, and perhaps the one that will prove most critical in moving away from "silo" risk management toward ERM, is the need to always consider both the "yin" or hard side of risk management (systems, reports, and limits) and the "yang" or soft side (culture, people, skills, and incentives). In the spirit of yin and yang, we'll take a summary look at the major drivers of change at the human and technological levels: the emergence of risk management as a professional discipline, and the way that technology supports many levels of convergence toward ERM. As we'll see, both starting positions ultimately lead to a point when the two overlap and intertwine—just like yin and yang.

I'll close by bravely making 10 predictions for risk management over the next decade. Those of you who want to take a (fictional) glimpse of what the future might look like are invited to read the epilog (Chapter

20), in which the travails of Pamela, a risk manager in the year 2010, are described.

THE PROFESSION OF RISK MANAGEMENT

As the practice of risk management has expanded from a "silo" approach to an ERM approach, so has the career path for risk professionals. In the past, risk professionals were defined by a specialization: actuary, auditor, credit analyst, asset/liability manager, market risk manager, and so on. These roles were largely independent of each other, with different educational and training programs, different qualifications, and different working practices, terminology, and trade bodies.

Given this specialization, there was only so far that a risk professional could rise within an organization. Expertise in buying insurance or pricing derivatives is not a board-level skill. At most, an ambitious risk manager might hope to become the head of a risk function, such as chief auditor or head of asset/liability management. However, even as the heads of these risk functions, it was unlikely that risk professionals were included in the executive committee of the company, and even if they were, their compensation was usually a small fraction of what their counterparts made in line units.

Since the mid-1990s, however, risk management has become more recognized as a professional discipline—one in which there are numerous specializations, all of which share a common set of core competencies, just as in accounting or law. Why should this recognition have arrived only now? A quick answer is that it is because of the successful demonstration of value-added at individual companies against the background of a rapidly changing business and regulatory environment. Companies today are under more pressure to perform well—without acting irresponsibly—than ever before, while the environment in which they operate is arguably changing more quickly than at any time in the recent past.

The core competencies of risk management can help with both of these goals. On the one hand, risk managers have made more effort to project themselves as custodians of shareholder value. On the other, risk management has been successfully presented as a compulsory component of change management—a discipline much in demand as technology has fuelled massive, sometimes disruptive, changes in the ways that many businesses work and compete.

Both of these contributions are much more in keeping with the mandate of executive management, so the risk professional today can aspire to become a chief risk officer (CRO) with responsibilities for all risk functions within a company. A CRO is usually a member of the executive committee and commands compensation that has risen rapidly over the past decade.

A Career in Risk Management

The kinds of people attracted by the CRO role—particularly those who are likely to succeed in achieving it—do not necessarily fit the profile of the traditional risk manager. A career in risk management has always been an attractive option for professionals with a quantitative background in a subject such as finance, accounting, or math. In risk management, quantitative methods—securities valuation, probability estimation, and covariance analysis—can be directly applied to solve real-world business problems. Today, the trend toward ERM and the acceptance of the CRO role have helped the role of the risk professional evolve from that of a quantitative analyst, focused only on models and analysis, to that of a senior executive who is also concerned about corporate strategy, product and development, performance measurement, and incentive compensation.

In short, the risk manager has evolved from a number cruncher to a full business partner. Unsurprisingly, the prospect of someday becoming a CRO is attractive to risk professionals. I led an Internet conference organized by ERisk in September of 2000, and polled the 175 professionals on whether or not they aspired to become a CRO. Nearly 70 percent of them said yes. The career path to CRO offers the risk professional the opportunity to think more broadly, learn new skills, and most importantly, add more value to the business.

As reflected in the rapidly rising compensation packages, companies have recognized the value that is added by risk professionals. Those with cross-functional skills are enjoying the lion's share of this increase, as highlighted by the rising compensation for CROs. Based on conversations with CROs and executive recruiters, the high-end compensation for CROs had increased from the mid-six figures in the early 1990s to more than seven figures by the end of the decade. Today, even those reporting to the CRO can command over seven figures. In addition to higher compensation, the role of a CRO offers the risk professional the chance to have a much greater impact on an organization.

A CRO often reports directly to the chief executive officer (CEO) and sometimes even to the board of directors. For example, CROs of Citigroup, CIBC, and Duke Energy report directly to their respective CEOs. In addition to being a "C"-level executive, CROs participate in the key business decisions of a company.

Today, a career in risk management is more exciting and challenging than ever before. But the widespread effort to improve risk management standards is not just about elevating risk managers. If an organization really wants to manage risk more effectively, it must disseminate understanding of risk throughout the business.

Today's employees are likely to know how the work of staff functions such as accounting or legal affects their business. Trading desk managers will know something about the tax and accounting of financial transactions; product developers will know something about liability issues. The greater the effects, the more they need to know and the more effort the company should expend on making sure they understand the issues involved. The same is true for risk management.

Education and Evangelism

Education is an essential part of almost any job, but it is of paramount importance in a rapidly changing field like risk management. In fact, it would be fair to say that the success of a company's risk management program can be greatly enhanced by a well-developed risk education program. Even the most sophisticated risk management tool will be rendered ineffectual if employees do not know how to use it to its maximum possible advantage.

A good education program is essential for equipping a company's risk professionals (and general staff) to carry out their current functions more effectively and also lays the foundation for new responsibilities that may be assumed in the future. The steps involved in setting up a risk management education program include determining what topics need to be covered, finding appropriate materials to use in covering these topics, and determining the mode of delivery.

The topics to be covered in the program must be tailored to the specific needs of the organization and the group being educated. While many programs focus on traditional risk management areas such as market risk and credit risk, a comprehensive program would include other topics. For example, an ERM educational program might include:

- *Market risk management.* Market risk methodologies are generally well developed relative to other types of risk management. Standard coverage of this topic includes topics such as asset/liability management, imposition of trading limits, and types of market risk.
- *Credit risk management.* Credit risk topics include credit ratings, exposure measurement, and limit management.
- *Operational risk management.* This is an area that is often vaguely defined and glossed over in risk management education programs. Topics to be covered include control self-assessments and risk process mapping.
- *ERM.* Coverage here should include establishment of risk frameworks, organizational structure, systems and reporting, and risk

culture. Risk analytics such as economic capital and value-at-risk (VaR) also should be included.
- *Risk transfer strategies.* Derivatives, insurance, and alternative risk transfer (ART) should be covered. This is an area of rapid change in risk management, so this portion of the curriculum will have to be updated on a regular basis.

Clearly, it is mandatory that industry practices, internal policies and procedures, and regulatory requirements be discussed for each of these topic areas. However, such rote learning tends not to grab the imagination of busy employees with other concerns, particularly when the subject, like risk management, is generally poorly understood and may be seen as a dull "house-keeping" function, rather than an active contributor to business performance.

As such, educators have to work doubly hard to ensure that their students find the material interesting. Fortunately, there is no shortage of illustrative—and interesting—stories about risk management. Specific examples and scenarios should be used throughout all phases of the curriculum to illustrate the principles being taught in a concrete and engaging manner. These case studies should include both best practices and debacles, followed by a discussion of "lessons learned" from these practices and situations. Using case studies will both demonstrate how the material being taught is relevant to real-life situations and maintain listeners' interest.

A comprehensive risk management education program will likely incorporate a variety of different modes of presentation. It is important to recognize that the educational effort should seek not only to inculcate new recruits in the company's approach to risk management, but also to provide for the continuing education of current employees. This continuing education takes three forms.

The first is the continuation of a formal training program (e.g., geared toward various levels of certification). The second is providing employees with a way to remind themselves of what they have learned, or look up an unfamiliar topic. The third is to provide forums for discussion of specific risk problems, allowing expertise gained by one employee to be shared by another.

The Internet and company intranets are especially useful for these latter aspects of ongoing education and awareness. Materials covered during official education sessions, along with supplemental readings and reference materials, including complete information on the company's risk policies and procedures, should be made available to employees via an intranet application. A division of one asset management firm, for example, has a "risk policies and procedures" help function that is a part of every employee's computer desktop.

TECHNOLOGY AND THE CONVERGENCE
OF RISK MANAGEMENT

Just as the profession of risk management has increased in importance, so too has the availability of tools that make the practice of risk management easier. Most notable among these has been the increasing emphasis on quantitative tools and techniques, from pricing models to portfolio simulation and beyond. As we saw in Chapter 10, the effectiveness of these tools and techniques, and of the risk managers using them, is intimately linked with the technology built to support them.

More generally, the great strides made in risk management over the past few years have been supported by great strides in technology, first in the form of exponentially increasing processor power and subsequently in the form of networks, most obviously the Internet. One does not have to be a fan of dot-coms or a cheerleader for the "New Economy" to recognize that professions dominated by information and technology—risk management among them—are changing rapidly and will continue to change radically for the foreseeable future.

Risk professionals, including risk managers, technology providers, market makers, and consultants, must find new ways to leverage the power of this technology, and in particular the distributive power of the Internet and related technologies. One of the most obvious network-related trends in risk management today is *convergence*.

Within an institution, convergence has meant enterprise risk programs that integrate the management of market risk, credit risk, and operational risk, often under the leadership of a CRO who can take a holistic view of an enterprise's total risks. Within the financial markets, convergence has meant innovative risk transfer solutions such as catastrophe bonds and integrated insurance/derivative products, which provide more complete protection, including hitherto unmanageable risks. And across industry sectors, and even across entire industries, convergence has meant a loosening of the traditional barriers between different institutions and organizations, as shared networks and protocols for the transfer of information allow companies to dynamically streamline and reshape themselves in the pursuit of business opportunities.

While convergence was an emerging trend even before "e" entered the business dialogue, the Internet and related technologies have added exponential speed to the process, and will continue to do so. This will happen in four ways: it will support the creation of a genuine risk management community; help establish common standards; enhance risk education; and improve analytics.

Develop a Community

The Internet will help unite the various risk management groups into a common community. As we've already seen, different groups have historically been responsible for market risk, credit risk, operational risk, and insurance risk, each operating as an independent "silo" within an institution. These silos extended beyond their institutions. Different risk professionals joined different associations, and purchased products and services from different providers.

As a highly efficient aggregator and distributor of content, the Internet will help develop a common community among risk professionals, allowing them to network with each other and share issues and ideas. The growth of the Professional Risk Managers' International Association (PRMIA) is a good example of this effect. Founded in January 2002, with no official headquarters or staff, PRMIA was established on the Internet as a virtual meeting place for risk managers. Today, it is one of the fastest growing risk management associations, with more than 5,000 members representing all risk disciplines around the world.

Establish Common Standards

In the past, risk professionals used different terminologies and methodologies when dealing with essentially similar risk concepts. Risk managers seemed to speak different languages when discussing the risks they faced. Consultants and regulators promulgated different standards designed for the "risk of the month." Likewise, software providers developed applications designed for specific products.

Over time, risk practitioners have grown to recognize that risk is risk, and that common standards must be established for measuring and managing all aspects of risk within an institution. The Internet will pro-vide an interactive medium that will help establish common risk standards and best practices for risk management. Regulators can put new supervisory proposals on their websites and get feedback from a wider audience of risk professionals. Academics can do the same for peer reviews. Risk managers can benchmark their loss experience and risk practices against industry best practices. These interactive processes will speed the development of risk standards. A good example of this effect was JP Morgan's decision to post RiskMetrics, a VaR methodology on the Web. RiskMetrics had an enormous take-up rate, quickly becoming a de facto benchmark for market risk.

Enhance Education

One of the major barriers to effective risk management has been the lack of good educational resources for the various risk disciplines, particularly for operational risk and ERM. While professional associations such as PRMIA, the Risk Management Association, and the Risk Management and Insurance Society each play a constructive role, there remains a significant void in risk education. The Internet will help fill that void. It is without peer the most powerful technology for developing, organizing, and distributing educational content; no less a figure than Cisco CEO John Chambers has suggested that the Internet's greatest value will be in education and "e-learning." As long as bandwidth continues to increase at its current rate and search engines become more intelligent, the Internet will play an ever-more effective role in providing risk education. The Internet will provide interactive videos, on-line conferences, e-magazines, and faster and cheaper access to risk experts. It will also provide better access to general risk knowledge, as well as specific case studies for lessons learned and best practices.

Improve Analytics

The Internet will improve risk analytics with respect to risk aggregation, risk monitoring, and risk technology. In terms of risk aggregation, the Internet will help corporate managers develop a consolidated view of risk, tracking losses, reporting incidents, and measuring aggregate exposures across the enterprise in real time. It will also provide the appropriate individuals with 24/7 access to critical risk information. In terms of risk monitoring, the Internet will do for risk professionals what My Yahoo has done for individuals. It will provide "risk dashboards" that integrate internal and external risk information. A risk manager will then be able to go to a single source and see the company's portfolio risk exposures, along with customized news, data, and early warning indicators.

The Internet will become the technological platform of choice, especially for small- to medium-sized institutions that cannot afford large information technology budgets. It will reduce prices for risk software and increase the number of users, resulting in significant cost economies with respect to software development, implementation, and maintenance. Today, leading providers of risk management software, whether in-house programmers or outside vendors, are quickly moving to web-enable their risk models. As risk models move from packaged software to an application service provider environment, "model risk" should decrease because risk managers will have greater access to different models. They can then more easily test the sensitivity of their portfolios according to various risk models and assumptions.

TEN PREDICTIONS

The future for risk management is bright. Regulators and managers are recognizing the importance of risk management as a way to minimize losses and improve business performance. Risk professionals are moving up in the business world in terms of both organizational level and compensation. Advances in risk methodologies and technologies are introducing a vast array of new tools for measuring and managing enterprise-wide risks, at a higher speed and lower cost than anyone could have imagined just a few years ago. Although there are many remaining challenges, one cannot help but think that the best is yet to come for the risk management profession. Against this backdrop I will look into my crystal ball and make 10 predictions of how risk management will change over the next decade.

1. *ERM will become the industry standard for risk management.* ERM will continue to gain acceptance as the best way to ensure that a firm's internal and external resources work efficiently and effectively in optimizing its risk/return profile. New financial disasters will continue to highlight the pitfalls of the traditional "silo" approach to risk management. External stakeholders will continue to hold the board of directors and senior management responsible for risk oversight and demand an increasing level of risk transparency. More importantly, leaders in ERM will continue to produce more consistent business results over various economic cycles and weather market stresses better than their competitors. Their successes will gain attention and other companies will follow. These trends, coupled with a stock market that is increasingly unforgiving of negative earnings surprises, will compel businesses in all industries to adopt a much more integrated approach to measuring and managing enterprise-wide risks.

2. *A CRO will become prevalent in risk-intensive businesses.* The rise of the CRO goes hand-in-hand with the trend toward ERM. Risk management is a key driver of success for financial institutions, energy firms, asset management firms, and nonfinancial corporations with significant risk exposures. Many market leaders in these industries have already created the position of a CRO. Others will follow suit. Companies without a CRO are faced with three perplexing questions: First, are we comfortable with diffused risk responsibilities, and if not, who is the de facto CRO—the CEO or chief financial officer? Second, are their necessarily part-time efforts sufficient in managing risk in an increasingly volatile business environment? Finally, will the company be able to attract and retain high-caliber risk professionals if a CRO career track is not available

to them? For an increasing number of companies, the logical resolution of these questions will be the appointment of a CRO and the
dedication of resources to implement an ERM program.

3. *Audit committees will evolve into risk committees.* As boards of
directors recognize that they have responsibilities to ensure that appropriate risk management resources are in place, they will replace
or supplement their audit committees with risk committees. A number of leading institutions, Chase and Export Development Corporation of Canada among them, have already established risk committees of the board. As we saw in Chapter 5, the board's
responsibilities for risk management have been clearly established
in regulatory and industry initiatives worldwide, including the Dey
Report in Canada, the Turnbull Report in the United Kingdom, and
the Treadway Commission Report in the United States. The result
of these and other similar initiatives is that board directors have
begun to realize that their responsibilities go beyond traditional audit
activities, and that they need to ensure that resources and controls
are in place for all types of risk. Going forward, companies will
establish risk committees of the board, and their audit committees
will either become subcommittees or independent committees that
have the traditional audit committee focus of ensuring accurate financial reporting and statements.

4. *Economic capital will be in; VaR will be out.* Managers and external stakeholders will demand a standardized unit of risk measurement, or common currency, for all types of risk. This way, they can
spot trends in a company's risk profile, as well as compare the risk/
return performance of one company against others. To date, VaR
has gained wide acceptance as a standardized measure for market
risk. However, VaR has three major flaws. First, it does not capture
"tail risks" due to highly infrequent, but potentially devastating,
events. Second, its inability to capture tail risks makes VaR a poor
measure for credit and operational risks (or even market risk positions with significant optionality). Third, VaR measures the risk,
not the return, of any risk position. Yet financial models that have
passed the test of time, such as the capital asset pricing model or the
Black-Scholes option pricing model, evaluate both risk and return.
The concept of economic capital is intuitively appealing because one
of the main reasons companies hold capital is to absorb potential
losses from all types of risk. Risk-adjusted return on capital extends
the concept and measures business profitability on a risk-adjusted
basis. The Basel Committee has already adopted economic capital
as the framework for international regulatory capital requirements
in the banking industry. Other industries will follow and adopt it as
a common currency for risk.

5. *Risk transfer will be executed at the enterprise level.* The integration of risk transfer activities has already happened as far as hedging and insurance strategies are concerned. For example, companies that hedge with derivatives realize they can save on hedging costs if they execute portfolio hedges rather than individual securities hedges. Companies that bundle their insurance coverage through multirisk multiyear policies are also realizing significant savings on insurance premiums. Alternative risk transfer, reviewed in Chapter 8, goes one step farther in combining capital markets and insurance techniques. The rise of ERM and ART products will mean that risk transfer strategies are increasingly formulated and executed at the enterprise level. In the past, companies made risk transfer decisions to control specific risks within a defined range, without being particularly thoughtful about the cost of risk transfer unless it was prohibitively high. In the future, companies will make risk transfer decisions based on an explicit comparison between the cost of risk retention versus the cost of risk transfer and execute only those transactions that increase shareholder value.

6. *Advanced technology will have a profound impact on risk management.* As discussed in the previous section, the Internet will have a significant impact on risk management and how information, analytics, and risk transfer products are distributed. Beyond the Internet, the increase in computing speed and decline in data storage costs will provide much more powerful risk management systems. Mid-sized companies will have access to sophisticated risk models that were once the privilege of large organizations. Even individual investors will be able to apply advanced risk/return measurement tools in managing their investment portfolios. Just as market risk measurement at large trading organizations is being conducted increasingly frequently, the time interval for enterprise-wide risk measurement and reporting will move from monthly to weekly to daily, and perhaps ultimately to real-time. Moreover, the development of wireless and handheld communication devices will enable the instantaneous escalation of critical risk events, and allow risk managers to respond immediately to emerging problems or new opportunities.

7. *A measurement standard will emerge for operational risk.* Today, there is considerable debate not only about the quantification of operational risk, but also how to best define it. Approaches to assessing operational risk range from qualitative assessment of probability and severity based on management judgement, to quantitative estimate of potential loss based on industry and company loss histories. The lack of consistent operational loss data, partially as a function of the infrequency of major operational risk events, has

led to the development of analytical models such as extreme value theory to come up with loss estimates. Other models borrow from total quality management techniques or dynamic simulations to quantify operational risk. More recently, there has been some support, and some encouraging results, from early experimentation with neural networks to recognize patterns in operational risk. As the practice of operational risk management gains acceptance, and as data resources become more available as a result of company and industry initiatives, a measurement standard will emerge for operational risk. However, the greatest challenge for operational risk will remain one of management, not measurement.

8. *Mark-to-market accounting will be the basis of financial reporting.* Over time, the risk management profession has recognized the importance of mark-to-market accounting versus accrual accounting in reporting the financial condition of a company. Although accrual accounting is adequate in reporting the value of physical assets, it can provide the wrong signals in reporting financial and other intangible assets. The use of mark-to-market accounting is widely accepted in the market risk field, and is gaining acceptance in credit risk management, where credit-based assets are mark-to-market given their probability of default (e.g., credit ratings or credit spreads). Given the demand for greater risk transparency from shareholders and regulators, it is likely that variability (i.e., risk sensitivity) will be much more integrated into financial reporting in the future, including the full use of mark-to-market accounting for all financial assets.

9. *Risk education will be a part of corporate training and college finance programs.* As companies recognize the need to train and develop their risk management staff, corporate training programs will increasingly feature risk management. These training programs will likely be a combination of internal and external resources, and include internal workshops, external conferences, and Internet-based training tools. Given the rising corporate demand for skilled risk professionals, professional organizations and colleges will continue to integrate risk management into their course offerings. Professional certification and college degree programs will gain popularity and acceptance. Similar to the development of the Chartered Financial Analyst (CFA) certification in finance and investments over the past decade, a widely accepted professional certification in risk management will emerge in the next decade. Colleges will expand their course offerings beyond derivative products and credit analysis, and offer courses in ERM, risk management applications in various industries, and integrated risk transfer.

10. *The salary gap among risk professionals will continue to widen.* The trend toward ERM and the appointment of CROs has created an exciting career path, and attractive compensation opportunities, for risk professionals. However, this new career opportunity will only be available to risk professionals who continue to develop new skills and gain new experiences, while the others will be left behind. The salary gap that has developed over the past several years will continue to widen in the next 10 years. On the one hand, the compensation for risk professionals with cross-functional skills will increase faster than other professions due to rising demand for their services. On the other hand, risk professionals with narrow skills or who serve limited intermediary roles will not enjoy above-average raises, and may in fact see their job security decline as their jobs become less relevant in the new world of risk management.

In the final chapter of the book, let's have some fun and see what risk management might look like in 2010.

CHAPTER 20

Everlast Financial

[It is the year 2010. Everlast Financial is a financial services company with global investment bank, commercial banking, and insurance operations. Pamela was appointed chief risk officer (CRO) two years ago, after spending five years as a trader and three years as a market risk manager.]

Pamela, the CRO of Everlast Financial, is enjoying breakfast at home when her cellular watch suddenly begins beeping furiously. She checks the digital display and notes the warning "Operational Risk Alert." She thinks to herself that, despite the many advances in risk management, an operational risk debacle is still every risk officer's worst nightmare. Using her wireless PC she logs onto the global risk management system to find out what is happening. Before she can so much as check the interactive risk monitoring program, Garrett, Chief of Staff, appears on the screen using the PC videoconferencing application. "We've identified a rogue trader," Garrett says. "While we were examining the traders' records to prepare for their annual compensation review, we identified a discrepancy in Rick Gleeson's accounts. Further investigation of the transactions in question revealed that they were fake transactions designed to conceal about $200 million in trading losses in emerging markets bonds over the past nine months."

"We need to move quickly on this to avoid additional losses and bad press. Let's call a videoconference with the CEO, and the heads of the audit committee, the trading unit, corporate communications, the legal department, and human resources. We need to clarify the details of what happened, why it happened, and what we should do to handle the situation," Pamela replies.

"I'll get right on it," says Garrett.

The next day, Brandon, the CEO of Everlast Financial Corp., has called Austin, the head of trading, into his office. "Your trading operations have generated nearly half of the corporation's profits over the past three years, but this is a very serious problem. Our investigation has turned up evidence that Rick was indeed involved in unauthorized trading and we have a zero-tolerance policy for unethical behavior. Austin, how did this happen under your watch and what should we do about Rick?" Brandon asks.

"I assumed our risk management systems would have picked this up. Also, Rick is one of our most talented traders," Austin argues. "He just had the bad luck to be trading bonds in emerging markets at a time when the market was a bit rocky. While we shouldn't condone what he did, the performance pressure here can be immense, and, if his gambles had paid off, we would be rejoicing right now rather than talking about this crisis."

"So what do you think we should do?" Brandon asks.

"Well, he should forfeit all of his bonus for this year, based both on the fact that he generated losses for the firm and that he violated risk management policies, which could cause us great embarrassment in the public eye."

"So you think that is the only punishment he should receive? You don't think he should be fired, which is the stated consequence for this kind of offense in our risk policies manual?" Brandon asks.

"I know that is what is recommended, but it would be such a shame to lose one of our best traders. I strongly encourage you to give him another chance," Garrett says.

"We have already determined in our company-wide risk policy that there will be no second chance for offenders of this magnitude. Your willingness to overlook such noncompliance in pursuit of higher profits poses a much bigger risk to the firm than the loss of a skillful rogue trader. We can easily replace him with another trader, but the damage he has done is irreversible. Since you have demonstrated a blindness to this basic risk management concept, you are both fired. I have plenty else to do to deal with this fiasco, so don't try to argue with me," Brandon states in his most assertive voice.

As Austin leaves, Brandon calls Jennifer, the head of Human Resources (HR), who comes into his office for a discussion. "I want you to personally take care of the dismissals of Austin and Rick. I also want to discuss what we can do from an HR standpoint to prevent these scenarios in the future," Brandon says. "Pamela informed me that one of the abnormalities that we discovered about Rick in retrospect was that he never took vacations longer than two days. Learning from this, I want HR to generate an annual report on employees' vacation time, flagging any employees who have not taken vacations of at least a week in length during the past year. Also, employees who consistently fail to use all of their allotted vacation days should be identified because they may either be hiding something or be candidates for burnout."

"That sounds like a good idea," Jennifer agrees, checking to see that the voice interface on her handheld PC has been recording all of these ideas. "I also think this situation and its consequences should be incorporated into one of our training videos offered through the risk intranet. It would be a valuable lesson learned for our new managers and employees."

"Absolutely. When we make that video, I want to speak in it to set the tone from the top and demonstrate how seriously we take breaches in our risk policy," says Brandon.

Meanwhile, Curtis, the chief operating officer, has been meeting with Peter, the company's head of risk transfer, to determine what coverage Everlast Financial Corp. has for this event. "Fortunately," says Peter, "the integrated risk policy that we have has specific provisions for operational risk failures such as rogue traders. After a $10 million deductible, we are covered for any losses up to $1 billion. For the future, though, I think we should consider looking into earnings per share insurance, since that way we would have much broader risk coverage and there would be no question as to whether or not our insurance policy covers specific losses."

"Yes, I know that EPS insurance has come down a lot in price since it has become more popular. Go ahead and get us some quotes," says Curtis. After his meeting with Curtis, Peter dials into risk.com, the Internet risk exchange, to get some quotes on EPS insurance. He submits a standardized term sheet for EPS insurance, attaches Everlast Financial's loss history and enterprise risk rating, and within 10 minutes his mailbox receives five quotes from prequalified insurance providers. Peter finds that two of the quotes represent a net cost of risk transfer that is below Everlast Financial's net cost of risk retention. His analysis on the on-line risk calculator shows that by executing an EPS insurance transaction, the company's market value should improve by 4 to 5 percent. After a brief conversation with Pamela, Peter executes the EPS transaction with a European insurance company.

Back in his office, Curtis calls Brandon to relay the good news that the trading losses will be covered by the firm's insurance policy. After speaking briefly with Curtis, Brandon calls Garrett again to exchange information with him and generate further ideas for using the situation as a learning experience. "I understand that besides not taking more than two consecutive vacation days, over the past year Rick's trading behavior was unusual in terms of trading volume and pattern. I've already spoken with Jennifer about identifying potential problem employees from an HR perspective, but I want you to consider creating other metrics to serve as early warning signals for possible rogue activities. Look at Rick's trading from as many different angles as possible to determine the ways in which it differed from other traders' activity. Maybe we can share data with trading units at other financial institutions to jointly identify patterns of trading that should serve as early warnings of irregular activity. I want you to start thinking about what we might want to include in a new operational risk report. That is the area where our risk reporting needs continuous improvement since operational risk can rear its ugly head in so many different ways. We need to work on that."

Brandon tells his secretary to set up an impromptu video conference with the board members as well as conference calls with the equity analysts who cover Everlast Financial Corp. Brainstorming the ideas that he wants to convey to these stakeholders, Brandon decides that key points should include ideas such as:

- State-of-the-art risk management can't ensure that bad events will never happen, but the investments that Everlast Financial has made over the past several years in ERM and risk technology have identified and corrected this problem at an early stage.
- The company has every intention of openly communicating the details and proceedings surrounding this situation as soon as they become available, since open communication and risk transparency is one of the tenets of Everlast Financial's risk management program.
- Based on the lessons learned from this fiasco, steps are being taken to reduce the likelihood of a similar event in the future, as much as this is possible. The soon-to-be-implemented vacation report from HR, the work in progress on better operational risk analysis and reporting, the incorporation of the situation into a case study for a training video, and the dismissal of both the rogue trader and the head of trading will all be discussed.
- The analysts in particular must be assured that the costs of the debacle will not substantially affect the company's earnings due to the insurance policy coverage. Additionally, the company has executed a broader EPS insurance coverage to protect itself from unforeseen events going forward.

As the day draws to a close, Brandon sits back and thinks about the risk management advances that have made this situation less explosive than it would have been 20 years ago—the real-time risk escalation that alerted him and Pamela to the situation that morning, coupled with technology-enabled instant response; and the insurance coverage for operational risk failures. Without this sophisticated risk monitoring, the rogue trading may have continued unnoticed for years, as was the case with a number of prominent rogue traders in the twentieth century. How did risk managers function in those days without the technology and risk transfer products that are now available? While the advances were substantial, there was still much to be done, thought Brandon as he shut off the lights to go home. With his highly competent risk management group and the technology that enabled him to stay abreast of business developments 24 hours a day, he could go home with the assurance that if any major new developments occurred, he would be among the first to know.